EYE OF THE STORM

The South and Congress in an Era of Change

Edited by
John C. Kuzenski, Laurence W. Moreland,
and Robert P. Steed

PRAEGER

Westport, Connecticut
London

Library of Congress Cataloging-in-Publication Data

Eye of the storm : the South and Congress in an era of change / edited by John C. Kuzenski, Laurence W. Moreland, and Robert P. Steed.

p. cm.

Includes bibliographical references and index.

ISBN 0-275-97114-7 (alk. paper)

1. Political parties—Southern States. 2. Southern States—Politics and government—1951– 3. Apportionment (Election law)—Southern States. 4. United States. Congress. 5. United States—Politics and government—1993– I. Kuzenski, John C., 1964– II. Moreland, Laurence W. III. Steed, Robert P.

JK2295.A13E84 2001

324′.0975–dc21 00–042787

British Library Cataloguing in Publication Data is available.

Library of Congress Catalog Card Number: 00–042787
ISBN: 0–275–97114–7

First published in 2001

Praeger Publishers, 88 Post Road West, Westport, CT 06881
An imprint of Greenwood Publishing Group, Inc.
www.praeger.com

Printed in the United States of America

The paper used in this book complies with the Permanent Paper Standard issued by the National Information Standards Organization (Z39.48–1984).

10 9 8 7 6 5 4 3 2 1

Contents

Part II: Ideology and Operations

Acknowledgments

This volume evolved from the Eleventh Citadel Symposium on Southern Politics held at The Citadel in March 1998. All of the chapters except the Introduction, the Epilogue, and those written especially for this volume by Charles S. Bullock III, Nicol Rae, and Ronald M. Peters, Jr., were originally presented as papers at that conference. The symposium itself, directed by the editors of this volume, was facilitated by the efforts of a number of people at The Citadel. Major General John S. Grinalds (USMC, retired), President of The Citadel, has supported the symposium throughout his tenure on campus. Former Vice President for Academic Affairs, Dr. R. Clifton Poole, and current Vice President for Academic Affairs, Dr. Harrison S. Carter, have both worked to promote an intellectual climate conducive to the pursuit of scholarship and professional development. We are grateful to all three for their encouragement and support. We are also appreciative of the support of our colleagues in the Department of Political Science and Criminal Justice at The Citadel. We are especially grateful to The Citadel Development Foundation, whose financial support has been indispensable for the continuation of the symposium since its inception in 1978.

In relation to the development of this volume we are indebted to the discussants and other panel participants at the symposium whose comments and observations were helpful in revising the papers for inclusion in this volume.

We also wish to thank those at Praeger who reviewed the manuscript and made valuable suggestions. We are indebted to Betty C. Pessagno, our production editor, and others on the production staff who worked diligently to smooth the publication process, and we wish to thank them for their invaluable assistance. We owe a special debt of gratitude to Dr. James L. Sabin, our general editor at Praeger, who has been a receptive editor for a number of our publication projects related to southern politics and who has shepherded them through the acceptance and publication process.

Introduction: The South and Congress

Southern politics scholarship has identified two broad ways in which attention to congressional politics helps advance our understanding of the region's political history, political processes, and political system. First, the South's special leverage in Congress has had profound policy consequences for the region and for the nation at large. Second, the changing composition of the South's congressional delegations is one important indicator of regional change, and especially regional partisan change, with its attendant implications for the national political system.

Interest in the policy process and political change is not limited, of course, to students of southern politics. It is not surprising, therefore, that those who study Congress and the legislative process have also been interested in the connections between the South and Congress. As Jack Bass and Walter DeVries (1995, 369) adroitly noted in their classic work *The Transformation of Southern Politics*, it has historically been in the U.S. Congress that the states of the old confederacy "have exerted the greatest influence. The legacy of one-party politics allowed incumbent southern Democrats to accumulate seniority and rise to power as chairmen of major committees . . . giving the South a dominance that greatly exceeded the region's share of membership" in the body. Spurred on by the increased powers given to committees and their chairs as part of the Legislative Reorganization Act of 1946 (particularly the expanded standing committee jurisdictions and the addition of considerable numbers of professional committee staff), senior southern members who did not have to worry about reelection from their solidly one-party states easily controlled the congressional agenda. Legislative process and southern politics were so intricately intertwined throughout this period, in fact, that a scholar who wished to work in one of these subfields of political science could not help but become at least something of an authority on both of them.

The southern Democratic stranglehold on power—which often, to the chagrin of northeastern liberals, also meant alliances with conservative Republicans on some key committee votes—was so great from the turn of the twentieth century to the early 1960s, in fact, that it gave rise to the formation of the Democratic Study Group (DSG) in 1959. The DSG was a band of Democratic liberals that was designed to combat the conservative Dixiecratic power structure in the House. Their record of success was mixed in the early years, but combined with reform of the seniority system in the House circa 1975 and the rapidly increasing defection of white Democrats to the GOP with the advent of the Great Society, conservative southern power began to break up dramatically for the remainder of the 1970s and well into the 1980s (Smith and Deering 1984; Ripley 1988). The forced southern retreat from the inner sanctum of legislative power during the latter 1970s may explain to some degree the dearth of available literature which explores the South-Congress connection during the close of the twentiety century, in fact; it appeared to be the case for better than some twenty-odd years to the professional audience as if the Yankees had once again put down those prickly but beatable Rebs in Congress as surely as they had taken Vicksburg a hundred-plus years earlier.

The results of the pivotal 1994 congressional elections—combined with the second-wave 1996 and 1998 races in which southern Republican voters solidified the power structure of a wave of new southern Republican members—may bear witness, however, to the idea that the importance of the South in Congress was too quickly buried and forgotten by scholars in both southern politics and legislative process, to say nothing of mass media political pundits. While some critical inquiry emerged during this time regarding the importance of the South in presidential contests (Black and Black 1992), it is perhaps only now after the dust has cleared from the legislative elections of the late 1990s that the need for scholarship on the new South-Congress connection can be fully appreciated. As Bullock and Rozell (1998, 6–8) have pointed out in a welcome attempt to bring the connection back to the attention of legislative scholars, the "key position of the South in GOP presidential success is now being paralleled in Congress. . . . In the 105th Congress, Republican House control rests entirely on the GOP's advantage in the South [and perhaps] there is no more compelling evidence . . . than what an examination of the leadership of both chambers reveals."

The purpose of this book is to present a number of studies that explore various aspects of this topic and that collectively advance the general proposition that understanding the connections between the South and Congress is necessary both to understanding contemporary southern politics and to understanding the contemporary Congress. In this introductory chapter, we will offer a brief review of the key developments in this relationship during the period between the end of World War II and the beginning of the twenty-first century in order to provide a foundation and context for the studies that follow. Inasmuch as these chapters focus on recent developments in both southern and congressional politics, we will pay special attention to the last decade. Finally, we will examine briefly the logic of the book's arrangement and the nature of the studies presented. We begin with an overview of the more significant changes that have transformed the politics of the South over the past half century.

THE CONTEXT: CHANGING SOUTHERN POLITICS SINCE WORLD WAR II

Post–World War II change in the South has been multi-faceted, affecting broad elements of southern society and culture and somewhat narrower elements of the region's legal system, political practices, and political institutions. The key societal changes have been associated with economic development, population movement, and educational improvement. The construction of military bases and related elements of the World War II economy were a boost to a South still suffering from the prolonged effects of Civil War devastation and the more recent impact of the Depression. When the war ended, the region's economic transformation continued under the impetus of the "bulldozer revolution," which steadily changed a predominately rural, agrarian economy into a more urban, industrialized one (Woodward 1960; Bartley and Graham 1975; Black and Black, 1987; Scher, 1997; see also chapters 1, 6 in this volume). As industry developed and reliance on farming declined, the South became increasingly urban, more affluent, and better educated, all of which contributed to the creation of conditions that would challenge the prevailing political order.

Closely related to the changing economic environment, dramatic population change also took place in the South during the post-war decades. One key source of this change was intraregional migration mainly from rural and small town areas into the growing urban centers. A second major source was interregional migration from outside the South into the region. The movement of people into the South was fueled largely by (1) the improved job opportunities in the region resulting from the economic changes noted above (with people often following jobs south as industries began to relocate from the Northeast and Midwest), (2) the large number of military bases in the region, and (3) the moderate climate, which made the region attractive to retirees (Black and Black 1987, 15–22). The increasing diversification of the region's economy and population created more pressure for social and political change.

Not surprisingly, the challenge to the South's system of racial segregation and exclusion, which peaked during the two decades following World War II, paralleled the early stages of sweeping economic and population change described above.[1] In the aftermath of a war fought, at least in part, to preserve democracy, it became more and more difficult to ignore the region's Jim Crow system, especially after so many nonsoutherners had seen it personally while training at military bases throughout the South. As Black and Black (1987, chapters 4–7) have described, the attack on segregation came in successive assaults on a series of color lines which resulted in removing most of the legal barriers to African-American participation in the South's economic, social, and political systems. The successes of the direct action civil rights movement—

with its demonstrations, marches, boycotts, and civil disobedience—were institutionalized in the 1960s both by the federal courts and by Congress. Of particular importance were the Civil Rights Act of 1964 (which forbade discrimination in such public accommodations as hotels, motels, and restaurants) and the Voting Rights Act of 1965 (which ended the last vestiges of the complex system of obstacles to black voter registration erected by southern states over a half century earlier). The *de jure* Jim Crow system had been essentially dismantled by the end of the 1960s, and the central position of race in the region's politics had begun to erode. While race continued to be an important issue, it was no longer true, as Key had observed at mid-century, that "[i]n its grand outlines the politics of the South revolves around the position of the Negro" (Key 1949, 5).

Given the importance of the race issue in southern politics in the two decades following World War II, it is not surprising that changes in race relations were associated with changes in other elements of the political system as well. This is seen especially clearly in the area of partisan change. Between 1948 and the mid-1960s, the state Democratic parties, overwhelmingly dominant in almost every southern state, fought a stubborn rearguard action aimed at stemming the national party's liberal tide on the race issue, but by the late 1960s African Americans had gained full access to the ballot. As black participation in elections increased and as the national Democratic Party succeeded in making African Americans one of its core constituencies, southern state and local Democratic Party leaders were forced to back away somewhat from the hard-line racial stances which had previously been common (see Black 1976). This, coupled with the general reform impetus which emerged in the Democratic Party after 1968, paved the way for increased efforts on the part of blacks to gain access to the party organizational apparatus, efforts which had clearly begun to succeed by the early 1970s (Steed 1990).

At the presidential level, substantial numbers of southern whites were becoming disaffected with the Democratic Party as early as 1948, when the national party was perceived by many southern Democrats as being too liberal on civil rights. However, the Republican Party was not the immediate beneficiary inasmuch as dissidents found an outlet for their unhappiness in the States' Rights Party, which ran South Carolina's Strom Thurmond for president. By 1952, however, with no viable third-party alternative, more southern voters than usual cast their ballots for Republican Dwight D. Eisenhower, who carried four southern states in the rim (or border) South (see, for example, Bass and DeVries 1995; Bartley and Graham 1975; Lamis 1984). From that beachhead, there developed a substantial presidential Republicanism in the region (Seagull 1975; Lamis 1999; see also chapter 1 in this volume). Southern Republicanism was further enhanced by the development in 1964 of a "southern strategy," which made the South the party's top regional target, often with spectacular success. In fact, a strong case can be made that in the years since 1968 there has been a partisan realignment, at least at the presidential level, in the South. Although, as will be addressed shortly, Bill Clinton was able in 1992 and 1996 to make the South more of a two-party battleground, it is still the case that a majority of the southern states have cast their electoral votes for the Republican ticket in seven of the eight presidential elections held since 1964. Only native southerner Jimmy Carter is an exception, carrying ten of the eleven southern states in 1976, and even he carried only one southern state (his own, Georgia) in his 1980 reelection bid against Ronald Reagan. In 1984 and again in 1988, the Republican ticket carried all of the southern states. (On presidential elections in the South, see Black and Black, 1992.)

The Democratic Party's 1990s strategy of nominating two southerners for president and vice-president has only partly overcome the Republican "lock" on the South's electoral votes. In 1992 Bill Clinton and Al Gore carried four southern states (their own states of Arkansas and Tennessee plus Georgia and Louisiana). In 1996, they again won four states, their home states plus Florida and Louisiana. These may be only temporary deviations, and it is too early to determine whether the Democrats regularly will be able to pick off a handful of southern states in presidential elections.

Republican gains at the congressional level came much more slowly, remaining relatively modest even in the landslide elections of Ronald Reagan in 1984 and George Bush in 1988. In 1992 the Republicans did make some clear gains, however, as they picked up two additional U.S. Senate seats and nine U.S. House seats. Finally, in 1994, the slow movement toward Republican voting gained significant momentum as southern voters swarmed to the GOP in proportions unmatched since Reconstruction. Republicans gained 16 seats in the U.S. House of Representatives and thereby became the majority in the region's House members (64 of 125). Prior to 1994 Florida was the only southern state with a Republican majority in its House delegation; following the 1994 elections, five southern states had Republican House delegation majorities (Florida, Georgia, Tennessee, North Carolina, and South Carolina). The GOP added enough seats in the U.S. Senate through a combination of electoral victories and party switches by incumbents (namely, Richard Shelby of Alabama) to emerge with a majority of the region's senators (12 of 22) as well. Following the 1996 elections, the Republicans retained a majority of the region's U.S. Senators (14 of 22—a net gain of two seats over 1994) and U.S. Representatives (71 of 125). While the Democrats retain a substantial presence in the region's political system, it is clearly different than even a decade ago, when that party maintained a significant majority status below the presidential level.

An additional factor in U.S. House races has been redistricting mandated by the 1982 extension of the Voting Rights Act, which resulted in the creation of as many black-majority districts as possible (beginning with the 1992 elections), sometimes referred to as "majority-minority districting." An unanticipated consequence of such districting, at least for Democrats, has been that Democratic strength has been concentrated in a small number of districts, leaving many others to be picked up by the Republicans. However, the U.S. Supreme Court has declared odd-shaped districts created solely on the basis of race to be unconstitutional,[2] and, as state legislatures and courts wrestle with which of these black-majority districts must be redrawn, the Republican advantage may be somewhat diminished as the new century develops.

At state and local levels of government, Republican gains have come more slowly and with more difficulty than at the presidential and congressional levels. Republican success in state and local elections has come only with vigorous and well-financed organizing efforts. As with congressional elections, the critical elections came in the early 1990s. In 1994, accompanying the Republican successes at the congressional level, Republicans gained 44 seats in southern state legislatures (31 in the state houses and 13 in the state senates). The most dramatic successes took place in North Carolina, South Carolina, and Florida, where the Republicans gained majorities in one state legislative chamber for the first time in this century. Additionally, Republicans picked up three new governorships, giving them six of the eleven in the region (Texas, Tennessee, Alabama, South Carolina, Mississippi, and Virginia). Republican candidates did well in other races as well, as, for example, in South Carolina where the GOP captured eight of the state's nine constitutional offices, including governor, lieutenant governor, and attorney general. Republicans in 1996 continued to do well in subnational elections with Florida, for example, becoming the first southern state in this century to have Republican majorities in both chambers of its state legislature (even while the state cast its electoral vote for Bill Clinton and Al Gore). Generally, in those areas targeted by the Republicans, their party organizations have surpassed those of the Democrats in terms of financing, use of technology, and organizational knowhow (direct mail and the like). One consequence has been a sometimes demoralized southern Democratic party as indicated, for example, in one recent survey that has shown that a majority of southern Democratic precinct officials see their party organizations as having declined over the last decade (Hadley and Bowman 1995).

Republican successes in the South have not been uniform. They have been affected by a unique combination of party switches (for example, Strom Thurmond, Phil Gramm, and Richard Shelby), economic growth, migration patterns, and national political issues, which have played to traditional southern values on conservative religion, roles for women, and support for the military. South Carolina, North Carolina, Virginia, and Texas have been among the most Republican states in the South, with Georgia, Louisiana, and Arkansas among the least Republican.

All the events sketched above have resulted in sweeping long-term consequences, some unexpected, for the southern party system. For example, V.O. Key, whose analysis of southern politics at mid-century (Key 1949) remains the seminal work on which all others build, anticipated that an emerging Republican Party in the South would be a moderate one, with the Democratic Party becoming the bastion of segregationist whites and of remnants of the never-say-die Confederate mentality. Almost the reverse has occurred, particularly in the 1960s and early 1970s, when many segregationist whites moved to the Republican Party. With the additional impetus provided by white in-migrants from outside the South who were often conservative and Republican (see, e.g., Campbell, Converse, Miller, and Stokes 1964), the Republican Party became increasingly competitive with the Democrats, and they found their strength in the burgeoning metropolitan corridors, especially in the white suburban areas of these corridors, that were rapidly emerging in virtually every southern state (Black and Black 1987). The Democratic Party, on the other hand, retains overwhelming support from the African-American electorate, supplemented by support from older whites, from relatively moderate-to-liberal whites, and from citizens of rural areas who were not as strongly influenced by the post–World War II trends noted above.

Finally, some mention must be made in this brief overview of change in the South since World War II of the institutional shifts that have occurred in southern state governments. Most notably, after the reapportionment decisions rendered by the U.S. Supreme Court in the 1960s—the key ones of which involved challenges in the southern states of Tennessee [*Baker v. Carr*, 369 U.S. 186 (1962)], Georgia [*Wesberry v. Sanders*, 376 U.S. 1 (1964)] and Alabama [*Reynolds v. Sims*, 377 U.S. 533 (1964)]—the southern states slowly reapportioned, thus breaking the lock formerly held by rural and small town areas. During this same period, efforts have been made to professionalize the legislatures in many of the region's states (Anderson 1994). Similarly, southern governors have experienced a change in the direction of greater pragmatism and heavier involvement in policymaking (Scher 1997, 401–4). Institutionally, then, as well as politically, socially, and economically, the South has modernized and has moved significantly away from the patterns that dominated the region before 1950.

THE SOUTH AND CONGRESS: THE EARLY HISTORICAL PATTERN

During the first half of the twentieth century, the South's pivotal position in the operation of Congress stood as a major weapon in the effort to protect and preserve the region's system of racial segregation and discrimination and to influence the direction of the nation's public policy in other topical areas as well (see Shannon 1972; Bass and DeVries 1995, 369; and Scher 1997, 74–75, 127, 356). The one-party system prevalent in the region often enabled southern Democrats in Congress to build the seniority which led to positions of power, especially as committee chairs.

In the early 1970s, W. Wayne Shannon detailed this situation in the House of Representatives for the 1950s and 1960s and demonstrated that the South's control of House chairmenships regularly ranged between 50 percent and 63 percent during these two decades even though the region held only about one-third of the seats in the House at the time (Shannon 1972). Inasmuch as the post–World War II decades witnessed a growing disaffection among southern members of Congress with the policy directions of the national Democratic Party (see Shannon 1972), it is not surprising to find that analyses of party loyalty scores revealed that southern chairs scored considerably lower on such measures than non-southern chairs. Indeed, in one study of the 90th Congress (1967–68) 83 percent of the southern House chairs demonstrated equal or higher opposition to Democratic Party positions on 30 selected key issues than did the average Republican (Democratic Study Group 1969). In addition to creating coalitional problems for the Democratic Party, this positioning of southern Democrats in power had policy consequences. Not only did it enable conservative southerners to hinder, if not entirely block, civil rights legislation, it allowed them the opportunity to exercise disproportionate influence on other policies such as labor relations, urban development, and agriculture (see Shannon 1972; Scher 1995: 74–75, 356).[3]

During the same period, southern Democrats followed a slightly different strategy to produce largely the same results in the Senate. As Merle and Earl Black (1990) have pointed out in their insightful analysis of Senate data from 1947 to 1972, southerners in the Senate were able not only to secure a disproportionate share of the key standing committee chairmanships, they were also successful in securing a disproportionate share of positions on these key committees. This strategy of achieving dominance in depth had the further advantage of avoiding service on those committees which were less important to regional policy interests, service that would waste southern representation. As they explain, "On the 'stacked' committees, Southerners would be well positioned to advance by seniority to chairmanships, as well as to replace other Southerners whenever they vacated leadership positions. And on committees where Southerners were proportionally represented, the absence of reelection challenges meant that the seniority system would give these Southerners disproportionate opportunities to acquire and maintain chairmanships" (Black and Black 1990, 7). The ultimate result here, as in the House of Representatives, was to allow for increased opportunities to influence policy in the directions most desired by southern (mostly) conservatives.

The South's importance in Congress in the decades immediately following World War II was, of course, not limited to its success in gaining more than its share of committee chairmanships. It was further enhanced by the institutional leadership of southerners such as Lyndon B. Johnson in the Senate and Sam Rayburn in the House of Representatives and by institutional rules (both formal and informal) that provided numerous opportunities for well organized, highly placed, and determined minorities to affect the legislative process.

THE SOUTH AND CONGRESS: THE TRANSITIONAL DECADES

By the mid-1970s, the patterns described above had begun to change in some important ways. For one thing, death, defeat, and retirement reduced the benefits of seniority for southerners in Congress. Not only did the numbers of southern committee chairs decline, the committees that were chaired by southerners were increasingly the less crucial committees (see Bass and DeVries 1995; Black and Black 1990, 14–20).

A second factor in the changing role of the South in Congress, related in part to the declining ability of the South to parlay seniority into influence, was the region's increasingly competitive party system. As outlined in the previous section, building on an extremely limited base dating back to the mid 1960s, the Republican Party slowly became more competitive in congressional (and other) elections in the South during the 1970s and the 1980s (Shannon 1972; Black and Black 1987, esp. chapters 11, 13; Bullock 1988; Black and Black 1990; Bass and DeVries 1995, chapter 15).[4] Inasmuch as the earlier construction of seniority was based in large part on the one-party system, this increased competition, coupled with the aging of the powerful Democrats noted above, eroded the South's power base during these transitional years. As Black and Black (1990, 14–15) have noted, in the Senate one clear result of these developments was that the Democratic Steering Committee became more broadly based and more representative of the prevailing regional balance of Democrats in that chamber.

A third factor was the reform effort in Congress itself during the 1970s (on congressional reform during this period, see, among others, Davidson and Oleszek 1977; Rieselbach 1986; Sundquist 1981; and Welch and Peters 1977).[5] For example, in 1975 House Democrats changed their mechanism for recommending assignments to standing committees from the Democratic members of the Ways and Means Committee to the Steering and Policy Committee, a committee chaired by the Speaker, which contained the other principal party leaders in the House, and which reflected a wider range of policy views in the party membership. This, in turn, allowed party leaders to take party loyalty more explicitly into consideration in awarding committee positions, especially on the part of non-freshmen (see Smith and Ray 1983). In the same year, House Democrats changed their method for selecting committee chairs so that the rule of seniority was less automatic. At approximately the same time, reforms to enhance the power of subcommittees served to further diminish the power of committee chairs and, hence, the importance of seniority (Ripley 1988, 153). This is not the place to review the entire range of reform, especially since reforms varied by party and by chamber, but this should serve to demonstrate that institutional change converged with demographic and partisan change in the 1970s to transform the South's power in Congress and to diminish the region's ability to influence the direction of national public policy from an institutionalized position.

The collective impact of these changes continued throughout the 1980s. Of special importance was the continued strengthening of the Republican Party, which resulted in increased electoral pressure on the Democrats. Moreover, aging Democrats continued to fall from the ranks of the southern congressional delegations, and those Democrats who remained tended to be less conservative and more diverse than their forebears. In the midst of this dramatic change, however, the foundation was being laid for a resurgence of the South's importance in Congress, this time under the Republican banner.

THE SOUTH AND CONGRESS: THE 1990s

The changes in the South's party system and its larger political and social systems which had altered the region's role in Congress in the 1970s and 1980s ultimately provided the basis for a renewal of southern influence in the 1990s. At the same time, those changes contributed significantly to the partisan transformation that occurred in Congress in 1994 which resulted in the emergence of Republican majorities in both the House and the Senate.

The Republican gains in the 1990s, outlined in the previous section, were significant. In the four years between 1992 and 1996, the Republican Party increased its percentage of southern House seats from 34 percent to 57 percent and its percentage of southern Senate seats from 32 percent to 68 percent (see the discussion in Stanley 1998). Thus, the South was important not only in helping to tip the partisan scale to the Republican Party in 1994, it was also instrumental in helping to retain that congressional majority in the years following.

The role of the South in Congress by the mid-1990s was not confined, however, just to the numbers of Republicans who contributed to pushing that party into the Congressional majority. It extended as well to the increased importance of the South in positions of leadership in both the House and the Senate. Southern Republicans such as Newt Gingrich of Georgia, Dick Armey of Texas, and Trent Lott of Mississippi emerged as highly important in defining the direction of the congressional GOP.

Thus, by the mid-1990s southern influence had resurfaced in Congress. While it was not identical to the patterns of southern influence during the days of the Democratic Solid South, it bore some marked similarities. Most notably, from an ideological perspective southern conservatives had once again emerged, albeit as Republicans rather than as Democrats, even though the specific configuration of issues was different (for example, the centrality of the conservative racial agenda had been largely replaced by equally conservative, but mainly social and economic, agendas). This development prompted some observers (such as Bass and DeVries) to suggest that these ideologically charged and impassioned southerners in Congress were leading a charge that would result—or maybe has already resulted—in the "Southernization" of the rest of the nation. States' rights, a "new federalism" that borders on confederation, a white backlash against equal opportunity programs (which, ironically, some of the most unsouthern states such as California, Washington, and Colorado outlawed in elections of the 1990s), and the emergence of the Religious Right from a southern regional movement into a national political force—to mention only a number of the more obvious developments—have been pushed onto the national stage largely by the cohesiveness and power of southerners in Congress.

ORGANIZATION OF THE BOOK

This book examines some of the key aspects of the changes in the South and in the Congress that have been discussed above. No claim is made that its treatment is comprehensive, either from the perspective of southern politics or from the perspective of congressional organization and operation. Rather, the analyses address selected elements of contemporary southern and congressional politics that shed light on both.

In part 1, Electoral Politics, five chapters examine the nexus between Congress and recent U.S. electoral patterns. As we have pointed out above, the congressional elections in the 1990s, and especially in 1994, were highly important to both change in the southern party system and to change in Congress. The House elections were particularly interesting because they elevated the GOP into a majority for the first time since the early 1950s and because in this process they revolved around an unusual statement of issue positions to which many of the Republican representatives subscribed, the Contract with America. In chapter 1, Ronald Keith Gaddie and Donna R. Hoffman analyze the twentieth-century history of the South and Congress within the context of partisan realignment. After exploring a variety of approaches to identifying if and when realignments have occurred, they utilize data on elections in the South for both the House of Representatives and the Senate, supplemented by analyses of data on state legislative elections, to search for evidence of party realignment in the region. Of particular importance in the context of the present volume is their focus on elections for Congress as a key indicator of significant party change, especially change related to shifting party strength in the region. In chapter 2, Stanley P. Berard and David W. Rohde are also concerned with party realignment. They focus on the recent trend toward Republican ascendancy in the South and in the House of Representatives with a view toward addressing the likelihood that the trend will continue into the near future. They are especially interested in the possibility of further Republican gains in southern congressional districts as a part of a broader realignment in the region. Indirectly, of course, their analysis has important implications for the partisan realignment of the Congress as a whole.

James M. Glaser continues this investigation of partisan realignment by examining the defection of Democratic office holders as a factor in Republican growth in the 1990s. In chapter 3, he utilizes data on southern Democratic defectors in Congress and in southern state legislatures during the 1980s and the 1990s to address a number of relevant questions: Does party defection lead to a change in legislative behavior? If the new party label does lead to such a change, how does one explain it? What is it about the change in allegiance that spurs a change in behavior? Is there a difference in how members of Congress and members of state legislatures respond to the switch? While Glaser wrestles with the issue of partisan defection as a factor in party change, Christine LeVeaux-Sharpe wrestles with the issue of racial-based redistricting as a factor in party and legislative change. More specifically, in chapter 4 she explores the relationship between racial-based redistricting and the emergence of Republican candidates to challenge incumbent Democratic representatives. Her findings relate not only to understanding congressional dynamics but to understanding party change in the South as well. Finally, the themes of party and congressional change in recent years are revisited in Charles S. Bullock's examination of the 1998 congressional elections in the South. In chapter 5, he describes key races and their electoral outcomes within the context of their meanings for the parties (and especially for the prospects of continued Republican growth) and for the partisan composition of Congress. Together, these five chapters help illuminate the nature of Republican resurgence in the South and in Congress over the past two decades and offer insight into the prospects for continued partisan change.

Elections are important, of course, well beyond the simple issue of which party wins the most seats in Congress. Ultimately, electoral victory matters because it presumably affects the policy directions Congress will take afterward. Indeed, much of the excitement over Republican control of Congress related to the expectation that this would usher in a significantly different (and more conservative) policy orientation exemplified by, but not limited to, the Contract with America. The five chapters in part 2, Ideology and Operation, address the connections among electoral outcomes, partisan balance in Congress, policy orientations, and internal operations.

Ronald M. Peters opens the section with an excellent detailed historical overview of the role southerners[6] have played in leadership positions in the House of Representatives. While not limited to the post–World War II period, Peters's discussion focuses on recent developments through the pivotal 1994 elections and the more recent changes in House leadership with the departure of Newt Gingrich and Bob Livingston. He concludes with some insights into the changing role of region in the House of Representatives.

In chapter 7, Nicol Rae examines some of the key reasons for Republican gains in the House of Representatives in 1994. Utilizing information from extensive interviews with many of those involved, he explores the impact of the southern members within the freshman class during the revolutionary 104th Congress, the elections of 1996, the continuing tensions between the sophomores of the class of 1994 and the leadership during the 105th Congress, and the election of 1998 and its aftermath. In this, he sees southerners in the class of 1994 acting as the "keepers of the flame" of the Republican "Revolution" of 1994. His perspective on this point, and on the role of region generally in the House, contrasts with Peters's conclusions in chapter 6 on the ideological role of southern representatives during the 1990s. The placement of these two chapters in proximity to each other should prompt continued consideration of these varying viewpoints.

In chapter 8, Frank B. Feigert and Michael Ault return to a broader historical perspective in exploring the evolution of ideology in Congress since World War II (specifically from 1947 through 1996). In this analysis, they pay special attention to the relative importance of party, region, and chamber as factors in congressional change. While these variables contributed to the regional and institutional shifts explored in this book, other factors such as congressional redistricting and religion have also been significant. Christine Sharpe examined the implications of majority-minority districting for southern Republican growth in chapter 4, and Allison L. Hayes and Kenneth A. Wink revisit this topic in chapter 9. Utilizing data from fourteen states (the South plus the border states of Kentucky, Missouri, and Oklahoma), they attempt to map the effects of majority-minority districting on African-American and Republican representation. They are particularly interested in the possibility of greater ideological polarization in the House of Representatives, and they explore the implications for coalition building in Congress.

The final chapter in part 2 deals with another important element in regional and institutional change in the 1990s: the role of the Religious Right. The entry of conservative Christians into the political process has had a significant impact on southern (and national) politics over the past decade. Organizations such as the Moral Majority and, more recently, the Christian Coalition have claimed success in influencing specific elections and in redirecting the issue orientation of the Republican Party, especially in the South. (On the political involvement of the Religious Right generally, see, for example, Hill [1972], Baker, Steed, and Moreland [1983], Hunter [1991], Baker, Steed, and Moreland [1991], Guth and Green [1991], Leege and Kellstedt [1993], Rozell and Wilcox [1997], and Baker, Steed, and Moreland [1998].) In chapter 10, Mark Caleb Smith discusses the connection between the Religious Right and Republican Party fortunes in congressional elections in the 1990s. He is especially interested in examining whether there is evidence that Republican House members are in any way "paying back" the Christian Right for its electoral support in 1994 and since. As with the other chapters in part 2, Smith's analysis addresses a significant topic in understanding the contemporary Congress, especially in light of the historical context offered by Peters, Rae, and Feigert and Ault.

Finally, the epilogue presents a summary of the key conclusions developed in the substantive chapters and places these in the broader context of contemporary regional and institutional change. We seek a better understanding of the South and the contemporary Congress at the turn of the century in light of what has been a remarkable era of political transformation.

NOTES

1. A large literature explores the civil rights movement and its impact on southern politics. See, among others, Lawson 1976; Watters and Cleghorn 1967; Wright 1987; Stern 1987; Stokes and Halpern 1994; Chappell 1994; Faircloth 1995; Bass and Terrill 1986; Williams 1987; and Black and Black 1987.

2. The relevant cases are *Miller v. Johnson*, 115 S. Ct. 2475 (1995), *Shaw v. Hunt*, 116 S. Ct. 1894 (1996), and *Bush v. Vera*, 116 S. Ct. 1941 (1996). For a discussion of the legal struggle over majority-minority districting, see Scher, Mills, and Hotaling 1997.

3. For a dissenting view that the impact of the seniority system on policy has been exaggerated, see Hinckley 1971. Even if Hinckley's argument is accepted in principle, it does not negate the broad conclusion that the South was able to utilize the seniority system to exercise far more influence than would have otherwise been possible. Clearly there were other factors, such as the method of making Senate committee appointments, which also enhanced southern influence, but the one party system combined with the seniority system in important ways.

4. A large literature explores the changes in the southern party system over the past three to four decades. See, among others, Lamis 1984; Black and Black 1987; Swansbrough and Brodsky 1988; Hadley and Bowman 1995; Steed, Moreland, and Baker 1997; Scher 1997; Steed Clark, Bowman, and Hadley 1998; Hadley and Bowman 1998; More-

land and Steed 1998.

5. Congress has, of course, undergone reforms from time to time throughout this century. Here we are primarily interested in those which Ripley (1988, 418–19) classifies as serving mainly to disperse power among individual members of Congress as opposed to those which serve to centralize power so as to increase the power of Congress as an institution. Within that category of reforms, we focus on those that had the most consequence for southern power in Congress.

6. We must acknowledge at the outset that the authors of the studies presented in this volume do not utilize consistent operational definitions of the South. While all include the eleven states of the former Confederacy in the South, some add one, two, or even three of the border states as well (usually including some combination of Kentucky, Oklahoma, and Missouri). While this reduces the comparability of the analyses marginally, we think it does little to alter the comparability of the major theses and conclusions of the studies.

PART I

ELECTORAL POLITICS

1

Critical Events in Contemporary Southern Politics: Dynamic Growth and Partisan Percolations

RONALD KEITH GADDIE AND DONNA R. HOFFMAN

> *Like five-year-olds at Christmastime, political scientists have been awaiting the coming of a partisan realignment.*
>
> —Charles S. Bullock III (1988a)

Realignment has dominated discussion of southern politics for over thirty years. In 1964 Barry Goldwater captured the electoral college vote of the Deep South states, becoming the first Republican to do so since Reconstruction. On his coattails rode several southern Republican representatives and other officials. The Goldwater candidacy doomed the GOP throughout the rest of the nation; outside the old confederacy, the Republicans lost every state except Arizona in the presidential contest and almost sixty House seats in congressional races. As this occurred, the South began to confront a new era of two-party competition. The combination of the influx of new and overwhelmingly black Democratic voters and the massive vote of Deep South whites for the Republican presidential candidate pointed to a fundamental shift in the partisan dynamics of the South—or so it seemed.

Over the next thirty years the South vexed the nation with seemingly inconsistent voting behavior. Southerners voted heavily for conservative independent and Republican presidential candidates, while returning large numbers of Democrats to the Congress and state legislatures. At no point before 1994 did the Republicans translate their dominance of the Southern presidential vote into majority success down-ticket. Then, in 1994, the GOP surged to majority status in U.S. Senate and House races, and also realized substantial gains in state legislative contests. Again, the cry of realignment has been raised by students of electoral politics, although some observers echoed Bullock's (1988a, 553) cry for caution that "only through hindsight can one distinguish between a major shift in partisan fortunes of sufficient persistence that the results of a particular election signal the advent of a pattern that prevails."

How, then, do we assess realignment? How do we place the shifting tides of partisanship in the South into a meaningful historical context, be it in terms of control of legislative government or within the southern electorate itself? There are a number of potentially useful approaches which may be suggested (see chapters 3, 4, 8 and 9, among others, in this volume). We take a "long-sighted" view of the aggregate patterns of partisanship in the South, with the goal of determining how secular trends and critical events have affected the development of Republican strength in the South. In particular, we seek answers to three questions in this introductory essay. First, what constitutes the necessary and sufficient evidence of realignment? We then turn our attention to whether the change in office-holding in the South has been structured by secular trends (Key 1959; Bullock 1988a), critical events (Key 1955; Burnham 1970) or both. Finally, we ask what secular trends or critical events which structure change in southern politics meet the criteria for realignment.

From this inquiry, we hope to construct a rhetorical and statistical profile of southern partisan change that defines the contours of realignment. By identifying those contours, we can indicate areas for further exploration in both the study of realignment and of southern politics. We obtain a better understanding of how the concept of realignment relates to the dynamic of partisan competition. We are also able to draw conclusions concerning the pivotal 1994 congressional elections in the South, and how they fit into the galaxy of "realignments" so often declared by the more recent social science literature on the subject.

WHAT IS REALIGNMENT?

Substantial confusion surrounds realignment. This confusion arises from three factors: (1) a lack of clarity in the definition of realignment, (2) the variety of political events that realignment has been called upon to explain, and (3) shifts and inconsistencies in the evidence used to determine whether realignment has occurred. Largely because of this confusion, there is a proliferation of realignment literature as scholars construct new forms and features of realignment. Since the mid-1960s, virtually every election has been hailed as some form of realignment by some scholar, somewhere. Everett C. Ladd (1990) has aptly pointed out that political scientists have been waiting for realignment to occur like Estragon and Vladimir were waiting for Godot in Samuel Beckett's play of the same name. Various authors have produced concepts such as critical realignments, step realignments, secular realignments, creeping realignments, nested realignments, top-down realignments, partial realignments, hollow realignments, incomplete realignments, dual realignments, regional realignments, rolling realignments, no-alignment realignments, and dealignments. Speak of realignment, in summary, and the hounds will be let loose.

V.O. Key (1955, 1959) argued in successive articles in the *Journal of Politics* that there were two types of realignments in American politics: critical and secular. The more formal form of realignment is the critical realignment. Critical realignments are dramatic changes in the composition of partisan coalitions that are long-lasting. These realignments are associated with dramatic or cataclysmic events that capture the attention of the electorate and divide voters along lines that redefine partisanship; for many, those new partisan attachments are long-term and become the basis of a new party system (Key 1955; Burnham 1970; Sundquist 1973).

THE CRITICAL REALIGNMENT

In the critical (or "step") realignment, there is a recognized partisan equilibrium to elections before the occurrence of a profound political intervention. Then, between the election at time t and the election at time $t+1$, this intervention occurs—an important issue or other epic event with political implications—and a shift occurs away from the existing partisan balance to a new equilibrium. The new equilibrium sustains itself over time and becomes a new partisan era.

The number of critical realignments that have occurred in American history is the subject of debate. Most scholars can agree on three critical realigning "eras" and the events surrounding them: the antebellum debate over slavery and the Civil War (1856–61); the Depression of 1893 and the eastern industrial response to the Bryan takeover of the Democratic Party (1893–96); and the New Deal realignment of 1928–36. There are arguments made in support of other realignments, but the support for those events is inconsistent. Some are not considered realigning, such as the 1824–28 breakup of the Democratic-Republican Party, which is often referred to as an aligning election (see also Sundquist 1973) or the emergent party system of 1789–1803 (Hoadley 1980).

The impact of critical elections is not always national in scope. Bullock (1988a) argued in his examination of shifts in partisan officeholding that dramatic partisan trends in different regions of the nation could be masked by aggregation. Nardulli (1995) demonstrated that many critical events were not truly national. His county-level analysis of presidential voting found only one "national" realignment—the New Deal realignment—and a variety of subnational and regional events. Among the critical realignments documented by Nardulli are southern realignments in 1948–52 and an urban New Frontier realignment in the late 1950s and early 1960s.

THE SECULAR REALIGNMENT

The other principal form of realignment is the secular or "creeping" realignment. Secular realignment is characterized by a substantial shift in the voting behavior of a region or group over an extended period of time, such as a generation or more. V.O. Key described secular change in his second article on realignment by saying "[some] processes operate inexorably, and almost imperceptibly, election after election, to form new party alignments and to build new party groupings" (1959, 198–99). Key's explanation relied heavily on analysis of voting trends in rural and industrial communities, primarily in the Northeast and Ohio. Research on secular change in the South has taken a more holistic approach by examining trends regionwide. These investigations typically characterize the political change in the South as "creeping" realignment; the phrase captures the spirit of Key's realignment theory while also describing the sustained shift to the GOP (Bullock 1988b; Stanley 1988).

REALIGNMENT CRITICISMS AND THE DYNAMIC GROWTH PERSPECTIVE

Realignment encounters criticism because of the expectation it places on the behavior of voters. The major studies of individual voter behavior that emerged subsequent to Key's realignment studies indicated that party identification was stable and difficult to disrupt (Campbell et al. 1960). The absence of issue voting in *The American Voter* further undermined the realignment argument: If voters did not pay attention to issues, did not vote on issue cues, and their partisanship was stable, how could they realign?

Erikson and Tedin offered an alternative perspective on the realignment thesis. Critical elections did not produce realignment because most existing partisans did not change their party identification. Instead, new voters—either first-time voters or previous voters who had fallen out of the habit but returned in the realigning election—overwhelmingly identified with and supported the new majority party in a realignment. Subsequent generations show less partisan bias, until some new event redefines partisan alignments. Critical realignment was in fact critical mobilization of new voters. Key (1966) offered a glimpse of this phenomenon in *The Responsible Electorate*, where he observed that new voters supported the winning presidential party at a rate as high or higher than the winning partisans.

A third perspective on realignment advanced more recently is the concept of dynamic growth. Advocated most effectively by Carmines and Stimson (1989) in their volume *Issue Evolution*, the dynamic growth model of political change holds that the effects of realigning issues might not be fully felt in one critical election. According to the dynamic growth model, the critical event will produce a sudden shift away from one party and toward another. The difference between this model and the step model is that the shift will be followed by continued secular growth of the party advantaged by the realignment; in graphical terms, it is a strong "jerk" toward the party opposite followed by a smoother but nevertheless upward-continuing growth of support.

The second dimension of Carmines and Stimson's model is how issues and events relate to political change. Issues, they argue, can be divided into two categories—"hard" and "easy"—based on the ability of voters to access and understand the issue. Easy issues are the issues around which realignments are built: they are more symbolic than technical and deal with policy ends rather than means. An easy issue has been present on the political agenda for a long time and represents "an unresolved conflict long in the public eye" (Carmines and Stimson 1980, 92). For easy-issue voting to occur, Carmines and Stimson argue, it must be presented to the electorate; if it is not presented, then voters cannot use it as a voting cue. Or, to reiterate Key (1966), an echo effect is present; the voters only reflect back what they have been offered in issue voting.

This concept of the easy issue nests nicely into the literature on realignment. When realignment occurs, there is necessarily some cause, some reason, that relates to a political issue. If the parties are differentiated on an easy issue, then the issue and the electoral environment are primed for political change. Voters have differentiated parties, they have few barriers to obtaining information, and they have the opportunity to act. As Carmines and Stimson observed, "Easy issue voting . . . requires neither cognitive ability nor attention to politics, and is free to vary with the availability of easy issues" (1980, 80). So the conditions of issue voting posited by the Michigan scholars are not necessary, and, further, the nature of easy issues make them accessible to the types of voters that Key (1966) and Erikson and Tedin (1981, 1986) say are important to the partisan change in critical elections: new and previously demobilized voters.

So what is realignment? For our purposes, a realignment is a dramatic change in the partisan expressions of constituencies and communities. The change is long-lasting, and it can occur suddenly or over time. Realignment is not necessarily a change in the actual partisan identification of individuals, but of the composition of partisan preferences and choices made by the electorate in constituencies or groups. In addition, realignment needs a catalyst—a substantive issue or event that sets change in motion—that is to say, an "easy" or differentiating issue that distinguishes the parties in the minds of the electorate.

ISSUE EVENTS IN THE SOUTH, 1954–94

Race—more specifically the relationship between black southerners, government, and society—is the easy issue around which critical events in the South are traditionally structured (Key 1949). The major civil rights decisions of the 1940s and 1950s were aimed at southern institutions, and the major civil rights and voting rights legislation brought the power of the federal government to bear on the institutions of segregation and racial discrimination. The extent that these major policy decisions affected the relationship between the races in the South contributed to their political salience. Further, the extent to which the parties are differentiated on the issue contributes to both the size and direction of any political shock related to the policy.

What are these events, and how do they relate to political change in the South? Two major events are explicit in their ties to the race issue: the 1954 *Brown* decision, as well as the high-stimulus summer of 1964 and the passage of the Civil Rights Act (to say nothing of the 1965 Voting Rights Act, which soon followed), fostering white support for the Goldwater candidacy and laying the groundwork for Lyndon Johnson's Great Society. These two events, however, are quite different in their impact on the partisan politics of the South. The other three events—Watergate (1974), the first Reagan landslide (1980), and the Contract with America election (1994)—are less clearly related to the race issue. Arguments have been made, nevertheless, in support of those elections as realigning, and empirical evidence indicates a response in the outcomes of legislative elections to those events.

1954: THE *BROWN* DECISIONS AND MASSIVE RESISTANCE

The reaction of the segregated South to the two *Brown* decisions of 1954 and 1955 was swift and singular: the South would not readily or enthusiastically comply with court decisions desegregating public schools. The political reaction was a circling of the wagons: southern congressmen prepared to block enacting legislation, using the tools available through committee assignments and the filibuster. In the states, legislators and governors fell in line with the massive resistance philosophy articulated by Virginia political leader Harry Byrd (see Black and Black 1987; Rodgers and Bullock 1976). Through the region's representatives in the Democratic Party, the white South acted to protect the institution that reinforced the segregated society.

If there is any impact by the 1954 *Brown* decision and the subsequent symbolic efforts at its enforcement—the Little Rock crisis, for example—it should reinforce the Democratic Party against the movement toward the GOP that began after World War II (Nardulli 1995). The political structure surrounding the *Brown* decision should not have threatened the Democratic Party below the presidential level. The *Brown* decision was handed down by a Republican chief justice appointed by a Republican president. That Republican president was ambivalent-to-quiescent on the enforcement issue, although efforts in Little Rock indicated a willingness to support integration with force. The leadership of the Democratic Party in the South was either silent on the issue or (more typically) vocally opposed to integration. The "no, not one" proclamation of Georgia Governor Ernest Vandiver regarding the prospects for black and white children attending school together indicated the staunch resistance to breaking down the outer color barrier. The Democratic Party therefore continued as a vehicle for southern conservative expression (Heard 1952).

THE 1964 CIVIL RIGHTS REVOLUTION

The next major intervention had greater potential for creating a political shift away from the Democratic Party. Civil rights emerged in the 1960s as a fully blown divisive issue within the Democratic Party. The national party had been receptive to the civil rights movement for some time—both Adlai Stevenson and John Kennedy had made overtures and statements that encouraged the movement against segregation (Black and Black 1992). Despite Kennedy's moderate stands, Catholic faith, and in particular his appeal to free Martin Luther King, Jr., from a Georgia prison during the 1960 campaign, the Southern electorate remained largely loyal, with Florida, Virginia, and Tennessee defecting to Nixon (but see Key 1966). Faithless electors in Mississippi and Alabama cast votes for Virginia senator Harry Byrd, continuing a presidential defection initiated in 1948 (Nardulli 1995; Black and Black 1992).

The civil rights events of 1963 and 1964 are too numerous to detail, and no individual event of the civil rights era can necessarily explain the exact moment that propelled southern whites away from the Democrats. However, the dramatic events of the early 1960s further wedged apart the national Democratic Party and the southern white voter. The defection of Rim South states in the 1920s and 1950s was well-known; however, the beginnings of the cracks in Democratic presidential hegemony in the Deep South also predated 1964 (Nardulli 1995; Black and Black 1992). Louisiana had followed Eisenhower's banner in 1956 over the disposition of offshore oil leases. Mississippi had been bolting for independent electors since the 1940s, as had South Carolina and Alabama. And in 1960 South Carolina had substantially increased its Republican presidential ballots. However, there had been no systematic move to the GOP, in part because the GOP afforded little relief to the pressure applied to the South on the race issue.

The events of 1964 laid open the divisions between the South and the national Democrats. The agitation for civil rights by southern blacks, the continued white opposition toward the civil rights movement, and the heavy-handed support of President Lyndon Johnson all facilitated the passage of the 1964 Civil Rights Act. This act, which bore all the characteristics of the "force bills" disdained by the South for almost a century, provided for the defense of basic civil rights for all citizens and authorized the federal government to intervene actively in defense of civil rights (Black and Black 1987; Bullock and Lamb 1985; Woodward 1966). The creation of this legislation, called for in a special address by a southern Democratic president and passed by northern congressmen against the virulent opposition of their southern colleagues, created the potential for a substantial, lasting break between the national Democratic Party and the southern white voter. As Alexander Heard observed in his classic *A Two-Party South?*:

> [Southerners] cannot reasonably expect to influence the making of national policy more than conservative southerners already do in Congress. It is precisely if and when they lose this avenue of political expression that they will feel the greatest compulsion to break away . . . [to] the Republican Party. (1952, 247)

The Deep South acted on exactly such a compulsion in 1964 by supporting Barry Goldwater's 1964 presidential campaign. The details of Goldwater's appeals to southern whites are recounted elsewhere (Black and Black 1992; Bartley and Graham 1975), but, in sum, his appeal can be described as a meeting of Goldwater's deeply felt libertarian convictions about limited government and the appeal of the limited government as a codeword for segregation and rolling back federal intervention. Earl and Merle Black's recounting of Richard Rovere's assessment of Goldwater's appeal makes the point nicely:

> [Goldwater] did not, to be sure, make any direct racial appeals. He covered the South and never, in any public gatherings, mentioned "race" or "Negroes" or "whites" or "segregation" or "civil rights." But the fact that the words did not cross his lips does not mean that he ignored the realities they describe. He talked about them all the time in an . . . Aesopian language—a kind of code, that few in his audiences had any trouble deciphering. In the code, "bullies and marauders" means "Negroes." "States' Rights" means "opposition to civil rights." "Women" means "white women." This much of the code is as easily understood by his Northern audiences as by his Southern ones, but there are words that have a more limited and specific meaning for the Southern crowds. (1965, 143–44)

Goldwater was the stealth segregationist candidate, and the GOP was a vehicle for expressing displeasure with the national Democrats and Lyndon Johnson over integration and civil rights. As Key (1966) and Carmines and Stimson (1989) would argue from both sides of this event, the parties were differentiated on a clear, important issue, and voters would make a choice on issue lines. While Goldwater's candidacy had limited immediate impact on outcomes, it did redefine the Republican presidential strategy (see Aistrup 1996; Murphy and Gulliver 1971) and energized the southern Republican Party. The limits to the Goldwater-GOP appeal came in parts of the South where race was not the overarching issue of the day. For example, Goldwater ran far ahead of Johnson when race was the important issue with voters and, absent other issues, they overwhelmingly supported the GOP nominee. Especially in the Rim South, however, the race issue was overtaken by Goldwater's ill-conceived statements regarding federally funded technology and farm assistance programs, and social security. Peace, prosperity, and pork overcame the race card. However, the spadework was done for other Republican candidates under different circumstances (Black and Black 1992; Murphy and Gulliver 1971).

A place where the civil rights events of 1964 did affect the Republican Party was in the emergence of GOP candidates down-ticket. Republicans had been competing regularly in some southern states since the Reconstruction era—most notably in North Carolina and Tennessee. Regionally, however, the GOP had only contested about 30 percent of congressional seats in the decade before 1964; the postwar high up to 1964 was half of southern districts contested in 1948. From the postwar low of 20 percent of seats in 1958, Republican contestation grew steadily to almost 70 percent of seats by 1964. Republicans would not fail to contest at least 55 percent of southern congressional districts for the next three decades; for the decade of the 1990s, Republicans routinely contested over 80 percent of them.

1974: THE WATERGATE BACKLASH

Richard Nixon carried the electoral college vote of every southern state in 1972 and won over three-quarters of the white vote; additionally, Republicans achieved record numbers in southern Senate and House seats in the congressional elections of that year. Then, as quickly as those gains were achieved, Nixon's presidency came crashing down—and in many southern constituencies the Republican Party came tumbling after. The impact was most evident in North Carolina, where Republicans in the legislature virtually disappeared, and in Tennessee, where just four years prior the GOP had sat on the verge of majority control of the state house. Republicans lost a net of six U.S. House seats in the South. Two years later, the Democratic nominee for president, Jimmy Carter, carried ten of eleven southern states and down-ticket Democrats held their own against a recovering Republican Party.

The long-term impact of Watergate is questionable. By 1980 the GOP had almost fully recovered from its losses in 1974, and the Watergate impact appeared to lack depth. Nixon's resignation soon removed him as an issue, and, further, the decline of the domestic economy and the anemic foreign policy showings of the Carter administration placed the Democrats on the defensive. The political action of conservative political organizations prompted the fielding of numerous and well-financed GOP candidates for Congress, especially in the South. By the end of the 1970s, the Republicans were poised for a comeback in southern politics.

1980: REAGAN REALIGNMENT?

The 1980 presidential election is often viewed as a watershed event in southern politics. A southern Democratic president lost ten of eleven southern states in pursuit of reelection. The GOP also captured a net of four southern U.S. Senate seats and nine U.S. House seats, and made gains in many southern legislatures. These gains have been hailed as the coming of the long-awaited realignment (Norpoth 1987). The Reagan candidacy brought a coherence and focus to Republican politics that had been lacking in the post-Watergate era. Reagan's previous 1976 challenge for the GOP nomination had intended to recapture the party, even if the effort so badly split the GOP as to cost it the presidency (Black and Black 1992). In 1980, as the Republican nominee running against an embattled and unfocused Democratic incumbent, Reagan articulated a political vision that was attractive to southern whites: economy, community standards, responsibility, and less government. While Reagan's campaign may not have explicitly sought to exploit underlying racial sentiments, it did tap into the rhetorical divide between white conservatives and the national Democrats. Reagan and his articulation of the Republican vision, when contrasted against Carter's record in office, created a clear choice for southern voters. This would seem to be the basis for realignment.

The subsequent performance of Republican candidates down-ticket indicated that such an evaluation was perhaps premature. Republican gains in the U.S. Senate during the 1980–82 elections quickly eroded. By 1986 the GOP had returned to its 1978 level; Republicans made some gains in the House through 1984, then stagnated at about 35 percent of seats. Congressional Republicans had reached a dissatisfactory equilibrium (Theilemann 1992; Stanley 1992) and had not effectively built on (or even maintained) their gains in the South. The condition of realignment—critical, sustained departure from past patterns of partisanship—was not met in the 1980s. Realignment would have to wait for another day; as Harold Stanley (1992, 136) expressed in *Social Science Quarterly*, it appeared that the Republicans in the South "had fallen and could not get up."

1994: THE "NEWT DEAL"

It is far too soon to declare the political events of 1994 to be realignment. However, the empirical evidence supports a critical shift: a change in the congressional majority, dramatic gains by Republicans in governorships and state legislatures, and a shift in partisan identifiers, even in the South. Concurrent to the events of 1994 was a concerted effort by the Republican Party, especially Representative Newt Gingrich, to define the campaign on a collection of issues under the mantle of the "Contract with America." Was the collection of issues embodied in the Contract sufficient to constitute the basis for realignment? On one level, the answer is no. The issues discussed in the Contract were relatively arcane, and many voters had little notion of its content. On another, more superficial level, the Contract embodied and tapped the frustration of many voters with incumbent government, the failing of federal programs, tax revolt, and the general disaffection many voters had with incumbent Democrat Bill Clinton. Are these the bases of lasting partisan change or indicators of a temporary partisan deviation, as was Watergate?

DATA AND METHODS

How do secular trends and critical events enter the patterns of partisanship in southern politics? To answer this question, we first must decide what constitutes evidence of realignment. As we argued previously, the basis for realignment has usually rested on analysis of voter decisions—votes and outcomes. Studies of voting behavior indicate increasing instabilities in the relationship between partisan identification and voting decisions (Campbell et al. 1960; Nie, Verba, and Petrocik 1976; Epstein 1986). Additionally, it should be noted that polls do not decide elections or run government—votes and officeholders fill those functions. If we want to see how partisan trends translate into the end consequence of realignment—namely governing (Brady 1988)—we need to examine electoral outcomes.

What outcomes do we examine? Presidential voting in the South is extensively studied and sufficiently documented to the point that we have little to contribute there (see Black and Black 1992); the GOP has been the predominant presidential party in the South since 1980 and has won a vast majority of the South's electoral vote since the 1950s (Bullock 1988a). The Deep South made a critical movement away from the Democrats between the 1940s and 1960s (Nardulli 1995; Glazer 1996), but those effects were not evident down-ticket.

Rather than stop our exploration at this disjuncture, we move beyond it to examine patterns of partisan change at the legislative levels: U.S. Senate, U.S. House of Representatives, state senates, and state houses. This approach, previously used by Bullock (1988a) in his study of regional realignment, focuses on the stability and change of election outcomes rather than on partisan identifiers in polls and allows us to emphasize the end-point of realignment—changes in government or governing coalitions—that is the logical consequence of long-term partisan change. Republican strength is coded as the percent of all seats held by the GOP at each level of officeholding for 1944–96. To facilitate comparison of our officeholding findings with other indicators of partisan change, we also obtained data on partisan identification and senatorial and congressional voting by white southerners from the National Election Studies and subjected those data to the same analysis.

The technique we use is an interrupted time-series regression analysis. The use of this technique for assessing the impact of interventions over time is well established (Lewis-Beck and Alford 1980; Lewis-Beck 1980) and should allow us to get a more rigorous statistical picture of realignment in the South. We rely on ordinary least squares regression to test our model; however, autocorrelation was detected in three of our time-series; in those instances we reestimated the analysis using generalized least squares regression to correct for the potential validity threat from autocorrelation.

ANALYSIS

How do political events and secular trends structure southern partisanship? Bullock (1988a) demonstrated that much of southern political change could be explained by secular trends over time. We replicate his time-series analysis of officeholding and extend the analysis through 1996. A cursory examination of those results indicates that Bullock's (1988a) hypothesis of secular realignment in the South is substantiated. A tremendous amount of variation is explained by time for every time-series.[1] However, the existence of a secular trend does not preclude the existence of critical events that affected partisanship in the long term.

In Table 1.1, we present analyses of each time-series of legislative officeholding which controls for both time and the intervention of potentially critical events in southern politics: the 1954 *Brown* decision; the 1964 Civil Rights Act and Goldwater's campaign; the 1974 Watergate aberration; the 1980 Reagan landslide; and the 1994 midterm election. The effect of time is represented by

Table 1.1
Secular Effects and Critical Events in the South: Officeholding Data 1944–96

	U.S. Senate	*U.S. House*	*State Senate*	*State House*
Intercept	- .02	-1.29	-7.93	-3.58
Temporal Counter	.005 (1.34)	1.52 (.34)*	2.01 (.51)*	1.43 (.26)*
1954 Event	1.96 (5.17)	-2.34 (2.41)	-2.88 (1.76)*	-3.41 (1.86)*
1964 Event	11.35 (5.46)*	9.02 (2.35)*	.28 (1.75)	2.21 (1.81)
1974 Event	.71 (5.17)	-3.67 (2.37)	-6.22 (1.76)*	-5.46 (1.83)*
1980 Event	9.08 (5.5)*	1.39 (2.5)	1.72 (1.87)	.08 (1.93)*
1994 Event	19.24 (5.74)*	12.59 (2.63)*	6.62 (1.95)*	7.96 (2.03)*
Adjusted R^2	.81	.97	.92	.97
Durbin-Watson	1.48	2.23	2.01	1.56

* $p < .05$, one-tailed test.
Note: N = 27; standard errors in parentheses.
Source: Calculated by the authors.

the counter initialized to zero in 1944 and increasing by one for each two-year election cycle. The critical interventions are represented by a series of dummy variables, coded zero before the intervention and one for the intervention and years after. This specification produces an interrupted time-series model.[2] The time-series for the U.S. Senate and state senates contained first-order autocorrelation, which was corrected using generalized least squares.[3] The model uncovers some interesting differences in the movement of partisan strength across the different levels of officeholding. We proceed by discussing the findings of our analysis for each level of officeholding.

CHANGE IN THE SENATE

The gains by the GOP in the South have been most dramatic in the U.S. Senate. It is here that the GOP has also demonstrated its greatest volatility. In 1960 there were no southern Republicans in the U.S. Senate. By 1972 Republicans held a third of southern seats; by 1982, that proportion was half. After the 1986 elections, Republicans were down to a quarter of southern seats. Currently about 68 percent of southern U.S. Senate seats are occupied by Republicans.

Bullock's (1988a) analysis indicated that the growth of the GOP in the Senate was secular in nature; Republicans were gaining seats gradually over time. Our analysis paints a very different picture. The results of the U.S. Senate regression analysis appear in Table 1.1.[4] The regression analysis explains over 80 percent of the variance—but the temporal counter has a nearly flat slope and is insignificant. Increased Republican Senate representation in the South thus appears to have been driven by two critical events: the 1964 civil rights intervention and the 1994 elections. The 1980 Reagan intervention fails to reach significance at conventional levels (t = 1.65), indicating that 1980 was not an important intervention.

What might explain this lack of a significant temporal effect? The research of Abramowitz and Segal (1993), Mann and Wolfinger (1980), and Abramowitz (1980b) offer similar, relevant explanations. The nature of Senate elections is that they are high-profile and more closely wedded to national political events than are U.S. House and local contests. The period 1964–68 was characterized by differentiation between the national and local Democratic parties, and Senate seats were more closely identified with the national Democrats. If partisan shifts are going to occur, and the basis of those shifts is found in national politics, it of course stands to reason that the impact of those changing partisan preferences will first be felt in the most national contests, in this case the Senate.

CAPTURING THE HOUSE

Nowhere was Republican frustration more evident in the South than in the U.S. House of Representatives. For almost two decades the GOP blamed a variety of factors—particularly campaign finance, incumbency, and redistricting—for its inability to obtain a majority of southern congressional seats. Now the GOP holds over 55 percent of southern seats, with almost half of these seats having been gained from 1992 to 1996. Southern GOP representation in the House has shown less volatility than the U.S. Senate. Southern Republican emergence in the House predates Senate representation by over a decade and, until 1972, the GOP held a greater proportion of southern U.S. House seats than U.S. Senate seats. The great gain of Senate seats by Republicans in the early 1980s was not replicated in the House; instead, southern Republicans were stuck at about one-third of southern seats through 1990. Then, during the period 1990–96 Republican House representation from the South increased almost 20 points.

Secular effects and critical event effects are evident in the U.S. House time-series. Controlling for critical events, the southern Republican caucus has increased by about 1.5 percent in every election; the relationship is highly significant. There are also two critical events at work in the House: the 1964 election and the 1994 election, just as we observed in the Senate time-series. We will return to the importance of this finding later in our discussion of the results of the analysis. It is interesting to note that no significant negative impact by Watergate appeared. Our initial suspicion was that multicollinearity had possibly inflated the error term for the 1974 intervention. A subsequent examination of variance inflation factors indicated that there was no substantive problem with multicollinearity; tolerances were within acceptable limits. Additionally, as we will observe below, Watergate did have an impact further down-ticket.

STATE SENATES AND STATE HOUSES

There have been very similar patterns of GOP officeholding in the two chambers of most state legislatures over time; GOP strength is virtually indistinguishable in the upper and lower chambers of these bodies except for the period between 1972 and 1992, when the levels of Republican officeholding in the House was consistently two to three points higher than in the Senate. Throughout that period, however, state house and senate seats follow an identical pattern. Republicans underwent a period of brief, rapid growth from the fringe in the 1960s, fell off during the mid-1970s, and in the 1980s began a sustained climb to the point where, by 1997, Republicans held 41 percent of seats at each level.

With one exception (explained below), the state senate and state house analysis are remarkably similar.[5] The secular realigning effects evident in the U.S. House are again seen here. The slope is more pronounced for upper chamber ($b = 2.01$ versus $b = 1.43$ for the state house) but the intercept (unrealistically negative) indicates that the GOP had greater ground to cover in the state senates.[6]

The state legislative analyses reveal a small but significant impact by the 1954 intervention on partisanship: Democrats actually realized a partisan shift to their advantage after 1954. Given the anemic levels of Republicanism in these states' localities, this small shift represents a near-total suppression of the GOP at the state legislative level. There is no significant impact by the 1964 intervention on state legislatures; the slope coefficients are quite small compared to the U.S. Senate and U.S. House analyses, and compared to their standard errors do not even begin to approach significance. No doubt the low level of GOP candidacies had much to do with this outcome, as Aistrup (1990) notes in his compelling presentation of Republican legislative competition.

In the 1970s the state legislatures start to respond to critical events. Watergate resulted in a falloff of over 6 percent in state senates and almost 5.5 percent in state houses. These impacts were not evenly distributed; for example, in North Carolina the Republican legislative delegations were virtually wiped out, while in the Deep South states the low levels of GOP officeholding ensured that the few GOP legislators were from Republican strongholds. The slope of the temporal counters indicates that it would take three to four elections for the GOP to recover to its pre-Watergate levels, or approximately until 1980. The Watergate-era intervention, in fact, set back Republican state legislative gains in the South by approximately a decade. The Reagan election of 1980 produced a significant, lasting shift to the favor of Republicans in state house seats. However, it was not until 1994 that a significant intervention occurred that affected both state house and state senate elections that also resulted in a representative gain for southern Republicans. The 1994 intervention also produced the greatest shift in state legislatures, producing a net shift of just under eight points in state houses and almost seven points in state senates.

ANOTHER PERSPECTIVE: CONGRESSIONAL VOTING

We also examine the available survey data, noting its limitations, to see if our hypothesis is substantiated with this less reliable data. The National Election Studies for the years 1956–96 provides some useful evidence. First, only the responses of white Southerners are considered; the 1960s represented a critical mobilization of black voters, and overwhelming numbers of black southerners still vote Democratic (Wolfinger and Hagen 1985; Black and Black 1987). The population most at risk for realignment to the GOP—southern whites—is our object of interest, and data on their voting behavior over time merits our attention. We therefore extend our temporal/critical events model to examine aggregate survey responses in order to see if the findings for officeholding are reflected in these other data over time. Two questions asked by the National Election Studies are used to operationalize southern partisan behavior for analysis: the voter's preference in U.S. House races, and the voter's preference in U.S. Senate elections.

As shown in our analyses in Table 1.1, there is support for the secular realignment of voter behavior. However, less variation in the survey data is explained by time, unlike in the officeholding analyses, indicating less initial support for secular realignment of white southerners.[7] The intervention dummy variables are then entered into the equations, the results of which appear in Table 1.2. This analysis, comparable to that for officeholding in Table 1.1, indicates support of our hypothesis that critical events and secular change may simultaneously be at work in the South.

NES survey data for the Senate is only available continuously for the years 1964–96. The regression analysis, with the 1974, 1980, and 1994 interventions, does a poor job of explaining the variance. The temporal counter is not significant and, in fact, moves in a negative direction. It should be noted, however, that the 1994 intervention is significant. In fact, 1994 is revealed as the sole significant explanatory variable. The 1980 intervention does not come close to being

Table 1.2
Secular Effects and Critical Events in the South: Survey Data 1956–96

	Votes for Republican in U.S. Senate 1964–96	*Votes for Republican in U.S. House 1956–96*
Intercept	34.65	19.0
Temporal Counter	-.24 (1.26)	.89 (.83)
1964 Event	—	3.53 (5.33)
1974 Event	5.58 (7.73)	-3.32 (5.3)
1980 Event	2.29 (8.39)	4.35 (5.7)
1994 Event	17.20 (8.58)*	18.84 (3.08)*
Adjusted R^2	.29	.78
Durbin-Watson	1.52	1.95
N	17	21

* $p < .05$, one-tailed test.
Note: Standard errors in parentheses.
Source: Calculated by authors from the National Election Studies, 1956–96.

significant, despite significant GOP gains in the Senate and evidence of a Republican spike in GOP voting in 1980. Apparently the change in white voter preferences in 1980 was transient, undercutting further the arguments that Reagan caused realignment. When we look at an analysis of the House, we detect similar results. Time is not significant in the multivariate estimate. Again, 1994 is the only significant explanatory variable, and the model explains 78 percent of the variance. One possible explanation for these results in both the House and Senate voting is the impact of multicollinearity in the time-series specification. The temporal counter is plagued by multicollinearity from the inclusion of several intervention controls. However, these controls have not precluded the counter from attaining significance in any of the officeholding analyses, so we must consider the possibility that realignment in voting is not about time.

OBSERVATIONS ON CRITICAL EVENTS

These findings lead to some observations about events and secular trends that will help frame our final discussion. When political analysts look for realignment, they usually search for step realignments, the sudden, long-lasting shifts in partisanship characterized by the New Deal. There has been a tendency to be impatient for realignment and to declare realignment at any partisan blip (see Norpoth 1987; Wattenburg 1987; McSeveney 1991; Meyerson 1992). The one certainty we have is that political systems are afflicted by shocks—political scientist John Sprague's term for critical events—that change the partisan balance.[8] Sprague's analysis of changes in the partisan balance of the U.S. House of Representatives between 1930 and 1970 assumed the existence of a steady-state equilibrium in the national political system. In the South, the steady state is not so easy to establish because at most levels of officeholding and party competition, dynamic change is the steady state: there is no static equilibrium. So how do critical events incorporate themselves into a secular realignment that is already under way?

This circumstance has implications for the impact of critical events on partisan change. Sprague assumes that a shock would initially throw the party system away from equilibrium, the decay of the impact of the shock would return the parties to the steady state. With the system in a state of dynamic change when significant events occur, the impact of the intervention may create a different response. The presence of a secular realigning trend means that the direction of the partisan shock will have different impacts on the political system. Shocks that run in the direction opposite to the secular trend have a short life; almost immediately the system resumes its secular course, and within a few elections the impact of the deviating critical events are overtaken by the original secular trend. These events are little more than speed bumps for secular realignment, and in fact have probably had their overall impact tempered by a counter-prevailing long-term trend. A stark contrast is the political shock that runs in the same direction as a secular trend. When a secular realignment is underway and additional shocks occur that reinforce the secular trend, the impact is an acceleration of the secular trend. These reinforcing critical events are the superchargers of political change. They jump the secular trend forward in a manner like step realignment, and then the secular trend resumes, thereby exhibiting a pattern similar to a dynamic change model.

The last type of event we could expect in the presence of a secular trend is one that is unobserved in our analysis: the true dramatic realigning event. The dramatic realigning event will not only disrupt the secular trend, as does the deviating critical event; it will actually arrest the secular trend or turn it in the opposite direction.

Our analysis supports this designation of political events and their impact in a dynamic system. Of the five events we identified and specified in the regression equation, all had some impact on the dynamic of partisan change. None of these events disrupted the long-term secular trend toward the GOP. Two of the events—the 1954 and 1974 interventions—created short-term deviations from secular trends; in all instances the secular realignment resumes within two elections. Of the other three events, two (1964 and 1994) had a substantial, significant enhancing effect of GOP growth. Of the eight significant enhancing interventions we observed, none was followed by a lasting falloff in GOP strength. These interventions were associated with prominent GOP gains.

REALIGNMENT AS GOVERNING

A roundtable discussion at the 1997 Southern Political Science Association meeting made its way to the question "What is a standard for realignment?" Earl Black, in his response to the question, indicated that we certainly could not hold up the level of domination enjoyed by Democrats before the 1960s as a standard for GOP success. The inclusiveness of the modern southern electorate precludes such domination. In the place of overwhelming dominance, Black brought a new standard to the table: the real evidence of realignment is governing, which the GOP is some distance from attaining in much of the South—or is it?

At the congressional level the jury is in, should current patterns sustain themselves—and there is no current indication that they will not. Not only does the GOP have a commanding majority in both the House and Senate from the South, but most congressional leadership is from the South, including the major floor leadership and several prominent committee chairmen. The change in majority party, dependent in large part on the sustained shift in partisan outcomes in the South, has led to a departure in the policy imperatives and options available in crafting legislation. The internal structure of the institution of Congress changed with a new majority party. The outcomes of the policy process—welfare reform, changes in the tax code, a balanced budget—resulted from the change in majority congressional party (Brady 1988). Whatever would constitute more compelling evidence of realignment as government at the federal level eludes us.

With regard to governing in the states, the Republicans control only six southern legislative chambers, including complete control of the Florida legislature. In the period 1994–96, the Republicans attained their highest level of state legislative success since Reconstruction in ten southern states (the only exception being Tennessee). In only ten of twenty-two chambers do the Republicans hold less than 40 percent of seats, and in only four are they at less than 30 percent. This is a substantial change from just six years earlier, when the GOP was below 40 percent of seats in 20 chambers and below 30 percent in 14 of them. Currently, a change of 12 or fewer seats in 13 legislatures would lead to Republican majorities; in seven of those chambers the seat change needed is six or less (see Table 1.3).

Table 1.3
Partisan Composition of Individual Southern Legislatures

	Percent GOP 1991	*Percent GOP 1997*	*Net Change 1991–97*	*GOP Seats for Majority*
House				
Alabama	21.9	33.3	+11.4	18
Arkansas	11.4	14.0	+2.6	37
Florida	39.2	55.2	+16.0	—
Georgia	20.0	43.9	+23.9	12
Louisiana	17.1	26.7	+9.6	25
Mississippi	7.3	29.5	+22.2	26
North Carolina	30.8	50.8	+20.0	—
South Carolina	33.8	56.5	+22.7	—
Tennessee	36.3	38.4	+2.1	12
Texas	25.6	45.3	+19.7	8
Virginia	39.0	48.0	+9.0	3
Senate				
Alabama	20.0	37.1	+17.1	5
Arkansas	9.0	20.0	+11.0	11
Florida	47.5	57.5	+10.0	—
Georgia	19.6	39.2	+19.6	7
Louisiana	15.3	35.8	+20.5	6
Mississippi	15.3	32.6	+17.3	10
North Carolina	28.0	40.0	+12.0	6
South Carolina	23.9	45.7	+21.8	3
Tennessee	42.4	45.5	+3.1	2
Texas	38.0	54.8	+26.8	—
Virginia	25.0	50.0	+25.0	1

Source: Data compiled by authors.

The likelihood of continued GOP gains are high. Our analysis indicates that there is a long-term secular growth of Republican representation at state legislative levels that has been isolated, until recently, from the major critical events that were supposed to help Republicans. Further, the nationalization of southern politics down-ticket opens up the door to enhanced effects by presidential coattails. Campbell (1986) and Chubb (1988) both found that state legislative seat swings were tied to presidential coattails and to surge and decline patterns. Chubb excluded southern states from his analysis, while Campbell analyzed trends in seven southern states and uncovered evidence of presidential coattails in five (Florida, Georgia, North Carolina, Tennessee, and Texas, but not South Carolina or Arkansas). It is reasonable to expect that the combination of increased Republican competitiveness down ticket and the convergence of Republican partisanship at different levels of analysis will lead to further responsiveness by state legislative elections to trends that favor Republicans, such as midterm elections when the president is of the Democratic Party.

CONCLUSION: TAKING 1994 IN PERSPECTIVE

Whether the 1994 elections truly mark a partisan realignment is an issue still far too early to declare definitively. Shifts in indicators of partisan strength in 1994 and 1996, however, when compared to the long time-series of southern politics, lends greater support for realignment than any previous election or series of elections. The 1994 election appears to be, at the very least, a reinforcing critical event. Is there evidence for declaring realignment in 1994? The following discussion sheds some light on the idea of a midterm regional realignment in 1994.

Top-to-Bottom Partisan Shifts. The 1994 election and its aftermath constitute the only intervention in the post–World War II era that had a significant impact on the senatorial, congressional, and state legislative levels respectively, in the South. The 1994 realignment also had a significant impact on Senate and congressional voting by southern whites. No other intervention in the time-series had an impact that reached this deep into the politics of the South, or did so with such consistency.

The Magnitude of 1994. Other significant interventions in southern politics have been to the benefit of the GOP; however, none had as substantial an impact as the intervention of 1994. The 1964 election had a significant and positive impact on the Republican presence in the U.S. Senate and House but did not impact down-ticket into state legislative contests. The 1980 Reagan election had a marginally significant impact on Senate elections and state house officeholding, but not on congressional or state senate races. The 1994 intervention is the largest, most significant intervention for every officeholding time-series. The magnitude of impact is greatest at the federal level, being most significant in U.S. Senate elections, followed by U.S. House contests. The impact on state legislative contests is less than in federal contests, but still represents the biggest impact on state legislative contests during the period under study.

Congruence and Sustainability. The effects of 1994 carried into 1996 at all electoral levels and brought GOP legislative representation in the South into high congruence. Republican state legislative officeholding still lags behind that in the U.S. Senate and U.S. House, by 27 and 15 points respectively; however, state legislative representation is in close congruence with partisan identification among southern whites,[9] indicating that southern white partisanship is expressing itself in consistent fashion up and down the ticket. To echo the work of Black and Black (1987), the GOP has finally moved out of the quiescent stage in southern politics at all legislative levels. Republicans are genuinely competitive on a regionwide basis at all electoral levels. While this shift is not necessarily a change to a new majority, the continuation of a shift in the partisan balance of at least thirty points at every level of legislative representation is consistent with the empirical expectations of realignment.

Critical Event or Critical Realignment? This last point is the one that is most vexing. Our historical perspective on realignment allowed scholars to select the great defining issues of the day to characterize realignments. Substantial scholarship has pointed to the dramatic role of the slave issue in defining the political shifts of the 1850s and 1860s (Burnham 1970; Nardulli, 1995). Similarly, the economic upheavals of 1893–96 are attributed to the combination of blaming the Democratic Party for the 1893 depression and the antipopulist shift in eastern U.S. politics. Also, the New Deal realignment was defined by the Great Depression and the subsequent demand for government intervention in the economy.

The elections of the 1990s defy this easy, definitive critical issue approach to categorizing realignment, even in the South. Was it term limits and incumbent dissatisfaction, or was it more likely the resurgence of race as an issue that was witnessed in several southern states after 1990? Perhaps the characterization of the Democratic Party as the "party of big government" finally took hold, prompting southerners to a reaction similar to that described in Black and Black's thesis on presidential elections. Alternatively, it may have been redistricting. The potential culprits in this mystery, in short, are numerous. If previous realignments have been characterized by big issues that created cross-cutting cleavages that undermined the existing party alignments, the elections of the 1990s might be characterized as realignment by a hundred cuts—none individually critical or harmful, but collectively representing a significant and enhanced threat to the Democratic Party and its legacy of power in the South.

NOTES

1. The bivariate regressions of time onto Republican office-holding produced the following results for 1944–96:

	U.S. Senate	*U.S. House*	*State Senate*	*State House*
Intercept	-9.02	-3.36	-5.61	-5.40
Temporal Counter	2.35	1.96	1.33	1.44
	(.21)*	(.11)*	(.12)*	(.09)*
Adjusted-R^2	.83	.93	.83	.92

The N = 27 for all of the time-series, and standard errors appear in the parentheses below the slopes. Asterisks (*) indicate significance at a .05 level using a one-tailed test.

2. The same model is used in each regression analysis.

3. Because the same independent variables are used in each analysis, for the same observations, the potential for multicollinearity is the same for all of the analyses. Variance inflation factors were examined to determine the impact of multicollinearity on the model. None of the VIFs exceeded a value of 5 for the intervention dummy variables, but the VIF for the counter was 26, indicating that the error term for the temporal counter was inflated, raising the possibility of a type 2 error. The counter attains significance in three of the four officeholding time-series, and, in the one series where it is not significant, the slope of the counter is virtually flat (b = .005). Because multicollinearity affects error terms, and not coefficients, the impact of multicollinearity is not sufficient to lead to erroneous determinations of significance in our analysis.

4. The U.S. Senate analysis contained first-order autocorrelation. Generalized least squares regression (GLS) was used to reestimate the regression parameters and correct for the impact of autocorrelation (see also Lewis-Beck and Alford 1980).

5. The state senate analysis was corrected for first-order autocorrelation using generalized least squares regression.

6. Again, we had to correct for first-order autocorrelation in the state senate analysis.

7. The results of those bivariate regressions are:

	Vote for Republican in U.S. Senate	*Votes for Republican in U.S. House*
Intercept	21.98	16.68
Temporal Counter	1.42	1.58
	(.31)*	(.26)*
Adjusted-R^2	.51	.65

N = 20 for Senate Vote, 21 for House vote. Standard errors appear in the parentheses below the slopes. Asterisks (*) indicate significance at a .05 level using a one-tailed test. Data sources are the National Election Studies, 1952–96.

8. Sprague's (1980) discussion of the long-term Democratic domination of the U.S. Congress rested on two explanations: the relative advantage of Democrats in retaining seats over time (incumbent security) and the direction and magnitude of shocks to the political system.

9. The 1996 NES indicates that, among white voters, the number of GOP leaners and GOP identifiers is roughly 41 percent of the electorate.

2

What You See Is . . . Essentially . . . What You Get: House Races in the Contemporary South

STANLEY P. BERARD AND DAVID W. ROHDE

The three-election sequence of 1992–96, together with party switches and special elections during the period, produced a net gain of 38 seats for the Republicans in southern delegations to the U.S. House. This shift was of historic proportions, bringing as it did the first Republican majority since Reconstruction to the southern House delegation. It is typically viewed as part of a long-term realignment of southern politics that is progressing inexorably from the presidential level to lower electoral levels. Projecting this trend to future elections, it is difficult to avoid the conclusion that the outcome will be the development of overwhelming Republican electoral majorities at all electoral levels everywhere, from presidential to state house elections, from Texas to Virginia. With regard to the House of Representatives, however, we come to a somewhat different conclusion: Partisan competition for House seats in the South has reached a point at which Republican seat losses are as likely as Republican seat gains, particularly over the course of several elections. That is, the distribution of southern House seats between Democrats and Republicans is now within range of a long-term equilibrium, around which it will fluctuate from election to election due to short-term factors.

Our conclusion rests on the nature of party competition in the South today. Described in the language of spatial approaches (Downs 1957), party primary constituents and activists are consistent across states and regions in their deviation from local medians—Democrats are consistently left of the median and Republicans consistently right. As a result, in congressional elections the opportunity to select a Democrat to the right of the district median or a Republican to the left is exceedingly rare. Within each party's nominating process, however, the potential exists to select candidates at varying distances from the district median. The Democratic nominee in a given district might be anywhere in a range from extremely liberal to moderate, and the Republican nominee might be anything from moderate to extremely conservative. In any congressional district, the attractiveness to the median voter of the two parties' candidates is interdependent because the candidates are evaluated in relation to one another. Candidates seen as more moderate relative to their district will have an advantage in the general election over those perceived as more extreme. These dynamics give the Democrats the capacity to continue fielding credible candidates and winning elections in a variety of districts, including many that appear most promising for Republican candidates.

In this chapter, we first explicate these dynamics and the district contexts in which they operate. Then, we report how these dynamics operated in 1996 in a number of congressional districts. Finally, we consider how long-term electoral and demographic trends reinforce our argument, and how short-term forces will produce fluctuations around the long-term equilibrium.

COMPETITIVE PARTIES AND ELECTORAL DYNAMICS

Theoretical Considerations

The rise of the Republican Party in the South is part of a change in the fundamental character of electoral choices in the region. This fundamental change can be described using the language of spatial models (Downs 1957), with which parties and candidates are described in terms of their distance from the median voter. We also apply the findings of Fiorina (1974) and others regarding the effect of the heterogeneity of constituencies on legislative behavior. A homogeneous constituency constrains candidates to support the constituency median position if they wish to be elected, and a representative from a homogenous constituency is constrained to take the constituency position if he or she wishes to survive future elections. Heterogeneous constituencies are more likely to generate party competition and more likely to produce party support coalitions occupying distinctive issue positions. In two-party competition, each party's median voter will deviate from the district median in a different direction. The more heterogeneous the district, the greater the likely deviation of the parties from the median voter of the district. Using the language of Fenno (1978), the median voter of a representative's "reelection" constituencies does not hold the same position as the median voter of the "geographic" constituency, and this deviation is likely to be greater in districts that support more sharply differentiated parties.

Taking this a step further, reelection constituencies—and primary electorates that are a subset of reelection constituencies—can also vary in their heterogeneity. Homogenous primary constituencies give candidates for the party nomination incentive to stay close to the preferences of that constituency and give incumbents clear cues as to the positions that will reduce the risk of a primary challenge. For incumbents representing heterogeneous primary constituencies, a ready-made base for a primary challenge is always present. In open-seat elections, heterogeneous primary constituencies will generate primary candidacies representing a range of issue positions. It is important to note here that a more heterogeneous party can produce nominees for office that vary in their distance from the district median voter and thus vary in their attractiveness to the general electorate.

The Rise of Competitive Party Politics in the South

The dramatic Republican gains in southern congressional elections of the 1990s are a culmination of a long transition from the one-party electoral structure of the Solid South era to two-party competition. Before the 1960s, the Democrats almost totally dominated congressional elections in the South. For instance, in 1960 Democrats won 111 of 120 southern House seats. As late as 1958, 85 Democratic incumbents had no opposition (Squire 1989, 283). Under these conditions, the primary electorate in many southern Democratic districts was almost identical to that for the general election. Factional competition within the party replaced two-party competition, but factional politics rarely provided the basis for a differentiation of the electorate into durable groupings with distinctive aggregations of issue attitudes (Key 1949, 11–12, 15–19). This undifferentiated electorate was largely conservative, owing to the active disfranchisement of blacks and the low rates of participation among lower-status whites.

In the 1990s, the undifferentiated southern electorate of the 1950s was transformed into one exhibiting competition between parties characterized by distinctive sets of issue attitudes among their supporters. A critical factor in this transformation was mobilization of African-American voters. By 1969 the voter registration rate among voting-age southern blacks had increased to 64.8 percent; it had been 35.5 percent in 1964, just before passage of the 1965 Voting Rights Act. In the same period, white registration increased from 73.4 to 83.5 percent (Lawson 1976, 331). While some have characterized the increase in white voter registration as a conservative countermobilization, Stanley (1987) concludes that the increase in white voting was due to increased levels of education among whites and not to a racial backlash. In any event, registration rates among African Americans approached those among whites by the late 1980s: In the eleven-state South in 1988, black voter registration was 63.7 percent, compared to the white registration rate of 67 percent (Conway 1991, 108). Given the substantial differences between blacks and whites in their attitudes on economic, social welfare, and race-related questions, black voter mobilization represented a substantial liberalization of the southern electorate on these issues (Black and Black 1987, 216–19; Lamis 1984, 218–21).

The mobilization of the southern black voters occurred mostly within the Democratic Party. In this regard, black voting behavior in the 1964 election fits the classic definition of a "critical election" (Key 1955). The clarity of the national parties' stands on civil rights issues was associated with a sharp increase among blacks in concern with the election. The ranks of black Democrats in the South were increased both by the mobilization of new voters and by the conversion of many voters from the Republicans (Campbell 1977b). The new partisan alignment among southern blacks has persisted through the participation gains that followed the Voting Rights Act and on to today. In elections since 1964, it has been typical for over 80 percent of blacks to report supporting Democratic candidates for president and Congress.

That black voters have predominantly Democratic loyalties is especially significant in light of the rise of the Republican Party. By the late 1970s, the Republican Party in the South had become transformed from a minor party, nonexistent in some areas, into a party of roughly equal strength in the white electorate with the Democrats. Initially, Republican growth in the 1950s and 1960s was attributable to upper-status northern migrants in urban areas, but over time in-migration accounted for an ever-decreasing proportion of Republican identification (Stanley 1988; Campbell 1977b). The changing party balance in the 1960s and 1970s was driven by the behavior of native white southerners (Beck 1977; Stanley 1988). White southerners' departure from their historic identification with the Democratic Party was partly contingent on their social status: In the new southern party system, the Republicans tend to be the party of higher status whites, and the Democrats tend to be the party of lower status whites. By the late 1980s, the Democratic advantage in party identification among whites was undermined even in the black belt of the Deep South states, which had been the traditional core of conservative Democratic politics (Nadeau and Stanley 1993).

The realignment of southern whites had consequences for the balance of issue positions represented by each party. During the 1970s and 1980s, people who considered themselves conservative constituted a steadily decreasing proportion of white southern Democrats (Black and Black 1987, 249–56). Southern conservatives were moving to the Republican Party: Democrats held an 11 percent advantage in party identification over Republicans among southerners who called themselves conservative in 1972, but by 1984 the Republicans held a 32 percent advantage among conservatives. Meanwhile, the Democrats retained a 34-point advantage among southern whites who considered themselves moderate or liberal (Carmines and Stanley 1990, 26). The movement of conservative white southerners to the Republican Party is also reflected on specific issues: In the South, as in the North, Democrats are likely to favor and Republicans are likely to oppose increased government social spending on items like welfare and education and government policies intended to increase employment and assist minorities. White southerners with conservative positions on such issues have gradually defected to the Republican Party (Carmines and Stanley 1990, 27–29).

A similar ideological sorting accompanied the realignment of southern party elites.[1] Attitudes on issues were found to be the best predictor of party switching in a study of delegates to southern state party conventions (Nesbit 1988). Among Republican precinct representatives, former Democrats were particularly conservative (Bowman, Hulbary, and Kelley 1990). In a 1991 survey, county-level party committee members who were converts to the Democratic

Party were substantially more liberal than lifelong Democratic activists on several issues: support for government aid to minorities, affirmative action, abortion rights, and opposition to school prayer and to increased defense spending. Among Republican activists, party switchers were substantially more conservative than lifelong partisans on abortion and school prayer. This was especially true of activists who became Republicans after 1979 (Prysby 1992).

Among southern contributors to political action committees, those who have switched to the Republican Party tend to be more conservative than those who have always been Republicans, especially on social issues. Contributors converting to the Democratic Party are more liberal than those they have joined in their attitudes toward abortion, gay rights, gun control, and federal welfare programs. New members of both southern parties among financial contributors tend to be more conservative than their northern counterparts, but these regional differences are much smaller than the differences between new and old party members within the South (Green and Guth 1990).

The effects of party switchers on the ideological composition of party activists are matched by the effects of newer generations of party activists. Among county party committee members, younger Democratic activists were less likely than older Democrats to give conservative responses to questions on aid to minorities, affirmative action, abortion, school prayer, and defense spending. Younger Republican activists were more likely than older Republicans to give conservative responses to questions on abortion, government aid to minorities, and affirmative action, as well as on government spending, the role of government in providing jobs, and government's role in financing health care (Shaffer and Breaux 1992).

In sum, party switching and generational change have increased the distance between the parties among politically active Southerners as well as among the broader electorate. The rise of party competition in congressional elections means that this ideologically differentiated electorate chooses officeholders in two stages—primary elections and general elections. In the typical southern state or congressional electorate, the reelection and primary constituencies of Republicans are distinctly more conservative than the electorate as a whole, and the reelection and primary constituencies of Democrats are distinctly less conservative. As a result, in districts with competitive parties, Democratic primaries should generate candidates who hold issue positions that are at least somewhat more liberal than those of the median voter, and Republican primaries should generate candidates who are at least somewhat more conservative than the median voter (see Aldrich 1995, 182–92).

Interparty Dynamics

The next step in the analysis is to recognize that the degree to which Republican nominees are conservative relative to their districts and to which Democratic nominees are liberal relative to their districts varies across districts and over time. The Democratic nominee in a given district might be anywhere in a range from extremely liberal to moderate, and the Republican nominee might be anything from moderate to extremely conservative. Voters evaluate candidates in relation to one another. Which candidate is more representative of the voter? Which candidate will be more effective in representing the district? The party nominee who can be portrayed as more moderate relative to the district will have an advantage in the general election over an opposing party nominee perceived as more extreme.

We are familiar with the portrayal of Democratic candidates as being "too liberal" for their districts and "out of touch" with the attitudes of their constituents. Theoretically, Republicans as well as Democrats can be defeated for such a reason. This could be practically, if not explicitly, an expression of the representative/candidate being "too conservative" for the district. One can insist that this possibility is only hypothetical: How could a representative or candidate be "too conservative" for a southern congressional district, particularly one dominated by native white voters? We answer that ample evidence exists of the interdependence of candidate evaluations working to the advantage of Democratic candidates.

Democratic candidates have successfully portrayed Republicans as "too conservative" for their districts in a variety of situations. When Democrat Bill Nelson of Florida decided to give up his House seat to seek the party nomination for governor in 1990, the Republicans considered it an excellent opportunity. The district was solidly Republican in presidential races and had sent Republicans to the House from its 1962 creation until Nelson's election in 1978. Their nominee was Bill Tolley, a conservative anti-abortion activist. Democrat Jim Bacchus portrayed Tolley as an extremist and won the race with 52 percent. After compiling a record as a more loyal Democrat than Nelson had been, Bacchus faced Tolley again in 1992 in a district that had been made less favorable to Democrats by redistricting. Bacchus won the rematch with 51 percent, again portraying Tolley as too extreme. Republicans were finally able to take the seat in 1994, when Bacchus did not seek reelection (Rohde 1996).[2]

In the Alabama Sixth District, former Democratic state representative Ben Erdreich managed in 1982 to take a seat that had been in Republican hands since 1964. The incumbent was Albert Lee Smith, who was serving his first term and who had developed a reputation for constituency service. Erdreich attacked Reaganomics and the amount of attention Smith devoted to an anti-abortion, anti-busing and pro–school prayer agenda. Not only did Erdreich win the seat (with 53 percent) in 1982; he defended it until 1992, when redistricting made the seat far less favorable to a Democratic candidate (Rohde 1991, 14; Rohde 1996).

The Fourth District of North Carolina was won from the Democrats in 1984 by Bill Cobey, a very conservative Republican who won a narrow victory in part due to the personal problems of the incumbent. In 1986 Cobey faced Democratic nominee David Price, who emphasized Cobey's "extreme" voting record (Rohde 1991, 14). Price won the seat with 56 percent of the vote. In 1994

Price lost to Republican Fred Heineman by fewer than two thousand votes but returned to defeat Heineman in 1996 by 54 to 44 percent.

In all of these cases, the portrayal of Republican nominees as too conservative was a central component of the Democrat's appeal. Of course, Democratic incumbents must also fend off the Republican charge that they are too extreme for their districts, but they have a record of success in doing so. They can often point to conservative positions they have taken, like support for a balanced budget amendment or strong positions on crime. Establishing visible links with other conservative Democrats, through the Conservative Democratic Forum or in recent years the "blue dogs," is another tactic. Compared to national Democratic leaders, southern Democratic representatives following this strategy are less easily portrayed as unrepresentative of southern voters (Rohde 1991, 15).

Like incumbent representatives, Democratic nonincumbents also have a record of success in positioning themselves closer than their Republican opponents to district median opinion by making conservative issue themes an important part of their message. Glaser (1996, 80–141) describes such efforts, all of them successful, by five white Democratic candidates in special elections during the 1980s: Wayne Dowdy in the Fourth District of Mississippi, Glen Browder in Alabama's Third District, Jim Chapman in the First District of Texas, L.F. Payne in the Virginia Fifth District, and Gene Taylor in the Fifth District of Mississippi. Democrats continue to have a measure of success in these districts. Taylor continues to be reelected to his Mississippi seat as a Democrat. Chapman and Payne retired in 1996, and Democrats were elected to replace them. Glen Browder also retired in 1996, and the Republicans took the seat in a close election. In 1981 Wayne Dowdy won in a district that had been represented by Republicans Thad Cochran and Jon Hinson, who had won five consecutive elections between them. Dowdy held the seat until 1988, when he retired to run for the U.S. Senate. Democrat Mike Parker won the seat in 1988 and was reelected as a Democrat in the elections of 1990–94. Parker switched parties after the 1994 election and was reelected as a Republican in 1996. He retired in 1998 as a prelude to a statewide race for governor in 1999 (where he lost to Democrat Ronnie Musgrove).

The case of Dowdy's election in 1981 is one of several reversals of Republican gains that occurred in the 1970s and 1980s, many of which are noted above. In fact, in only three states of the eleven-state South did the landmark 1994 election mark a peak in the share of seats won by Republicans. In eight southern states, Republicans had achieved at some time prior to 1994 a share of congressional seats at least as great as their 1994 share, but those previous gains had been reversed during the 1970s and 1980s. An especially striking case is Virginia, where Republicans had virtually dominated the House delegation by 1980, when Democrats retained only one of the state's ten seats. The Democrats staged a resurgence in the 1980s and won seven of the state's eleven seats in 1992 (Rohde 1996). Such Democratic competitiveness in the face of widespread Republican gains suggests that the dynamics of electoral choice we have described, dependent as they are on competitive party politics, can have ample opportunity to operate in the future.

Intraparty Heterogeneity and Interparty Dynamics

The occurrence of contested primaries is indicative of at least one and possibly two conditions. First, a contested primary indicates that the primary winner's chance for victory in the general election is sufficient to make the nomination worth contesting. Second, contested primaries may indicate that the primary electorate is heterogeneous in its preferences. In such a circumstance, candidacies may emerge that appeal to different segments of the primary electorate. Primary challenges to the incumbent are indicative of unhappiness with the incumbent within the party, which is often stated as a question of the fit between the incumbent and elements of the party.

Heterogeneity of preferences within the parties is the source of potential variation in the distance of party nominees from the district median. A homogeneous party will consistently generate candidacies for the party nomination that are clustered closely about the party's median voter. Over time, such a party will nominate candidates who closely represent the party median, and who are thus about the same distance from the district median. Heterogeneous parties, on the other hand, will generate candidates for the party nomination who vary in their closeness to the district median. In a heterogeneous primary electorate, variation in outcomes will depend on the size and level of mobilization of various groups within the party. Over time, a heterogeneous primary electorate has greater potential to produce party nominees who vary in their proximity to the district median than does a homogeneous primary electorate.

Several factors introduce preference heterogeneity into southern primary electorates. Within the Democratic Party, race is the most obvious correlate of issue preferences, at least on economic and civil rights issues. Not only did the mobilization of African Americans render the general electorate more heterogeneous, it also had the same effect on Democratic primary electorates. As conservative whites defected from the Democratic Party, the role of African Americans in Democratic primary and election constituencies and the issue differences between black and white Democrats became more central to election outcomes. The balance that Democratic incumbents and candidates try to achieve between conservative and liberal issue themes is most typically an effort to balance their attractiveness to white and black constituents. A Democrat viewed among whites as too closely tied to black concerns may lose white votes, while being viewed among African Americans as unsympathetic to black concerns will also be detrimental to the Democrat's electoral chances.

Other sources of issue diversity are sometimes important to Democratic nomination politics as well. In some districts, labor unions have enough organizational strength to make a difference in mobilizing voters. Teacher organizations and local Democratic officials can also be reliable sources of electoral support. Adherence to the agendas of these groups among the Democratic electorate is not universal, but they are frequently important building blocks of a winning coalition. National interest groups representing pro-choice, environmental, and labor concerns also are potential influences on primary politics. Here it is important to note the preference heterogeneity among party activists that we cited above: Among Democrats, newer activists are typically more liberal than longtime activists, especially on noneconomic issues. The interaction of these various issue concerns and preferences within Democratic primaries can produce a variety of results in terms of the nominees' placement relative to the median voter in the geographic constituency.

In Republican nomination politics, the most important source of issue heterogeneity is the potential for conflict between elements of the Christian Right and party regulars who emphasize economic over social conservatism (Schneider 1997). The level of intraparty conflict between old guard Republicans and the Christian conservatives varies across states. Judging from recent relations within state party organizations, accommodation has been easiest in Mississippi, Kentucky, and perhaps Tennessee, while open differences occur between the regulars and the newer conservative activists in most of the other Southern states. Christian conservatives have varying levels of influence in the state party organizations. Where the Religious Right holds more party positions, they do not necessarily control primary outcomes. The result is that Christian Right party activists and party-regular elected officials are at odds with one another within in some states, like Texas, Virginia, South Carolina and Louisiana (See *Southern Political Report* 1997, 468).

In some states, like Mississippi and Alabama, the organizational advantage gained from the support of Christian Right organizations can offset the potential impact of such endorsements on a Republican nominee's attractiveness in the general election. In states like Florida, Texas, and Virginia, on the other hand, candidates of the New Right lose some support that Republicans have come to count on in suburban middle-to-upper class areas (Aistrup 1996, 143–66). How the outcome of intraparty nomination politics influences the dynamics of choice between the parties depends in part on the district context.

VARIATIONS IN DISTRICT CONTEXT

The dynamics of partisan choice operate in a variety of electoral contexts in the South. To express it in the spatial language we have used above, the variety of contexts creates a variety of party and district medians and varying levels of heterogeneity among primary and reelection constituencies. For the moment, we will simplify the great variety of contexts in the South by applying a fourfold typology of congressional districts based on two critical demographic characteristics: each district's level of urbanization and the size of its African-American population. These contextual characteristics are by no means the only factors at work in producing variation in electoral environments across the South, but they do provide a point of reference for some broad comparisons.

The historic bedrock of southern Democratic conservatism was the "black belt," which consists of those areas that supported large-scale plantation agriculture. Not by happenstance, these regions also had the largest populations of blacks in the South. The white leadership in these areas had the greatest interest in maintaining the racial, social, and economic status quo (Key 1949). Southern whites living in the old black belt areas persist in demonstrating more conservative attitudes on matters related to race (Glaser 1994), and racially coded messages in congressional campaigns appear to be more salient to whites in districts with higher proportions of African Americans (Glaser 1996).

In the Solid South era, the politics of the black belt contrasted with that of the uplands and mountains. Race was not as salient an issue in the hills, which historically could not support extensive plantation agriculture and consequently were populated by small farms, less wealthy white farmers, and far fewer blacks than was the black belt. Counties in such areas were most likely to deviate from the regional pattern of solid support for Democratic presidential candidates. In a few areas, like the mountain regions of North Carolina, Tennessee, and Virginia, the numbers willing to deviate from solid Democracy were sufficient to support local Republican organizations and elect Republicans to House seats. In the states where all politics was confined to the Democratic party, populist candidacies tended to have their origins in the hills, where economic and welfare policies that would be called liberal today found substantially more support than among the whites of the black belt (Nixon 1949). (We might add that the hills traditionally were more likely to support moral stands like the prohibition or restriction of alcoholic beverage sales. On all of these points, see Key 1949.)

To understand what makes southern politics "southern," it is important to keep in mind these traditional variations among local areas that are correlated with the local proportion of African Americans in the population. The variation across these contexts in the salience of race as a political issue is perhaps most crucial. The South is not unchanging however. Together with the effects of black voter mobilization and the rise of Republicanism, the urbanization of the South stands out as key to understanding the alteration of traditional southern political patterns. Apart from its effects on the distribution of incomes and education, the urbanization process represents change in the context in which political attitudes are formed and represented. As urbanization reflects a transition away from the traditional context of southern politics, perhaps it is accompanied by a reduction in importance of the racial composition of the population as a predictor of political attitudes. If anything, we might expect that among urban whites, conservative attitudes are more prevalent in predominantly white suburban areas than in center cities where more blacks live (see, for example, Voss 1996).

Urbanization has had a second transformative role in southern politics. Through the 1990 election, the major catalyst for Republican gains in southern congressional elections was their organizational strength in urban areas resulting from the exploitation of beneficial demographic changes—in-migration of northern Republicans and the rise of a professional and managerial class. These changes were especially apparent in states like North Carolina, Texas, and Florida, outside the Deep South (Strong 1956, 1960; Seagull 1975; Black and Black 1987, 264–77). In contrast, the whites of the black belt, even as they contributed substantially to the emergence of a Republican presidential majority (Cosman 1966; Seagull 1975), continued to participate in Democratic primaries for Congress and other offices, assuring continued success for Democratic conservatives. As long as Democratic candidates could distance themselves from the liberalism attributed to their national party, little incentive existed for voters, candidates, or activists to concern themselves with supporting or building a Republican Party. (See, for example, Bartley and Graham 1975, 111–35.)

We have created a surrogate measure of white presidential Republicanism to show the persistence of black belt voting patterns through the early 1990s. We cannot determine the actual distribution of white presidential votes in each congressional district. In creating our measure, we have taken advantage of the very low level of support for Republican presidential candidates among African Americans and among non-Cuban Hispanics concentrated in several districts in Texas. From a bivariate regression of district Republican presidential vote in 1992 on percent black population (combined with percent Hispanic population for Texas districts), we use the residual as an indicator of the degree of Republican support among white voters.[3] The higher our residual measure, the more conservative were the preferences of white voters in the 1992 presidential election.

Table 2.1 reports the mean value of this indicator for each of the four types of congressional district.[4] Consistent with the geographic distribution of white conservatism that we would expect, the "low urban, high black" district type is characterized by the highest rate of white Republicanism. Whites in rural districts with relatively few blacks are less Republican than those in districts in the "high urban, low black" category. A similar pattern holds for presidential elections in the 1980s.

From Table 2.2, one will note that Republican congressional gains from 1980 to 1990 occurred in the "high urban, low black" district type, which we might consider to be the most "suburban." No net Republican gains occurred in the decade in any of the other district types. This is consistent with earlier patterns of Republican growth. The Republican gains of 1992–96, however, were disproportionately in rural districts. Of the total 38 seat net gain from 1990 to 1996, the Republicans gained 32 seats in the combined rural categories. Today in the South, congressional Republicanism is tied far more closely than ever before to white presidential Republicanism. This is the culmination at the congressional level of the Republican strategy of "top-down advancement," tying local Republican candidates to the good fortunes of the national ticket by linking local Democrats to the policies of the national Democratic Party (Aistrup 1996).

Table 2.1
Residual Estimate of White Republican Presidential Vote—1992
By Demographic Type of District

District Type	*Mean Residual*	*N*
Low Urban, Low Black	-1.38	44
Low Urban, High Black	3.77	27
High Urban, Low Black	.65	44
High Urban, High Black	-3.16	22

Source: Compiled by the authors.

Table 2.2
Partisan Division of House Seats, by District Type,
after the Elections of 1996, 1990, and 1980

	Post-1996			*Post-1990*		*Post-1980*	
District Type	*White Dems.*	*Black Dems.*	*Reps.*	*Dems.*	*Reps.*	*Dems.*	*Reps.*
Low Urban, Low Black	11	0	29	22	11	20	13
		(27.5% Democratic)		(66.7% Dem)		(60.6% Dem)	
Low Urban, High Black	9	4	18	27	4	25	5
		(41.9% Democratic)		(87.1% Dem)		(83.3% Dem)	
High Urban, Low Black	12	0	32	17	21	19	12
		(27.3% Democratic)		(44.7% Dem)		(61.3% Dem)	
High Urban, High Black	7	12	3	19	8	14	13
		(86.4% Democratic)		(70.4% Dem)		(51.9% Dem)	
Totals	39	16	82	85	44	78	43
		(40.1% Democratic)		(65.9% Dem)		(64.5% Dem)	

Source: Compiled by the authors.

Differences among the types of district in which Republicans have been successful suggest ways in which district context can shape the parameters in which interdependent evaluation of candidates will operate. Districts vary in the mix of issue positions that will best fit the median voter, and in the potential heterogeneity of preferences in the district and within each party. With regard to the operation of interparty electoral dynamics, we should observe that the districts where whites demonstrate greatest conservatism are also those where African-American voters are a larger proportion of the population. Fewer white votes are required for Democrats to win such districts than in the suburbs or the hills. In rural districts with fewer blacks, Democratic candidates begin with a smaller base of African-American voters, but the median white voter is likely not to be as conservative as the median white voter in a black belt district. In different ways, both of these contexts provide Democratic candidates with the potential to gain enough of the middle ground to achieve electoral success in less urban districts.

Another contextual comparison that may be of importance is that between the older centers of Republican strength in the suburbs and the newer, more rural centers of Republican gains. The extension of Republican success to more rural districts has come at a time of greater prominence of conservative social activists and the Christian Right in Republican Party politics. Republican success in the rural South has come to some degree through nationalizing congressional elections with respect to social and cultural issues. In more urban contexts, Republican success has more often been based on appeals related to economics, and there is somewhat less cultural consensus on social issues. The ascendance of Republican activists or candidates who link local campaigns to the national (or southern) party's positions on social issues could result in some marginal loss of votes for Republicans in suburban-type districts.

These district types are a useful way to conceptualize how context might condition the workings of interparty electoral dynamics. Given that congressional districts function within state electoral systems, it is also useful to divide the southern states into three subregions. The subregions represent different mixtures of local political context. For instance, the Deep South states are at the core of the traditional political South. The black belt counties were traditionally dominant in state politics in South Carolina, Georgia, Alabama, Mississippi, and Louisiana. Today these remain the southern states with the largest percent black population, and all except Georgia are in the bottom half of the South in population growth.

In the peripheral South, strands of political culture that deviate from the black belt norm play a larger role in the states' politics. Sufficient pockets of "mountain Republicans" existed in North Carolina, Virginia, and Tennessee to regularly elect Republicans to Congress in the Solid South era, contrary to the Deep South norm. In more recent years, urbanization has been the more crucial factor in undermining the dominance of the traditional southern Democratic political mindset. Texas and Florida were the states where in-migration and urbanization initially had the largest impact, and all five of these states are in the top seven in the South in estimated population growth from 1990 to 1996. (We group Arkansas with the Deep South here because its rate of population growth and the persistence of Democratic Party strength at the state legislative and county levels indicate that it has been less affected by change than the states grouped in the peripheral South.)[5]

The two border states, Kentucky and Oklahoma, have the smallest black populations among the southern states (both about 7 percent), which is indicative of their having been least like the Deep South historically. Yet the border states also have the lowest rates of population growth among the thirteen. Urbanization is an even less potent force in these states than in the Deep South. The border and Deep South states provide contexts in which Republican growth has adapted to traditional modes of politics, and thus they are interesting cases. The peripheral South states, on the other hand, provide illustrations of a fuller variety of political contexts in the South—black belt and hills, traditional and urbanized. More importantly, current demographic trends will give the peripheral South increasing weight in defining southern politics in the coming years.

FUTURE PROSPECTS IN LIGHT OF THE 1996 ELECTION OUTCOMES

In the previous sections, we discussed the dynamics of the nomination process and aspects of the political context in the South that have influenced the growth of GOP success in contests for the U.S. House. Before turning to a consideration of how those influences are currently manifested in the results of the 1996 congressional elections and what the likely prospects are for the Republicans in the future, it is important to emphasize that these are not the only factors that have affected, and will affect, election outcomes. In addition to these influences, which are to varying degrees South-specific, more generic forces also have an impact. Specifically, the outcomes of individual races in a particular election year will be affected by things like whether the race involves an incumbent or an open seat, how well funded the respective candidates are, the "quality" of candidates (that is, their skills and abilities related to electoral competition), and the district-level impact of national electoral forces (Jacobson 1990; Abramson, Aldrich, and Rohde 1995; Herrnson 1998). These short-term factors played a substantial role in producing the current pattern of partisan control of House seats, and they will continue to influence future outcomes.

The results of 1996 were considerably less damaging to the Democrats than the 1994 results were, and they also brought less success to the Republicans than they had hoped. The shift of seats to the GOP in 1994 was substantial (as it was in other regions except the Northeast), while in 1996 the shift was relatively small. The results were, moreover, not uniform across the region.

Table 2.3 presents the breakdown of partisan control of House seats in 1996 and also presents the results of 1980 (the high point of GOP southern strength until 1994) for comparison. Overall the GOP held about one-fourth more of the House seats in 1996 than it had sixteen years before, with the Democrats' share just shy of 40 percent. While, however, the Democrats in 1980 held approximately equal shares of the seats in the three subregions, in 1996 there was considerable variation.

Table 2.3
Partisan Division of Southern House Seats after the 1996 and 1980 Elections

	Post-1996			*Post-1980*	
District Type	*White Dems.*	*Black Dems.*	*Reps.*	*Dems.*	*Reps.*
Deep South					
Alabama	1	1	5	4	3
Arkansas	2	0	2	2	2
Georgia	0	3	8	9	1
Louisiana	1	1	5	6	2
Mississippi	1	1	3	3	2
South Carolina	1	1	4	2	4
Total	**6**	**7**	**27**	**26**	**14**
		(32.5% Democratic)		(65.0% Democratic)	
Peripheral South					
Florida	5	3	15	11	4
North Carolina	4	2	6	7	4
Tennessee	3	1	5	5	3
Texas	15	2	13	19	5
Virginia	5	1	5	1	9
Total	**32**	**9**	**44**	**43**	**25**
		(48.2% Democratic)		(63.2% Democratic)	
Border States					
Kentucky	1	0	5	4	3
Oklahoma	0	0	6	5	1
Total	**1**	**0**	**11**	**9**	**4**
		(8.3% Democratic)		(69.2% Democratic)	
All South	**39**	**16**	**82**	**78**	**43**
		(40.1% Democratic)		(64.5% Democratic)	

Source: Compiled by the authors.

Deep South and Border States

In the border states, the Democrats' ability to win House seats had completely collapsed. In 1994 Republicans gained a net of three seats, giving them nine of twelve in the two states, and in 1996 the shift nearly reached the theoretical maximum when the Republicans gained two more, one in each state. Only one of the twelve seats—Kentucky's Sixth District—still belonged to the Democrats. One of the 1996 switch districts was Oklahoma's Third, one of the two best in the state for the Democrats on the basis of 1996 presidential results. There a recruiting coup created the optimal situation for the GOP when Wes Watkins (who had represented the district as a Democrat from 1977 until 1990, when he tried for the governorship) agreed to switch to the Republican Party. Watkins faced a Democratic state senator, Daryl Roberts, and was able to outspend him by more than two to one. Against a different Republican, Roberts might have had a better chance. As it was, with his advantages, Watkins secured a 51–45 percent victory.

Meanwhile, in Kentucky's Third District, the GOP defeated the only Democratic incumbent it was able to beat in the entire South. Democrat Mike Ward had won in 1994 by only 400 votes because the Republican Party had divided over abortion. The GOP candidate that year was a pro-choice woman, and a pro-life independent had polled 12 percent of the vote. In 1996 the Republican nominee was a pro-life state representative, Anne Northrup, who outspent the freshman Ward, and edged him by 300 votes. The future implications of the border-state results are simple: given that the GOP holds eleven of the twelve seats, the contribution the two states can make to Republican growth is tiny or none. Prospects of a significant Democratic rebound are low, but—both because of their current dominance and the low probability of additional seats coming to these states through reapportionment—the GOP will have to look elsewhere for gains.

The Deep South had been particularly fertile ground for Republican gains in 1994. They netted five seats in the six states in the election by beating two incumbents and taking three Democratic open seats, and then got four more seats through party switches during 1995. The progress continued in 1996; the Democrats lost a net of three open seats, two in Alabama and one in Mississippi. The Mississippi candidate won by a substantial margin, and that was no surprise. It occurred in the Third District, the strongest GOP district in the state based on 1996 presidential vote (Dole won it by nearly 20 points). The Republican candidate was "Chip" Pickering, a legislative aide to Senator Trent Lott, who had handily won nomination over eight other candidates The Republican contenders included populist conservative state senator Mike Gunn, who allegedly had ties to David Duke (*Congressional Quarterly Weekly Report,* February 24, 1996, 478). Pickering spent more than a million dollars in the race—almost twice the funding of his Democratic opponent—and polled more than 60 percent of the vote. This was surely a district that the GOP expected to win and hold; it had remained in the Democratic column only because of the personal popularity of conservative Democratic representative G.V. "Sonny" Montgomery, the longtime chairman of the Veterans Affairs Committee.

The Alabama districts tell a different story. The two districts (the Third and Fourth) were less strongly tilted to the Republican Party; Dole carried each by five points. Neither of the GOP candidates had previously held significant office, while both of the Democratic nominees had been state senators. The Republican nominees both hewed to a strongly conservative line, especially on social issues, and they had strong ties to the Christian Right. Similarly, the Democratic candidates also adopted conservative positions on social issues, while trying to tie their opponents to the more unpopular aspects of the record of the 104th Congress. The nominees of both parties were quite successful in fund-raising; the GOP had a small advantage in the Third District, while the reverse was true in the Fourth (Duncan and Lawrence 1998, 14–17). The experienced and well-funded Democrats with conservative platforms made both races close, but in the end the Republicans carried the Third District by four points, and the Fourth by two points.

Yet not all the open districts in the Deep South states went against the Democrats. Two open Democratic seats in Arkansas (the First and Second Districts) were held by the party, albeit not without difficulty. In the First District, the Democrats nominated a moderate, Marion Berry, who opposed abortion and gun control and supported a balanced budget, matching his GOP opponent (*Almanac 98*, 118). Despite the fact that the Republican nominee (a former city attorney) had won 47 percent against the former incumbent in 1994, and that Berry had no elective office experience, the Democrat was able to outspend his adversary by about $300,000, and won by nine points. In the Second District, on the other hand, the Democratic nominee—Vic Snyder—was a reform-oriented state senator with a liberal reputation. He supported the ban on semiautomatic assault weapons and had tried to repeal the state's sodomy laws. Snyder began the race with a substantial lead in the polls against a GOP candidate with no electoral experience, but the two were about equally well-funded (Duncan and Lawrence 1998, 73). In the end the gap closed, and Snyder survived by only four points. Consistent with our earlier argument, in two relatively similar districts, the more liberal Democratic candidate had the more difficult time.[6]

As a result of 1996, the Deep South had six white Democrats and seven black Democrats. While, with recent redistricting, not all of those black Democrats are *certain* to be free of danger of general-election defeats, it seems pretty clear that as Republican targets they rate between poor (Sanford Bishop of Georgia) to impossible (John Lewis of Georgia). The remaining white Democrats in the subregion are surely less secure, but there are not many of them, and there is little likelihood that reapportionment will add many seats for these states in the next few censuses, so there is not a great prospect for GOP growth here either.

The Peripheral South

Given the discussion above of the eight southern states outside the peripheral South, it appears that whatever additional growth in southern House seats the Republican Party is to experience will have to come largely from the remaining five states. These could come from two sources. First, these states have experienced considerable growth in population (and, thus, in total House seats) in the past. As Table 2.3 shows, the number of seats they were entitled to grew from 68 after the 1970 census to 85 after 1990 (while the total seats in the other eight states *declined* by one). The prospects for further increases are good.

Second, there are still a substantial number of districts held by white Democrats that the GOP could conceivably contest and win. Let us see what the 1994 and 1996 races tell us about the Republicans' recent experiences in these districts and what that might bode for the future.

The peripheral South states were a bonanza for the GOP in 1994. The party gained 11 seats net in the election (from defeating five incumbents and winning six Democratic open seats) and then added one more seat from a party-switcher in 1995. The Republicans gained at least one seat in each state, with a high point of plus four in North Carolina. The aggregate result in 1996 offered a striking contrast: only five seats changed partisan hands, and the net shift was a one-seat gain for the Democrats. The GOP lost three of the freshmen who had taken Democratic seats (two in North Carolina and one in Texas), while the GOP won two open Democratic seats in Texas. This was a striking outcome, particularly because the Democrats had so many open seats (twelve) at risk in the five states. (The GOP had three open seats, all of which they successfully defended.)

Space will not permit an account of all of these open-seat races, so we will focus on five that we think are particularly instructive regarding our theoretical argument. First we will consider the three open Democratic seats in Florida. The Second District had been held by Pete Peterson, a moderate Democrat and former Vietnam POW (who is now the U.S. ambassador to that country). The Democratic nomination contest was a three-way race, and the two who made the runoff were Allen Boyd (a moderate state representative) and Anita Davis (an African-American county commissioner). Boyd won the runoff by nearly two to one. The Republicans had strong hopes for the district, since George Bush had carried it with 60 percent of the vote in 1988, and Clinton had won by only four points in 1992. Their primary was also a three-way race, with Bill Sutton (a former bank president) and Carole Griffin (the pro-life 1994 nominee) (*Southern Political Report* 1996, 3). Sutton won the runoff handily. Thus both parties nominated relatively moderate candidates, but in the general election Boyd was able to spend more than $800,000, while his opponent was limited to less than $300,000. Boyd won with a comfortable 59 percent.

Republican hopes were, if anything, even higher for the Eleventh District of Florida. Clinton had won the district by only two points in 1992, and in 1994 the GOP nominee, Mark Sharpe (a former naval intelligence officer), lost to long-term Democratic incumbent Sam Gibbons by only 52–48 percent. When Gibbons retired, Sharpe again sought the nomination and received it unopposed. Among the Democrats, there were four candidates, but the clear favorite was former Tampa mayor Sandra Freedman, who was endorsed by EMILY'S List, a group that funds liberal Democratic women candidates. Freedman finished first in the primary, but short of a majority, and the second-place finisher was state representative Jim Davis. Davis was a mainline Democrat, who focused on education and crime issues, and was perceived as less liberal than Freedman (*Southern Political Report* 1996, 3). In the runoff, Davis secured many endorsements from groups and won by 12 points. In the general election, Republican

Sharpe had high name recognition and was able to raise over $750,000. He attacked Davis (who spent $935,000) as a tax-and-spend liberal, but Davis ran as a moderate New Democrat, supporting a balanced-budget amendment and the Defense of Marriage Act, while opposing property "takings" legislation and school vouchers (*Almanac 98*, 370). Davis won 58 to 42 percent.

The final Florida open seat (the Nineteenth) offered a very different situation from the previous two. It was one of two South Florida districts that had a strong Democratic tilt despite the lack of a significant minority component (the Nineteenth was only 1 percent black). Both districts, however, do have a high concentration of Jewish retirees who maintain their previous allegiance to the national Democratic Party (Duncan and Lawrence 1998, 359). Clinton had carried the Nineteenth District by 22 points in 1992 and had increased his margin to 37 percent in 1996. The four Democratic primary candidates included three state legislators, plus the 1994 Republican nominee who switched parties to run. The eventual winner of the nomination and the election (by nearly two to one) was state senator Robert Wexler, who ran as a national Democrat like his predecessor, Harry Johnston.

Thus the Democrats easily held on to their three open seats in Florida, in one instance because the preferences of the constituency made the district virtually impregnable, and in the other two cases because they nominated experienced candidates who were not from the extreme liberal wing of the party. By contrast, the only incumbent of either party in Florida who had a difficult race was freshman Republican David Weldon of the Fifteenth District, who is closely identified with the Christian Right. Despite the strong GOP tilt of the district (Bush won it by 12 points in 1992) and a more than two to one spending advantage, Weldon was held to 51 percent of the vote by a former naval officer who attacked him as too conservative for the district (Duncan and Lawrence 1998, 348).

The two Texas open seats we want to focus on are the First and Second Districts. Both are largely rural districts in East Texas, with black percentages about the southern average. The First District divided almost equally between Clinton and the Republican candidates in 1992 and 1996, and the GOP had carried it in recent statewide elections (Duncan and Lawrence 1998, 1368). The Democrats nominated moderate Max Sandlin, a county judge, who emphasized his support for a variety of targeted tax cuts. The GOP nominee was an attorney with no political experience. Both candidates tried to paint the other as being from the extremes of their respective parties, but Sandlin was able to draw on his personal fortune and ties with business to produce a spending advantage of more than three to one. He triumphed in November, 52–47 percent. The Second District also split evenly in the 1996 presidential race. The Democratic candidate was Jim Turner, a longtime state legislator and fiscal conservative who backed the balanced budget amendment and expansion of the death penalty (Duncan and Lawrence 1998, 1370). In the Republican primary, the GOP candidate in the previous three elections was defeated by Brian Babin, a dentist who was strongly supported by Christian conservatives (Duncan and Lawrence 1998, 1370). Turner was able to use his legislative record to counter Babin's charges that he was an "elitist liberal," while pushing for more support for education and tying Babin to the GOP budget and Medicare "cuts" (*Almanac 98*, 1346). He also outspent the Republican candidate by 1.5 to 1, and won 52–46.

Thus in these two similar rural Texas districts, relatively similar circumstances led to the Democrats retaining the seats. In both districts, moderate Democrats faced inexperienced Republicans and they had a significant advantage in campaign money. Here it was fairly conventional political advantages that supported Democratic wins, although in the Second the Republican was also more strongly identified with the populist conservative wing of the party than was the candidate in the First. Compare this with the two Democratic open seats in Texas that the GOP took away. In the Fifth, Pete Sessions (the son of the former FBI director), who had been the party's candidate in 1994, outspent the former Dallas Democratic Party chair by almost two to one to win the race by 53–47 percent. In the Twelfth, Kay Granger (the former mayor of Fort Worth)—a moderate abortion-rights supporter—won a massive victory in the GOP primary. She then parlayed that, plus spending more than twice the amount of her Democratic opponent (also a former mayor), to a 58 to 41 percent victory. Here the conventional advantages were with the GOP candidates in both districts, and the ability to paint them as extremists was neutralized.

Finally, the reader should note that the three instances where Democratic challengers in the peripheral South defeated GOP freshmen all involved Republicans who were identified with the more extreme conservative positions of the "revolution" of 1994, coupled in each case with some serious personal political disadvantages.[7] In addition, all three Democratic winners were politically experienced and well funded, and at least the two North Carolina candidates were identified with the party's moderate wing.

A Summary Picture

A more general picture of the prospects for the two parties in light of 1996 can be obtained by employing the presidential vote in each district as a relative measure of the underlying preferences of voters.[8] We computed the difference in the percent of voters supporting Clinton and Dole in 1996 in each district, then grouped districts according to the result of that computation, and counted the number of districts in each category that were won by each party. The results are displayed in Table 2.4.

Overall, we see that most of the marginals for each category are consistent with the idea of the measure. In the 29 districts with a presidential vote difference of -16 percent or less, the GOP controls 27 of them. In the opposite situation (a vote difference of +16 percent or more), the Democrats hold 26 of the 28 seats.

Table 2.4
1996 Presidential Vote Difference in House Districts and Partisan Control

*Presidential Vote Difference in District**	*Deep South*		*Peripheral South*		*Border South*		*All*	
	D	*R*	*D*	*R*	*D*	*R*	*D*	*R*
-16% or less	1	9	1	16	0	2	2	27
-6% to -15%	1	6	4	11	0	4	5	21
-5% to +5%	2	8	10	14	1	2	13	24
+6% to +15%	1	3	8	2	0	3	9	8
+16% or more	8	1	18	1	0	0	26	2
Total	13	27	41	44	1	11	55	82

*Clinton vote percent minus Dole vote percent. Thus, positive values indicate relatively pro-Democratic districts while negative values indicate pro-Republican districts.
Source: Compiled by the authors.

The pattern of the data also appears to be in accord with our basic argument. The number of districts that have a solid Republican presidential advantage but are currently held by Democrats are few: only two with an advantage of more than 15 points, and five more with an advantage between 6 and 15 points. On the other hand, there are two districts with a Democratic presidential advantage of more than 15 points that have Republican representatives, and another eight districts with a Democratic presidential advantage of 6 to 15 points are also represented by the GOP.[9] While the Democrats may not have a good chance of winning these ten districts that are relatively favorable to their party while the current incumbents continue to seek reelection, they should offer decent prospects for the party when they are open (and of course the parallel argument holds for the seven pro-Republican districts when they are vacated by their Democratic incumbents). Thus again from the perspective of a different kind of data, we reach the conclusion that both parties have similar prospects for losses and gains in the near term.

LOOKING BEYOND 1996: HOUSE ELECTIONS IN THE SOUTH

The core of our analysis is that the partisan split in southern House seats is near or at a long-term equilibrium. That is, Republican losses in congressional races are approximately as likely as Republican gains, although one party or the other may benefit from a confluence of election-specific, short-term forces that could result in deviations around the equilibrium. Our intent in this section is to summarize and embellish our argument for this view, and to briefly discuss the short-term forces that have the potential to produce deviations, as well as more long-term factors that may affect the equilibrium itself.

Long-Term Considerations

First, it is important to emphasize again that we do not claim that the current partisan division of seats is precisely an equilibrium. The balance of opportunities may still tilt a bit toward the GOP, leaving some expectation of limited further gains. With that caveat, the set of factors we think are most relevant to consider—population growth and its relationship to reapportionment and redistricting—do not seem to offer particular advantages to the Republicans relative to the Democrats.

Looking toward the census of 2000 and beyond, overall population growth in the South will likely continue to be greater than the national average, leading to the shift of more House seats to the South. These prospective gains are not, however, evenly distributed across the region. Recent estimates show projected seat gains for Georgia, Texas (two each), and Florida (one), and projected losses for Mississippi and Oklahoma (one each) (*Congressional Quarterly Weekly Report*, June 21, 1997, 1436). Since future Republican seat gains must come either from winning the dominant share of new seats or from taking existing seats away from the Democrats, these trends place limits on the likelihood of such future gains. The border states offer no chance of gains because of GOP saturation and the projected loss of a seat. The next redistricting may reinforce or undermine current Republican dominance. In the Deep South, only Georgia projects gains, and whether they offer a boon to the Republicans will depend on both voter preferences and the location of the population growth. In these states, there are some, but very limited, prospects for GOP gains. Given the current distribution of seats, redistricting cannot offer a significant advantage to the Republicans beyond reinforcing their current hold, but it could undermine their control in some states like Georgia.

It is only the peripheral South that offers the prospect of notable Republican gains. These states have the best prospect of gaining seats after the census, and they still have a significant number of current Democratic seats that the GOP can plausibly contest. Moreover, given the large number of seats in each state, there is the potential for the next redistricting to have a significant impact on party fortunes. The population trends in these states do not, however, seem clearly one-sided in their partisan implications. In particular, there are a couple of developments that offer some hopes to the Democrats although they may be effectively counterbalanced by pro-Republican factors. One potential Democratic advantage is the continued faster growth among Latinos compared to other segments of the population, coupled with the recent reinforcement of Latino inclination to vote Democratic (Gugliotta 1998). The latter development may not persist, but the former surely will. The effects of this are largely confined to Texas, but there it could lead to the Democrats maintaining control over a half dozen of their current seats plus adding a couple more.

More widespread in impact are the population trends among African Americans. Nationally, the numbers of black citizens have tended to increase much faster than those of white, but the southern impact of this growth has been mitigated by migration patterns. During the first seven decades of the 1900s, the number of African Americans moving out of the South substantially exceeded the number moving in (Vobedja 1998). In the late 1970s, this trend reversed, but net migration of blacks to the South was small. By the early 1990s, however, the pace had picked up, with a net migration of 369,000 between 1990 and 1995. The effect of black population growth is not, moreover, evenly distributed around the region. For example, the largest net gain in black population among southern metropolitan areas was in Atlanta, with an increase of 159, 830 since 1990 (Vobedja 1998). This could have a pro-Democratic effect on the drawing of districts, especially since the Supreme Court's decisions on racial gerrymandering in *Shaw v. Reno* (1993) and *Miller v. Johnson* (1995) mean that the Justice Department will no longer compel the production of the maximum number of majority-minority districts.

Beyond the population trends among African Americans and Latinos, the consequences of the next redistricting will depend on the relative positions of the parties, state by state, and the strategies they pursue. Certainly the Republicans will have a stronger voice than ever before because of their gains in governorships and legislatures, but there is still the probability that much redistricting will be governed either by compromises negotiated between the parties or deadlocks that turn the matter over to the courts. Relative to possible Republican gains, the population trends and their districting impact will be most important in the peripheral South. Developments elsewhere can largely lead only to maintenance of the status quo or an undermining of GOP seat control.

Short-Term Forces

Even if we are right about the existence of a long-term equilibrium between the parties at approximately the current level, there is always a probability that the results in particular elections will depart from that equilibrium due to the effect of short-term forces. As noted earlier, these are generally relevant to congressional elections rather than South-specific, although their effects can vary regionally.

Candidate Emergence. For decades, Republican fortunes in House races were undermined by limits on the ability to recruit strong candidates. As GOP fortunes have improved generally, and in state legislative races in particular, this problem has largely disappeared. Both parties currently have lower-level officeholders and capable amateurs from whom they can recruit House candidates although the supply will vary for both parties from district to district and over time. Clearly this will continue to be true for the GOP, but it will probably also persist for the Democrats. The same kinds of factors that we have discussed above regarding congressional races will maintain a significant pool of lower-level experienced candidates. Their willingness to run in particular races and specific years will be affected by the other short-term factors we will discuss (thus we will address 1998 candidate recruitment below).

Money. As with the supply of candidates, the GOP's chances in the past were mitigated by difficulty in funding candidates who did run. With the growth of the party in the South and the achievement of majority status in the House, their position is vastly improved although we saw above a variety of races in 1996 where the Democrat had a significant spending advantage. It seems likely that the partisan balance will continue to equalize although it does not seem plausible for the near future that it will become significantly reversed.

Election Margins. Whether candidates run and money is forthcoming for them depends in large measure on the perceptions of candidates' and parties' prospects in individual districts. One widely watched indicator is the margin by which the district was carried in the previous election. This is particularly true if the results are not believed to be artificially inflated, as were so many Democratic margins in the past when they were not really contested. The results from the most recent round of congressional races indicate that there is no pronounced asymmetry between the parties in the vulnerability of their representatives on this measure. Among incumbents who won reelection in 1996, there were only four representatives in each party who won with less than 55 percent of the vote. Expanding the inspection to the next level of vulnerability—victories by 55 to 59.9 percent—the numbers are still very close: ten Democrats and seven Republicans. Similarly, each party had five freshmen who won with less than 55 percent; within the next category the partisan division was two Democrats and three Republicans. Thus each party has a nearly identical number of vulnerable districts by this conventional measure.

Open Seats and Freshmen. Other indicators of the vulnerability of a candidate or district include whether the seat is open, or if the incumbent is in her or his first term. It is easier in most instances to take a district from the opposition party if there is no incumbent, and it is generally perceived to be easier to defeat an incumbent at the first attempt at reelection than later. One of the reasons the Democrats suffered so badly in the 1994 elections was that they had 31 open seats, and the GOP won 69 percent of those races (Abramson, Aldrich, and Rohde 1995, 318–19). In addition, among the 34 Democratic incumbents defeated, fully 14 were freshmen. In 1998, the balance of southern open seats for 1998 was three for each party. Also, the number of freshmen was relatively closely divided at 16 Democrats and 12 Republicans. Of course, in any given election the number of first-term members of each party will be a function of their respective success in the previous election, while the incidence of open seats will depend partly on expectations about the upcoming election. Given, however, the large number of retirements among southern Democrats in the last few election cycles, it is unlikely that their party will have a disproportionate number of open seats in any election in the near future.

National Tides. Another relevant short-term factor is if there is a national (or regional) electoral tide in favor of one party, or whether individual races are determined just by local forces. This consideration interacts, of course, with the other factors. The 1994 Republican gain of 53 seats nationally was due to the combination of an electoral tide in their favor coupled with the contextual weaknesses of the Democrats, like many open seats and freshmen. Neither of these variables alone would have produced a GOP majority. It is the influence of national tides that has produced the historical pattern of midterm losses for the president's party. There is nothing inexorable about midterm losses; it is just that off-year elections have been strongly related to negative public reactions to the president's party, often because of bad economic conditions. Those negative views both directly influenced voters' choices and influenced whether strong potential candidates of each party were willing to run for Congress (Jacobson and Kernell 1983). Furthermore, presidential elections used to routinely produce gains for the winner's party, creating a group of freshmen who would be particularly vulnerable in the following midterm (Oppenheimer, Stimson, and Waterman, 1986). Neither of these contingent events occurs invariably. When there is a midterm with a bad economy and an unpopular president whose party has many vulnerable seats (for example, in 1964), midterm losses can be devastating. On the other hand, when the economy is in good shape, the president is positively evaluated, and there are few vulnerable seats (for example, in 1986), losses will be few to none.

The current situation regarding these variables offers little prospect for a national tide either way. Now the economy is in very strong condition, and Clinton's approval ratings are decidedly positive, even high by historical standards; and, as this is written, Vice President Al Gore may run well in at least parts of the South in the 2000 presidential election. Moreover, the Democrats' gains in the House were small in 1996, so their "exposure" is low. Thus there is no indication of a pro-GOP national or regional tide for 1998 and beyond.[10] Most analysts expect few incumbents to be seriously threatened nationally, and the ones in danger are fairly evenly divided. This is causing both parties some difficulties in recruiting (*Congressional Quarterly Weekly Report*, October 25, 1997, 2625–29), and that makes changes even less likely. In a summary evaluation of House races that were to some degree expected to be competitive in 1998, *The Rothenberg Political Report* (January 23, 1998) listed only twelve southern seats, and six are held by each party.

Thus there is little expectation that the next few elections will produce a significant shift in southern House seats. In the longer term, the GOP has minimal prospects for gains outside the peripheral South. In those five states, some currently Democratic seats (like Charlie Stenholm's in Texas) may be particularly vulnerable, but many of those seats have either strong incumbents or a strong Democratic tilt to them, which offer good prospects of Democratic retention. New seats, as they are added after the 2000 census and subsequently, are likely to appear in areas that both parties can contest. Moreover, open seats due to retirements or representatives seeking higher office are likely to come disproportionately from the Republicans in the future. Each election cycle will offer a set of potentially competitive races, the outcome of which will depend on a set of factors, in particular where each party's candidate stands on the issues that are important to the voters. Where only one party nominates a candidate who can be portrayed as deviating significantly from the constituency's preferences, the other party will have the advantage. As our earlier discussion indicated, it is in the peripheral South states where the interaction of growing urbanization with the increasing power of the Christian Right within the Republican Party may cause the GOP the most problems in their nomination process. Overall, however, there seems to be little prospect of any sharp change in the current division of southern House seats between Republicans and Democrats.

Epilogue: The 1998 Elections

The previous analysis was completed before the 1998 elections, and we decided that it would be better to let the presentation above stand largely unaltered rather than completely rewrite the discussion in light of the 1998 results. This seems particularly desirable given that the results in the South produced several illustrations of the interparty and intraparty dynamics we have discussed, and thus the outcomes serve as a check on the accuracy and applicability of our arguments. Illustrative and relevant cases were not confined only to House races; gubernatorial and Senate races were especially noteworthy. In the South Carolina and Alabama elections for governor, Democrats defeated Republican incumbents who had strong Christian Right support. In Alabama, Governor Fob James faced opposition from Alabama's business-oriented conservatives for being unaggressive in pursuit of new business for the state. He defeated businessman Winston Blount in a Republican runoff on the strength of votes from black belt areas. In turn, James was defeated in the general election by lieutenant governor Don Siegelman who had campaigned for a state lottery to fund college scholarships. Democrat Jim Hodges similarly emphasized support for gambling and education and defeated incumbent Republican governor David Beasley in South Carolina (*Congressional Quarterly Weekly Report*, November 7, 1998, 3000). Meanwhile, the Republican incumbent Governor George W. Bush in Texas and Jeb Bush in Florida won victories in part by delivering a message of "compassionate conservatism" and appealing to minority voters who do not typically support Republicans. The example of Jeb Bush is particularly instructive. He is credited with delivering a more inclusive message in 1998 than he had in his 1994 gubernatorial loss to Lawton Chiles (*Congressional Quarterly Weekly Report*, October 24, 1998, 2876).

In the North Carolina Senate race, incumbent Republican Senator Lauch Faircloth was defeated by Democrat John Edwards. Edwards asserted his support of the death penalty and took a "tough on crime posture," winning the endorsement of the state's largest organization of police officers. Edwards also favored local control of education while attacking Faircloth for voting against some spending bills containing Head Start funding (*Congressional Quarterly Weekly Report*, October 24, 1998, 2872; *Congressional Quarterly Weekly Report*, November 7, 1998, 2982). In Arkansas, former representative Blanche

Lincoln retained the seat of retiring senator Dale Bumpers for the Democrats. Lincoln associated with the "blue dog" Democrats while representing the First District in 1993–97. Her opponent, state senator Fay Boozman, had strong support from religious conservatives and is noted for his strong anti-abortion stance. The race for the Kentucky Senate seat vacated by Democrat Wendell Ford was a fiercely competitive contest between two incumbent House members: Republican Jim Bunning and Democrat Scotty Baesler. The outcome was a Republican gain, but by less than 8,000 votes (49.8 to 49.1 percent). Baesler defeated five other candidates in the Democratic primary with 34 percent of the vote. Although the top Democratic candidates rallied around Baesler, the tough primary put him at a financial disadvantage against Bunning, who had only nominal opposition in the Republican primary (*Congressional Quarterly Weekly Report*, July 11, 1998, 1862).

A comparison of the House seats vacated by Bunning and Baesler provides a striking example of the interparty dynamics we have discussed. Bunning's Fourth District, in northeastern Kentucky, had not elected a Democrat to the House since the 1960s. A former Boone County judge, Ken Lucas, was the Democratic candidate against Republican state senator Gex Williams. Lucas opposes abortion rights and supports school prayer; he was endorsed in the primary by the "blue dogs" and House New Democrats. Williams is identified closely with Christian conservatism, and he made campaign appearances with such leaders as Ralph Reed, Gary Bauer, and James Dobson. While ethics questions did not help Williams's chances, the result—a 53–47 percent Lucas victory—is consistent with our view of the workings of interparty dynamics.

In the Kentucky Sixth District, former state representative and Baptist minister Ernest Fletcher was renominated by the Republicans. (He had been Baesler's opponent in 1996.) The Democratic nominee was state senator Ernesto Scorsone, a candidate viewed as more liberal than Baesler. In the primary, Scorsone was supported by the Kentucky Education Association and the AFL-CIO (*Congressional Quarterly Weekly Report*, November 7, 1998, 2982; *Congressional Quarterly Weekly Report*, May 9, 1998, 1221). A relative liberal facing an experienced and familiar Republican candidate, Scorsone lost with 46 percent to Fletcher's 53. With Republican Mike Parker retiring, the Mississippi Fourth District was captured by the Democrats. State transportation commissioner Ronnie Shows won a 53–45 percent victory over Delbert Hosemann. Despite his extensive political experience, Shows had to overcome a fundraising disadvantage in order to win. In this district, which is 41 percent African American, Shows emphasized his working-class roots and stressed Social Security, the minimum wage, and trade protection as important issues. He is suitably conservative for his district on issues like abortion, gay rights, and gun control (*Congressional Quarterly Weekly Report*, July 11, 1998, 1865; *Congressional Quarterly Weekly Report*, October 17, 1998, 2815; *Congressional Quarterly Weekly Report*, November 7, 1998, 2982).

In summary, key 1998 results reflect the continued operation of interparty dynamics across the subregions of the South. The aggregate outcome in the House, no net gain for either party, is further confirmation of what appears to be the foreseeable long-term effect of the interdependence of candidate evaluations: to keep the division of southern House seats at something close to the current Democratic and Republican shares.

NOTES

1. In fact, the issue evolution approach to partisan political change would hypothesize that party elites take the lead in partisan reorientations of the mass electorate, because of their role in communicating party stands on salient new issues. See Carmines and Stimson (1989).

2. In 1994, the Democrats nominated a former Republican woman with a pro-choice platform. Republican David Weldon won the race with 54 percent of the vote and successfully defended the seat in 1996 by 51 to 43 percent against Democrat John Byron's attacks that he was "an extremist with a narrow agenda" (Rohde 1996; Almanac 1998, 378).

3. This follows Fleisher (1993), who uses the residual values from the regression of 1984 Democratic presidential vote on district percent black as an indicator of the level of white liberalism in congressional districts.

4. The four types are defined according to two dimensions: whether the district is above or below the mean percent urban of all southern districts, and whether the district is above or below the mean percent black. The mean percent urban is 55.02 percent, and the mean percent black is 18.11 percent. One will observe from Table 2.1 that 88 of 137 districts fall into the "low black" category. This is the result of a highly skewed distribution, in which 116 districts are below 30 percent black but 17 have at least 50 percent African-American population. Contrast this to the 1970s round of redistricting, which produced a distribution of 64 districts below the mean of 18.96 percent black and 57 districts above the mean.

5. See Aistrup (1996, 87–88, 95–105) for cross-state comparisons of Republican advances below the congressional level through the early 1990s.

6. The Democrats also won one of the open seats in Louisiana with a moderate-conservative state representative, Chris John. Because of the redistricting before the 1996 election, there is some definitional problem in calling this a Democratic open seat, but it is true that of the two open seats in the state, one was Democratic and one Republican before the election and the same was true after. Also, due to the state's all-party primary system, both John and his opponent in the November final were Democrats.

7. The losers were David Funderburk (NC 2), Fred Heineman (NC 4), and Steve Stockman (TX 9).

8. Leogrande and Jeydel (1997) have raised questions about using these data to measure district preferences, but their analysis relates mainly to use in longitudinal research. We share their reservations on that score, but we believe that the presidential-vote data are a valid and useful measure for cross-sectional analysis. The marginal results in Table 2.4 are certainly consistent with that view.

9. We want to emphasize that there is no certainty that the presidential differences translate directly; that is, we cannot tell that a district with a positive advantage is pro-Democratic, and one with a negative difference is pro-GOP. We only contend that the former is more favorable to the Democrats than the latter.

10. There could also be "state tides." For example, most observers believe that Governor Bush of Texas is headed for an enormous landslide in his reelection campaign. While there is little evidence for gubernatorial coat tails in congressional races, there could be some spillover effect.

3

When Legislators Change Sides: The Implications of Party Defections in the South

JAMES M. GLASER

In the year following the 1994 midterm elections, six southern members of Congress (and a Coloradan as well) left the Democratic Party and joined up with the Republicans. Party defections such as these are important events in the ongoing realignment of the South,[1] for they carry great symbolism as well as another vote for the GOP.[2] When high-level officials abandon the party, it speaks volumes to voters back home. Moreover, defectors often use their decision to switch parties to actively bring voters with them to the other side. When Louisiana representative Billy Tauzin changed parties, for instance, he sent out thousands of letters with voter registration cards to encourage constituents to formally make the switch with him. Little wonder that with each defection, pundits eulogize the Democratic Party in the South.

For obvious reasons, defections are an important part of the growth strategy of the Republican Party. The six southern members of Congress who left the Democrats in 1994 and 1995 are only part of the flow of politicians out of the party. Since Ronald Reagan's victory in 1980, large numbers of politicians have changed sides. In Congress, there have been ten defectors to the GOP in the 1980s and 1990s.[3] In southern state legislatures, 77 sitting Democratic legislators have become Republicans during this period. Hundreds of state and local officeholders also have joined the GOP parade, though it is difficult to gauge exactly how many since such decentralized information is so hard to come by.[4] Though the entire picture cannot be painted, Table 3.1 does give some sense of the timing and the geography of the movement of officials to the Republican side. As the table shows, over 80 percent of state legislative defections occurred in the Deep South states of Alabama, Louisiana, Mississippi, and South Carolina, and most of them occurred in the wake of the Republican sweeps of the South in the 1984 and 1988 presidential elections and after the 1994 midterms.

Table 3.1
Southern Defectors in Congress and in State Legislatures, 1980–97

	1980–1981	*1982–1983*	*1984–1985*	*1986–1987*	*1988–1989*	*1990–1991*	*1992–1993*	*1994–1995*	*1996–1997*	*Total*
Congress	1	0	1	0	2	0	0	6	0	10
State Legislatures	2	8	17	2	19	7	10	31	20	116
Alabama	0	0	0	1	5	1	0	2	2	11
Arkansas	0	0	0	0	0	0	0	0	1	1
Florida	0	0	1	0	0	0	0	1	3	5
Georgia	0	0	1	0	0	0	0	1	5	7
Louisiana	0	5	11	0	1	1	1	6	3	28
Mississippi	0	2	1	1	7	4	6	5	4	30
N. Carolina	0	0	0	0	0	0	1	1	0	2
S. Carolina	1	0	1	0	5	0	2	11	2	22
Tennessee	0	0	1	0	1	1	0	2	0	5
Texas	1	0	1	0	0	0	0	2	0	4
Virginia	0	1	0	0	0	0	0	0	0	1

Source: Compiled by the author.

The figures in Table 3.1 do not account for those who left the Democratic Party before they ran for office, and, certainly, large numbers of southern Republicans have been Democrats at one point in their lives. My focus on those who change parties while in office, however, is purposeful, for these individuals set up a research opportunity, a natural experiment with built-in controls. The idea here is to look at the voting behavior of partisan switchers over the time preceding and following their change in allegiance. The beauty of this strategy is that the only attribute of these legislators that changes is their party affiliation. Their personal attributes, or at least those attributes that might be meaningful, remain constant. Except in years following redistricting, the attributes of their districts and their constituents remain constant.[5] These individuals thus offer an opportunity to test ideas about legislative behavior and the role of partisanship in the votes cast by southern legislators.

There is much reason to believe that the voting behavior of southern conservative Democrats should not change or change that much after a defection to the other side. For several decades, many southern congressional Democrats have been very conservative, even while sharing the party with northern liberals. Indeed, while in recent years southern Democrats and Republicans in Congress have become somewhat distinct, particularly on issues of civil rights (Bullock 1981; Fleisher 1993), there are still quite a few Democrats who are as conservative as the average Republican (Bullock 1985). These, of course, are the legislators most likely to defect and, one might expect, these are also the individuals least likely to change as a result of such a defection. Here is how Mickey

Edwards, a former Republican congressman from Oklahoma, described the behavior of Texas defector Greg Laughlin. "[Laughlin] had always been a sore thumb in the Democratic Party. . . . [He] did not shift his positions" to switch parties, but rather switched to the party that fit his positions. When the Republicans took over Congress, "Bingo, he switched to the party that had always been closer to his ideological heart" (personal correspondence). Or as Representative Cynthia McKinney described her colleague Nathan Deal after his defection, he already was a "Newtie," and his departure meant the loss of "excess weight" for the Democratic Party (Gruenwald 1995, 1084). Again, by her logic, the change of party labels should not mean that much given Deal's original conservative disposition.

In southern state legislatures, there is even less reason to believe that changes in voting behavior should accompany a change in party label. It is not just that large numbers of very conservative legislators resided easily in the Democratic caucuses in southern legislatures over the years, but in these legislatures, there is little evidence that party is a major reference point, either in terms of intraparty cohesion or interparty differentiation (Graham and Whitby 1989). Where the parties do not demarcate ideological lines well, where they do not provide any pressure on individuals to fall into line, one would not expect individuals to change much after a partisan defection.

In this work, I investigate whether a party defection leads to a change in legislative behavior. If, in this natural experiment, the new party label does lead to such a change, how might one explain it? What is it about the change in allegiance that spurs a change in behavior? And is there a difference in how members of Congress and members of state legislatures respond to the switch?

DATA

The data for this project come from several sources. Material on members of Congress is easy to gather. Information on state legislatures is more difficult to locate. Even figuring out which legislators have defected is a large task, particularly given that state party records are not uniformly good and given that many states, with so few Republicans in their legislatures over the years, have not even included party in their public records). I thus use the biennial *State Elective Officials and the Legislatures*, put out by the Council of State Governments, to determine who has defected. I compare legislative rosters year-to-year and note changes in parties. Those legislators who left the legislature immediately after their defection, as in a recent case in Louisiana (*[New Orleans] Times Picayune* 1995), cannot be identified given this method. To pick them up, I have checked my list of defectors against lists acquired from state Republican parties, where I could obtain such a list, and the list posted by the Republican National Committee. After 1992, then, this identification issue is not a problem.

To study the voting behavior of legislators, I do not analyze roll-call votes given that, particularly in the case of state legislatures, my ability to distinguish important votes from unimportant votes is limited. I therefore rely upon ratings put out by various organizations interested in legislative outcomes. For Congress I use the ratings given to representatives and senators by the organization Americans for Democratic Action. I also use scores published by the weekly *National Journal*, which analyzes votes along three dimensions (economic issues, social issues, and foreign policy issues). The data I use here go back to 1980.

Finding over-time ratings for southern state legislatures is much more difficult, and I use legislative ratings put out by various conservative and business political action committees in those states with the largest number of switchers—Alabama, Louisiana, Mississippi, and South Carolina. In one case—Louisiana—the ratings are calculated year-by-year using a consistent formula. In two other cases (Alabama and Mississippi), the ratings have been calculated by session, not by year, and the organizations doing the rating occasionally have changed the formula they use to grade the legislators, usually by counting missed votes in different ways. As much as possible, I have standardized these ratings over time. South Carolina legislators were not rated for a long enough period of time to include in the analysis. The ratings were acquired from the Business Council of Alabama, the Louisiana Association of Business and Industry, and the Business and Industry Political Education Committee of Mississippi. An additional rating was acquired from the Christian Coalition of Louisiana, though only three years worth of ratings (1993–95) were available. In the case of Louisiana, the ratings go back to 1980. In the other two cases, the economic ratings start in the mid-1980s, but as there were few defections in Mississippi and Alabama before this, the ratings acquired permit a look at almost all the defectors in these states from the past 15 years. The data collected on state legislators are not as complete as the congressional data, and I use these data mostly to bring the congressional findings into greater relief.

DO DEFECTORS BECOME MORE CONSERVATIVE?

Is there pressure of some kind that leads the new Republicans to become more conservative? The data in Table 3.2, based on Americans for Democratic Action (ADA) scores for members of Congress, suggest this is the case. The scores in Table 3.2 are calculated by averaging, for each defector, the ratings three years prior to the switch and the ratings three years after the switch (including the rating for the year of the switch in this "after" score).[6] The "before" scores and the "after" scores are then averaged across the ten southern switchers. The average "before" ADA rating for these congressmen is 24, the average "after" rating is eight. The difference in means has a highly significant T-value over four. Clearly, members became more conservative after taking on the Republican label and, given the nature of the comparison, there is little else that would explain this change.

One factor not held constant in this experiment is the behavior of other members of Congress, and I also attempt to account for the scores of these other

Table 3.2
Average ADA Scores of Congressional Defectors Before and After Switch

	Before Mean	*S.D.*	*After Mean*	*S.D.*	*Diff*	*T-value*
Ave. ADA Score	24	(13)	8	(10)	16	4.64*
% of the way between all Democrats and all Republicans	.90		1.07			
% of the way between all southern Democrats and all southern Republicans	.66		.96			

* < .01

Note: The before score is the average ADA score of the member in the three years prior to the defection. The after score is the average score in the three years post-defection (including the year of the switch). For some members, three years of data are unavailable due to short tenures and the averages are thus based on one or two scores. For each defector, the average ADA score for all/southern Democrats/Republicans was calculated in each of the three before/after years. The percentages are averages of the average distance of the defector from his Democratic/Republican colleagues. The defectors included here are Gramm, Ireland, Grant, Ireland, Shelby, Deal, Laughlin, Tauzin, Parker, and Hayes.

Source: Compiled by the author.

members. How were other Democrats and other Republicans voting in these same years and where do the switchers fall in comparison? To answer this question, I have calculated the average Democratic ADA score and the average Republican ADA score, as well as the average for all southern Democrats and Republicans. For each defector I have calculated, for each of the three "before" years and each of the three "after" years, where he fits vis-à-vis all Democrats and all Republicans, averaged these three scores together, and then averaged this average across all ten switchers. Compared to all Democrats and all Republicans, the changed behavior of defectors does not seem very dramatic. These defectors are clearly the most conservative Democrats in their chambers before they leave the party, and they have ratings almost comparable to the rating of the average Republican in the years before their switch. After the defection, they are even a bit more conservative than all Republicans. The scale for southern members of Congress is shifted to the right, however. Defectors are two-thirds of the way between all southern Democrats and all southern Republicans before their switch. After the switch, their average is 96 percent of the way between all southern Democrats and all southern Republicans. Clearly the voting behavior of these defectors undergoes some change because of the switch.

To make this point even sharper, I compare the behavior of switchers before and after their switches to the behavior of individuals identified as potential switchers by *Congressional Quarterly* after the 1994 defection of Richard Shelby. *CQ* identified a dozen legislators who could follow Shelby's example given their conservative records. Seven of those on the list did not change parties in 1995, and it is instructive to compare the 1994 and 1995 ratings of those who stayed put (Pete Geren, Ralph Hall, Jimmy Hayes, Sonny Montgomery, Charles Stenholm, Gene Taylor, and Charles Wilson) with those who jumped sides (Nathan Deal, Greg Laughlin, Mike Parker, and Billy Tauzin).[7]

In 1994, there was little perceptible difference in the scores of the four switchers and the seven southern "stayers." Indeed, those who changed sides the following year were a bit more liberal in 1994 than those who stayed Democratic: switchers averaged a 25 on the ADA scale while their colleagues averaged a 22 rating. A comparison of the two groups in 1995, however, shows a difference. The four who changed sides averaged a rating of four from the ADA. Laughlin and Deal, who switched earliest, got zeroes from the liberal organization. Those conservative Democrats who did not change parties in 1995 looked about the same in 1995 as they did in 1994, averaging a 26 score from the ADA. Clearly, these two groups are completely comparable, and the comparison shows that the impact of a move across the congressional aisle is direct and immediate.

HOW TO EXPLAIN THE CHANGE

If Democratic defectors do become more conservative after their defections, what accounts for this change? I pose and test three alternative explanations for the apparent postdefection change in ADA ratings. The three explanations are not necessarily mutually exclusive, but there are some opportunities to pit them against each other, which I do below.

The New Colleagues Explanation. The first explanation is that one might expect that the influence of new colleagues might lean heavily on the new Republicans. Congressional voting behavior, as John Kingdon (1989) argues, is heavily influenced by those colleagues that legislators look to and interact with in the process of deliberating and voting. Kingdon notes in discussing a social psychological explanation for congressional voting behavior that "the position of the fellow congressmen to whom the deciding congressman turns is a perfectly splendid predictor of his vote" (Kingdon 1989, 74). And, he finds in his survey of members of Congress, colleagues are the most important influence on voting decisions, if one measures importance by how frequently members spontaneously mention a particular influence on their vote. If this is the case, one might expect switchers to respond to their new "points of reference" by moving to the right.

The New Constituents' Explanation. This explanation centers on how a representative who has changed sides must anticipate the response of those back home. It is not the case that a sitting representative is going to face a new constituency. In fact, the beauty of these tests is that this factor remains constant. Those who change, however, are going to have to face a new primary constituency and defend themselves and their record to Republican voters. These new voters can pose a problem to a new Republican. As former Representative Glen Browder (D-Alabama) said to me, "Switchers have a difficulty. [In addition to the fact that] Democrats are mad at them for leaving, Republicans fault them because they're a Johnny-come-lately. Their old friends hate them and their new friends don't trust them."[8] If this is right, one might expect switchers to change their voting behavior to shore up support from new Republican constituents and to fend off primary challenges, particularly from the right. These defectors may, after all, have some Democratic votes in their past that are not popular among those who are likely to turn out in primary elections.

The Liberation Explanation. It may not just be new influences on a defector's vote that is leading to the phenomenon shown here. It may have been something about their situation before they switched that caused them to be artificially liberal before their change in allegiance. In other words, perhaps they were always more conservative, but because of their position in the Democratic Party, they were constrained and had to position themselves more to the middle.

To test the first of these explanations, the new colleagues explanation, I use some different ratings. If new colleagues have influence, one would expect that influence to be uniform across issues. That is, there is little reason to believe that new colleagues would shape or influence the votes of switchers on some issues and not others. On the other hand, the new constituency explanation might lead to such a prediction. Given the strong and growing presence of the religious right and other social conservatives in the Republican Party (Green et al. 1995) and the increasing political savvy and effectiveness of this "formidable party faction" (Rozell and Wilcox 1996), the imperative to move right on social issues may be more pressing than the pressure to move right on economic issues or foreign policy. Fending off primary opposition from the Religious Right may be a necessity for a new Republican because one might suspect that this is the part of the Republican base that is most likely to punish a newcomer for an errant vote or two from the past. Or it may be that switchers are just like all newer southern representatives who are likely, as Bullock (1995, 152) notes, "more sensitive to the preferences of the coalitions critical to the success of their parties." In any case, the two explanations lead to two different predictions.

Using *National Journal* scores to tap different dimensions of congressional voting, the new constituency explanation appears to be more persuasive. *National Journal* calculates voting scores for economic, social, and foreign policy issues. The scores are somewhat different from the ADA ratings because they represent not the percentage of the time a legislator takes a liberal or conservative position, but rather how much more liberal or conservative a particular legislator is vis-a-vis the entire House or Senate. A score of 25 on the economic policy ratings means that a representative is more liberal than 25 percent of her colleagues (thus, like the ADA scores, a 100-point scale running from

Table 3.3
Average *National Journal* Scores of Congressional Party Defectors Before and After Switch

	Before Mean	*S.D.*	*After Mean*	*S.D.*	*Diff*	*T-value*
Ave. Social Policy Score	32	(8)	11	(8)	21	6.14*
% of the way between all Democrats and all Republicans	.74		1.20			
% of the way between all southern Democrats and all southern Republicans	.50		1.01			
Ave. Economic Policy Score	39	(16)	25	(10)	14	3.35*
% of the way between all Democrats and all Republicans	.57		.94			
% of the way between all southern Democrats and all southern Republicans	.41		.79			
Ave. Foreign Policy Score	33	(14)	14	(13)	18	4.82*
% of the way between all Democrats and all Republicans	.71		1.12			
% of the way between all southern Democrats and all southern Republicans	.51		.81			

* < .01
Note: The before and after scores are calculated as above.
Source: Compiled by the author.

conservative to liberal). Like above, up to three years of scores are averaged together to create before and after scores, and defectors are compared to all partisans and all southern partisans.

The findings in Table 3.3 are intriguing. Replicating the ADA results, on all three dimensions, defectors appear more conservative after their switch than before it. In support of the new constituency explanation, the defectors appear to change most in their voting on social issues, both in absolute and in relative terms. Prior to their switch, the average *National Journal* social score is 32; after the switch it is 11. This difference in means is highly significant. There are statistically significant differences in the expected direction in the means on economic and foreign policy issues as well, but they are a bit smaller. Looking at the defectors in the context of the entire House (or Senate, in the case of Richard Shelby) further supports these findings. Comparing them to all southern Democrats and all southern Republicans shows that they moved considerably closer to Republicans from the region after their switch on the economic and foreign policy scales. On social issues, however, the difference is most dramatic. Switchers fall right in between southern Democrats and southern Republicans on social issues before their defection. After the defection, they are fully in line with southern Republicans.

Inconsistency is something members of Congress have to defend against in reelection campaigns. "Flip-flopping" is among the more common charges leveled against incumbents. Inasmuch as the changes in these scores reveal inconsistency, there is the potential for reelection difficulties. But the electoral risk of not adjusting one's positions after changing parties may be greater, especially as these data indicate, on social issues.

The third explanation for the change in voting behavior is the liberation explanation. As many of these defectors tell it, they were somewhat constrained before their switch, serving under national party leadership that was much more liberal than they were and belonging to a legislative caucus that had a much more liberal center of gravity. Under this explanation, the observed change in congressional voting behavior is not as much a change in conviction as a greater ability to express true convictions.

To test this hypothesis, I again examine new evidence, this time from three state legislatures. If this national party explanation has value, one should see a postdefection change among members of Congress, where the national party and its leadership exerted a liberal force on legislative behavior. Changes in voting behavior should be less apparent in state legislatures, where the national party is not a factor, or at least much less a factor, in pre-switching behavior. In other words, there are far fewer constraints on southern Democratic state legislators prior to their switch.

In Table 3.4, the mean before and after scores are displayed for state legislative switchers in Alabama, Louisiana, and Mississippi. As above, the switches studied in this table occurred since 1980 (through 1995). As above, the before and after scores are multiyear averages, where more than one year of data is available. Again, these ratings were calculated by an outside organization, though obtaining and standardizing them proved to be a difficult task.

State legislative switchers do not appear to vote much differently after their defection than they did before it. The results are somewhat different in the different states, and this is probably a function of some differences in the organizations that came up with the scores and their methods. Nonetheless, evidence of change is weak. In two cases, the change is in the expected direction—switchers

Table 3.4
Average Conservative Organization Scores of State Legislative Party Defectors Before and After Switch (A score of 100 is liberal)

	Before Mean	*S.D.*	*After Mean*	*S.D.*	*Diff*	*T-value*
Alabama (n=4)	33	(10)	30	(14)		
Louisiana (n=16)	13	(9)	17	(9)		
Mississippi (n=12)	32	(13)	25	(11)		
Combined (n=32)	23	(14)	22	(11)	1	.59

Note: Compiled by the author. Data come from the Business Council of Alabama (BCA), the Louisiana Association of Business and Industry (LABI), and the Mississippi Business and Industry Political Education Committee (BIPEC). Some ambiguities as to the timing of defections means that some cases had to be rejected. Because the organizations have used scales where 0 is liberal and 100 is conservative, I have subtracted each score from 100 to make them comparable to the congressional scores reported in Tables 2 and 3. Where the organization changed its method of calculating scores, the scores are standardized across years.
Source: Compiled by the author.

becoming more conservative—but the changes are small (four points in the Alabama case, seven points in the Mississippi case). In Louisiana (the case where the best data were available), switchers appeared more *liberal* after the defection, a surprising result, though the difference is small enough to write off as meaningless. Putting all the cases together (though calculated in different ways, the different states would be weighted equally in the before and after scores) shows a tiny and insignificant difference in the conservative direction after defection.

The state legislative scores used here are put out by organizations interested mostly in issues that affect business and industry. The Louisiana Association of Business and Industry (LABI), for instance, rates legislators on their votes on labor, consumer, environmental, and tax issues that in some way affect the business climate in the state. Some of these issues are not strictly "economic," but for the most part, these ratings are most comparable to the congressional economic ratings analyzed above. This may mute the change observed here. After all, the economic ratings for congressional defectors changed less than the other ratings, particularly the social ratings. Unfortunately, meaningful over-time ratings on social issues for state legislators are not available.[9]

The explanation I offer for the fact that there is so little observed change in pre- and post-switch behavior is that Democrats in the state legislatures are not nearly so constrained by their position in a more liberal party as members of Congress. Further evidence of this continuity is that there are still large numbers of very conservative Democrats in southern state legislatures. In Louisiana in 1995, 45 percent of Democrats in the legislature received a more conservative rating from the Christian Coalition than the average Republican's rating (77.5). Over 13 percent of Democrats in the legislature that year received an economic rating from LABI that was more conservative than the average Republican rating (86.2). Certainly there is nothing comparable to this in the U.S. Congress. If these numbers are representative, and there is good reason to believe that they are, the party lines are still rather fuzzy in state legislatures in the South. Democrats are all over the political spectrum, and the forces of a more liberal national party do not operate fully in these chambers. When southern switchers refer to the difficulties of serving in a more liberal caucus under a more liberal leadership, and when they talk of how the switch has liberated them, there is likely something to it.

CONCLUSION

Since 1980 a large number of officials have left the Democratic Party, and there promises to be more. What do these changes mean for the political parties in the South? Do the new members change the balance of ideas within the parties? With each switch, the Democratic delegation from the South gets a bit more liberal overall. Without its most conservative members, the party's center of balance creeps leftward, perhaps even making more defections likely. This is less likely in state legislatures than in Congress; as the Louisiana data show, there are still many very conservative members of the Democratic Party in the state, and the balance of the Democratic Party is still rather conservative. What do defectors mean for the Republican Party? Will they moderate their new party or will they adjust themselves to their new party's norm? The evidence here points to the latter. As Democrats turn Republican, at least in Congress, political forces are likely to encourage them to the right.

Perhaps the most important lesson to be learned from these analyses is that party is beginning to matter more to southerners. This may not seem to be a great epiphany, but prior to the filtering down of the realignment in the region, there was plenty of comfortable room in the Democratic Party for true conservatives. In Congress, not only are partisans increasingly distinct, but there are forces within each party driving them further apart. That defectors in this natural experiment are compelled to move further to the right to protect themselves is some indication of this. Partisan fuzziness still characterizes several southern state legislatures. As recently as 1996, one Mississippi organization rating conservatives could leave the party affiliations of legislators off the scorecard because, as its director said, "It just doesn't matter down here." But southern legislatures are growing more Republican by the year and as they move toward majority status, as is happening on the Atlantic Seaboard, the incentives to switch parties will change and the internal dynamics of the institutions will change. One would expect at that point that the same forces operating on southern switchers in Congress would operate on new Republicans in the state legislatures.

NOTES

I am grateful to Seth Aframe, my research assistant, who did an outstanding job collecting data for this project, keeping me organized as it was under way, and helping design a research plan that would yield these results. I also would like to thank Dick Wilcox, executive director of the Mississippi Business and Industry Political Education Committee (BIPEC), for providing me with insight on the process by which rating systems are devised, and John Clark, for his helpful reading of an earlier version of this work.

1. The South is defined here as the states comprising the former Confederacy: Alabama, Arkansas, Florida, Georgia, Louisiana, Mississippi, North Carolina, South Carolina, Tennessee, Texas, and Virginia.

2. Phil Gramm (Texas, 1982), Andy Ireland (Florida, 1984), Bill Grant (Florida, 1989), Tommy Robinson (Arkansas, 1989), Richard Shelby (Alabama, 1994), Nathan Deal (Georgia, 1995), Greg Laughlin (Texas, 1995), Billy Tauzin (Louisiana, 1995), Mike Parker (Mississippi,1995), and Jimmy Hayes (Louisiana, 1995).

3. Up to the beginning of 1998.

4. Though, with wonderful publicity in mind, the Republican National Committee kept track for a while. According to RNC records, posted in early 1998 on a crowing page at their web site, 357 elected officials across the country have switched parties since Bill Clinton's election, 80 percent of them from the South and 26 percent of them (91) from Texas. The large number of defections in Texas is especially notable as it has been almost entirely at the county and local levels. Democratic state legislators there have stayed put, only four of them switching parties between 1980 and early 1998.

5. Redistricting is not an issue in any of the congressional cases studied here.

6. In some cases, where a legislator was not in office for three years pre- or post-switch, the average is based on one or two years of ratings.

7. Deal switched in April, Laughlin in June, Tauzin in August, and Parker in November. Hayes switched in December. I include Parker's scores in the switchers' averages as he prepared for his switch well before November, returning campaign money to the Democratic National Committee and the Democratic Congressional Campaign Committee and quitting the "blue dog" coalition in July (Espo 1995; Sheffner 1995). I do not include Jimmy Hayes with the1995 switchers as he switched at the end of the year and did not ready for his switch as Parker did.

8. Representative Greg Laughlin's 1996 loss in a Republican primary to a former Republican congressman, Ron Paul, illustrates well this danger in switching.

9. Usable ratings were only located for the Louisiana legislature. Only since 1993, however, has the Louisiana Christian Coalition been evaluating legislators on issues of "Crime, Term Limits, Gun Control, Gambling Reform, Homosexuality, School Prayer, Abortion, & More!" as the front cover of their scorecard puts it.

4

Congressional Responsiveness to Redistricting-Induced Constituency Change

CHRISTINE LEVEAUX-SHARPE

One of the major goals of the 1990s redistricting was to increase the representation of minorities in the United States Congress. Achievement of this goal was attempted in large part through the creation of majority-black congressional districts.[1] These districts were formed by concentrating at least 55–65 percent of blacks in a district in order to insure the election of a black candidate. By most accounts the policy worked as expected. Of the 23 African-American members in the 1980s, only one-sixth of those members represented southern districts. Between 1991 and 1993, the number of African-American members of Congress grew from 27 to 40, largely as a result of the creation of several majority-black districts. The strategy of the redistricting was aimed at the southern states, and accordingly this is where the impact was the greatest. Of the 27 African-American members in 1991, only five of them were from the South. In stark contrast, 13 of the 17 African Americans elected between 1992 and 1994 were from the region.

Although the numbers of African Americans in Congress have increased, the 1990s redistricting may ultimately threaten the overall representation of African Americans. There have been many claims made both by scholars and political pundits that the creation of the majority-black district has led to a more conservative Congress in terms of voting behavior and partisan membership. Although there is increasing diversity in the political interests of blacks, as a group they still remain overwhelmingly liberal and Democratic.[2] Therefore, a more conservative Congress is seen as jeopardizing the overall representation of black interests rather than enhancing it. Many studies have focused on the direct relationship between the creation of majority-black districts and increased conservatism in the House (Bullock 1995; Overby and Cosgrove 1996; Lublin 1997). This direct relationship focuses on the voting behavior of the House member—or more simply put, the change in black population in a district leads to change in the roll-call voting behavior of that member. In this chapter, I contend that there is also an indirect relationship between the creation of majority-black districts and increased conservatism in the House. This indirect relationship focuses on the partisan makeup of the House.

Republicans took control of the House in 1994, with one popular media explanation for that drama being that the creation of majority-black districts influenced the shift in party control. The theory generally posited in support of that explanation is that majority-black districts are formed by removing blacks from surrounding districts. These districts are subsequently "bleached"—they become substantially more white—and by the simple fact that a large liberal voting bloc has been pulled from these districts, they are now more conservative and thereby more attractive to prospective Republican candidates. Thus, the creation of majority-black districts makes aggregate white members of the House more conservative in their voting behavior, which is considered the direct effect of redistricting. The creation of these districts also, however, attracts quality candidates who believe the incumbent is more vulnerable because of the demographic changes in their district—which is claimed to be the indirect effect of redistricting.

Political observers claim that the loss of large numbers of Democratic House seats in 1994 can be attributed to the creation of majority-black districts. In 1992 there were three Democratic incumbents defeated as a direct result of the creation of majority-black districts. The 1994 election marked the first time since Reconstruction that Republicans made up a majority of the southern congressional delegation. Many techniques have been used in an attempt to determine how many of the Republican victories were results of the creation of majority-black districts; other chapters in the current volume, in fact, use race as one possible explanation for the mammoth shift that has occurred in party control of Congress (see chapter 1, in particular). Perhaps more important than the actual number of majority-black districts created, however, is determining what factors within the redistricting process itself could have caused such an upheaval. As Bullock (1995, 22–23) explains, better Republican "candidates, Democratic incumbents trying to defend their records before more conservative constituents, and perceptions that winning might be possible" all played a role in making Republican candidates competitive. Thus, the "bleached" districts that resulted from the 1990s redistricting process in many states may have attracted more experienced and qualified Republican candidates than at any time since the preclearance procedures of the Voting Rights Act took effect.

This chapter focuses on the emergence of quality challengers in the 1994 congressional elections in the eight southern states that underwent race-based redistricting in the 1990s: Alabama, Florida, Georgia, Louisiana, North Carolina, South Carolina, Texas, and Virginia. Specifically, the hypothesis tested is this: In southern states where race-based redistricting occurred, House members who experienced a decrease in the percentage of black population in their districts were met with Republican challengers of a substantially higher campaign quality in the 1994 congressional elections. The formulation of this hypothesis is based on the fact that in order to create the majority-black district in the South, several other district boundaries were altered. Due to district changes, both anticipated and actual, I contend that the electoral vulnerability of incumbents increased in southern states that underwent specifically race-based redistricting during this period.

EFFECTS OF THE "BLEACHED" DISTRICT

The small number of studies on this subject tend to focus on the impact of majority-black districts on Democratic seat losses by observing whether districts that lost significant numbers of black voters were won by a Republican candidate (Hill 1995; Bullock 1995). Although these studies have significantly impacted our understanding of the phenomenon, this research attempts to refine that understanding by exploring the degree to which the emergence of higher-quality challengers in those districts made them more competitive. Gary Jacobson (1981) has noted that incumbents who appear vulnerable attract higher quality challengers; so, too, Charles S. Bullock III (1995, 22) argues persuasively that these so-called bleached districts may attract "more formidable Republicans than would have emerged had the racial proportions remained unchanged." I empirically test this proposition.

STRATEGIC POLITICIANS

The discussion of candidate emergence—and more importantly, quality candidate emergence—in congressional elections is part of a larger debate on the influence of national and local forces on determining the presence of a quality challenger in an election. Jacobson and Kernell (1983) integrate national and local forces to develop a model of the strategic politician. The authors argue that career politicians are sensitive to both local and national conditions when calculating their probability of electoral victory. In fact, it is not the voters who consider national forces when choosing a congressional candidate; it is rather the strategic politician who incorporates national factors into his or her decision to run for office, which in turn colors the campaign and the outcome of the election.

The "utility calculation" idea espoused by Jacobson and Kernell is a concept that has commonly been applied to the impressive body of literature on candidate emergence. Many studies have focused on whether the local or national political climate has a larger influence on the decision of quality challengers to enter a congressional race (Bond et al. 1985; Born 1985; Krasno and Green 1988; Squire 1989b; Lublin 1994). National conditions are generally believed to have played a role in the outcomes of the 1994 election. The main concern in this chapter, however, is the effect that local conditions had on the emergence of quality challengers and outcome of the elections.

Prospective challengers are profit maximizers. Quality challengers are likely to choose not to compete in an election that they have no chance of winning. Instead, they will wait until the national and/or local political environment is more favorable for their candidacy. As Kazee (1994) explains, prospective candidates must ask themselves when is the right time to run. Timing is a contextual factor important to a potential candidate's decision to enter a House race.

Ambition theory, first presented by Schlesinger (1966, 7–8), argues that "potential candidates behave rationally, that is, they assess the costs and benefits of alternative courses of action and choose the course that they perceive to be most consistent with their political ambitions." The theory also asserts that "politicians are rational decision makers and do not hanker after offices they cannot hope to attain." Thus, it is not cost-efficient to seek an office when the probability of winning is low or nonexistent. After redistricting, prospective challengers examine the new political environment in order to see if the time is right for them to run and if electoral success is possible—the desired goal, of course, being election to office. Behaving rationally, prospective candidates will search for the electoral atmosphere in which the possibility of electoral victory is high. It is due to this fact that many potential candidates, especially the higher quality candidates, were not willing to organize a campaign in 1992, when the demographic makeup of their home districts was uncertain because of redistricting (Canon et al. 1996). Instead, tougher challengers waited until the 1994 congressional elections.

As part of the strategic calculations that go into timing a candidacy, potential challengers ask questions such as how the districts have changed in terms of partisanship and race. They may also be concerned with what the final geographic map will look like, and when the redistricting fracas will be completed with little likelihood of further judicial challenge—such as was the case throughout the 1990s in South Carolina (Kuzenski 1998). In several of the states under analysis in this study, redistricting plans were not finalized until shortly before the 1992 elections, making it impossible or unattractive for a candidate to run in the election.

The redrawing of congressional lines signals an important change in the opportunity structure that is part of a potential challenger's utility calculation in seeking office. In many districts, the incumbents are considered so electorally safe that their House seat is actually not considered part of this opportunity structure. When district lines are redrawn, however, the incumbent may become more vulnerable electorally. The degree of danger an incumbent faces in this process may also rise substantially as the redrawing takes increasingly more dramatic form. With the creation of majority-black districts in a number of the states included in this study, several congressional districts were restructured in such dramatic form. These restructured districts attracted more quality challengers who hoped that shifts in district boundaries would lead to a decline in incumbency advantage. Incumbent House members who previously relied on their name recognition, their record of service, and their voting behavior to the known commodity of their constituency were effectively thrust into a "new" district.

The Challenger Quality Model of Elections

There has been substantial debate in the professional literature on how challenger quality should be measured (Jacobson and Kernell 1983; Bond, Covington and Fleisher 1985; Abramowitz 1988; Krasno and Green 1988; Squire 1989; Lublin 1994). In their 1983 study, Jacobson and Kernell measure challenger quality by whether a candidate has ever held elective office. Those challengers who have previously held elective office are classified as "quality" challengers, whereas those who have not held elective office are not so labeled. Jacobson and Kernell's measure, however, has been considered somewhat crude; there may be significant gradations of challenger quality that are not captured in a measure of this nature. Because of this concern, many scholars have attempted to refine Jacobson and Kernell's measure of challenger quality (Bond et al. 1985; Krasno and Green 1988; Lublin 1994).

In his effort to improve the measure, Lublin (1994) has created a measure that can be justified on empirical grounds. In a study examining the U.S. Senate, Lublin offers a measure of challenger quality that ranks the impact of holding one type of political office versus another. Thus, there are *levels* of challenger quality based on an ordinal scale depicting different types of political service. Following Lublin's technique, I initially constructed a hierarchical scale of challenger quality for House members; using the hierarchical scale versus the dichotomous dependent variable, however, the results of coding challenger quality were too similar to justify using the scaled dependent variable in this analysis. Also, following the lead of previous studies, I do not include challenger spending in my explanation of challenger quality due to the circularity of the measure (Bond, Covington, and Fleisher 1985; Krasno and Green 1988; Squire 1989b; Lublin 1994).

Model of Analysis

The dependent variable in this study is challenger quality, which is based on whether a challenger held previous political office. The variable is dichotomous, with 1 representing challengers who have previously held political office, and 0 representing challengers who have not previously held political office. There are several independent variables that determine whether a quality challenger emerged in the 1994 congressional elections. I use a LOGIT regression model to test the relationship between challenger quality and several independent variables, defined as follows:

Challenger Quality = a + b1 (Incumbent's Margin of Victory in Previous Election) + b2 (District-Level Presidential Vote in 1992) + b3 (Challenger party) + b4 (Change in Black Population proportion)

The incumbent's margin of victory in a previous election (b1) is used to measure what effect the local environment may have on whether a quality challenger emerges. If the incumbent won by a large margin in the previous election, the more quality challenger may opt not to enter that particular House race. Thus, there should be a negative relationship. The higher the previous incumbent's vote, the lower the level of challenger quality.

The second independent variable is the district-level presidential vote in 1992 (b2). The presidential vote is based on the percentage of the district vote the president received in the most recent election. This variable will be multiplied by 1 if the incumbent House member shares the same party as the president and -1 if the incumbent House member is of a different party than the president. It is expected that there will be a negative relationship between this and the dependent variable. If the party of the president and the incumbent House member is the same, and the president's percentage of the district vote in 1992 was high, then the quality of the challenger will decrease. Quality challengers are less likely to compete against a member of the president's party if the president is popular in the district.

The challenger party variable (b3) identifies whether the challenger is a Republican or Democrat. This variable is coded -1 for Republican challengers and 1 for Democratic challengers. The expected relationship is negative, signifying that the more quality challengers in the eight race-based redistricted states in the 1994 congressional elections were more likely to be Republican. It is believed that in the southern race-based redistricted states, the creation of one majority-black district led to the subsequent creation of several more conservative surrounding districts. These more conservative districts would be expected to attract formidable Republican challengers.

The redistricting-resultant change in black population proportion variable (b4) takes into account changes in black population from 1991, before redistricting, to 1993, when the process was completed. In a subsequent model, a variable measuring losses in black population due to redistricting is substituted for the change in black population variable. The focus of this chapter is on those districts that lost a portion of their black population due to the fact that blacks were removed from their district in order to create a majority-black district. My contention is that when House members lose a substantial portion of their black liberal voting bloc, it changes the makeup of the district which in turn makes sitting House incumbents more vulnerable to the threat of a quality challenger.

It might be expected that small changes in black population would have little effect on candidate emergence because such changes would not change the makeup of the district drastically. Therefore, a more accurate measure of the effects of racial changes should focus on large changes in black population. In those districts that lost 10 percent or more of their black population, it is expected that the strategically-minded challenger recognizes that the large drop in black population makes the incumbent House member more vulnerable, and therefore the prospective candidate is more apt to run in these districts.

REGRESSION ESTIMATES FOR QUALITY CHALLENGER EMERGENCE, 1994

The regression estimates for the 1994 quality challenger model are presented in Table 4.1. Each variable has a directional hypothesis; a one-tailed test is therefore used to identify coefficients that attain statistical significance. Model 4.1a includes 213 incumbent House members whose congressional seat was challenged in 1994. Model 4.1b includes incumbent House members who faced a challenge in 1994 in the eight southern states that underwent redistricting (N=38). Model 4.1c includes 170 incumbent House members who faced a challenge in 1994, in all states excluding the eight southern states. Model 4.1d includes only white incumbent House members in the eight southern states who were met with a challenge in 1994 (N=36).

First, in Model 4.1a, the coefficient for incumbents' previous margin of victory is negative and significant at the .10 level. This finding indicates that as House incumbents' margin of victory in the last election increases, the quality of the challenger decreases. As should be expected, a House incumbent who wins by a large percentage in the previous congressional race will, barring scandal, retain that popularity in the following election, and thus will not attract a formidable challenger. This result is consistent with the strategic politician theory. More calculating prospective candidates run for office in congressional races that they believe they can win. A high level of incumbent popularity, reflected in a large prior margin of victory, discourages the strategic politician from challenging the incumbent. Strategic prospective candidates will not waste precious time and resources on a campaign they cannot win. However, it appears that this factor was not as important as the president's popularity and the challenger's party.

The coefficient measuring the district-level presidential vote is negative and significant. When the party of the president and the incumbent House member are different, the larger the presidential vote in the district, the more likely a high quality challenger will run. In other words, if a president's level of popularity in a district is high, and the incumbent House member is not a member of the president's party, it is likely that the incumbent House member will face a high quality challenger in 1994.

Third, the coefficient measuring the party of the challenger is negative and significant. This suggests that Republicans were the higher quality challengers in 1994. It is important to keep in mind that this is the full model, including northern and southern states and states that were and were not affected by the 1990s race-based redistricting. In the 1994 congressional races throughout the

Table 4.1
Parameter Values for Logit Models of District Level Challenger Quality in 1994

	All		Redist		Nonredist		Redist/white	
	(a)		(b)		(c)		(d)	
	b	t	b	t	b	t	b	t
Incumbent Margin of Victory 1992	-0.026	-1.482*	0.038	1.207	-0.044	-2.183**	0.036	1.141
District Level Presidential Vote 1992	-0.139	-3.467***	-0.068	-0.671	-0.185	-3.555***	-0.055	-0.466
Challenger Party	-5.461	-3.322***	-2.400	-0.664	-7.755	-3.485***	-1.951	-0.473
Change in Black Population	-0.062	-1.407	-0.181	-1.401	-0.031	-0.334	-0.186	-1.408
Constant	-1.112	-2.222**	-3.836	-2.428***	-0.514	-0.957	-3.872	-2.398***
Pseudo R^2	0.180		0.225		0.250		0.214	
N=	208		38		175		36	

*** significant at .01 level; ** significant at .05 level; * significant at .10 level
Source: Calculated by the author from census and election data.

nation, Republican challengers were the higher quality challengers. This fact manifested itself in the form of more Republican victories and a majority Republican House after the election.

Fourth, the coefficient measuring the change in black population proportions does not attain statistical significance in the model including all House members met with a challenge in 1994. For the most part, districts not affected by the 1990s race-based redistricting did not experience substantial changes in their black population proportions. Therefore, it is not surprising that this variable does not seem to have an effect in the full model.

Model 4.1b focuses exclusively on House members in the eight southern states that experienced race-based redistricting. The variables that attain significance in the full model are no longer significant. In fact, the variable measuring change in black population proportions does not attain statistical significance either. This finding is interesting due to the hypothesis that incumbents in districts that experienced changes in black population would attract high quality challengers. At this point, the hypothesis is not supported by the data.

Model 4.1c includes all other states. Again, the coefficients measuring previous incumbent vote margin, presidential vote in 1992, and challenger party are all significant and in the expected direction. The level of significance for the coefficient measuring previous incumbent vote increases in level of significance when the eight southern states are excluded from the model. This suggests that the popularity of the incumbent in the previous election is more important in states not affected by the race-based redistricting.

The coefficient measuring change in black population does not attain significance. It is expected that in these districts, where race was not a focal point of the redistricting, race would not play an important role in a prospective challenger's decision to run for office.

Model 4.1d includes only white incumbents in the eight southern states. The difference between this model and Model 4.1b is the focus on white incumbents. This modification only changes the number of observations by two, and the findings are very similar to Model 4.1b, with no variables attaining significance.

Respecification of the Model: Changes in Black Population

In Table 4.2, the model is re-specified substituting losses in black population for changes in black population. The focus of this paper is on the effect that losses in black population had on the prospective candidate. It is useful to recall that my contention is that the creation of majority-black districts played a role in the increased conservatism in the House due to the subsequent creation of less black, more conservative districts. Thus, including increases as well as decreases in black population may mask the true impact of black population losses. The criteria used to select models 4.2a–4.2d are the same for models 4.1a–4.1d. Again, the only difference is the substitution of the variable measuring black population loss.

Table 4.2
Parameter Values for Logit Models of District Level Challenger Quality in 1994—Including Decrease in Black Population

	All		Redist		Nonredist		Redist/white	
	(a)		(b)		(c)		(d)	
	b	t	b	t	b	t	b	t
Incumbent Margin of Victory 1992	-0.026	-1.478*	0.039	1.242	-0.045	-2.191**	0.037	1.171
District Level Presidential Vote 1992	-0.139	-3.464***	-0.063	-0.619	-0.184	-3.539***	-0.048	-0.395
Challenger Party	-5.462	-3.321***	-2.248	-0.621	-7.546	-3.477***	-1.731	-0.411
Decrease in Black Population	-0.056	-1.203	-0.200	-1.445*	-0.019	-0.298	-0.207	-1.454*
Constant	-1.124	-2.209**	-4.064	-2.427***	-0.500	-0.914	-4.114	-2.391***
Pseudo R^2	0.174		0.232		0.242		0.222	
N=	213		38		175		36	

*** significant at .01 level; ** significant at .05 level; * significant at .10 level
Source: Calculated by the author from census and election data.

Model 4.2a includes 213 incumbent House members. The coefficients measuring previous incumbent margin, previous presidential vote, and challenger party remain significant and in the expected direction. In the full model, the loss in black population does not have an effect on the emergence of quality challengers in 1994. In order to determine the effects of redistricting, however, it is important to disaggregate the models. With this in mind, the model is divided, with Model 4.2b including only the eight southern states, and Model 4.2c including all other states.

In Model 4.2b (N=38), the coefficients measuring previous incumbent margin, presidential vote in 1992, and challenger party all fail to attain statistical significance. However, the coefficient measuring decreases in black population achieves significance. It appears that in states that underwent race-based redistricting, the effect of losing a substantial proportion of black population overshadowed the other variables that would normally be expected to affect a prospective challenger's decision to run for office. This finding, along with the findings in Model 4.2c (N=175), support the hypothesis. Model 4.2c presents findings for all states other than the eight southern race-based redistricted states. The coefficient measuring previous incumbent vote margin is significant at the .05 level and in the expected direction. Also, presidential vote in 1992 and challenger party are significant and in the expected direction. However, the variable measuring decreases in black population proportions does not attain significance. This suggests that in nonsouthern states and states that did not experience race-based redistricting, challengers considered more traditional factors when deciding whether to run for office. However, in southern states experiencing race-based redistricting, black population losses played an important role in the quality of challenger that emerged in the 1994 congressional elections.

Finally, Model 4.2d includes 36 white incumbent House members from the eight southern states. These are the incumbents that would be expected to be most affected by the race-based redistricting. The results are presented in the last column of Table 4.2. This model differs from 4.2b due to the inclusion of only white members. Again, this distinction only changes the number of cases by two. Consequently the findings are similar to 4.2b, with black population loss being the only variable attaining significance.

Large Decreases in Black Population

The model is also re-specified substituting large decreases in black population for the variable measuring raw decreases in black population. The findings are presented in Table 4.3 and are very similar to the findings in Table 4.2. However, the level of significance of the coefficients for decreases in black population is higher when focusing on large changes. Large decreases in black population have a significant effect for the models focusing on all districts, redistricted districts and redistricted districts with white House members, but the effect of this variable for nonredistricted states is not significant. This is exactly what one would expect. The effects of raw decreases in black population barely attain statistical significance in Table 4.2. In Table 4.3, however, the results are starkest and most clear. In states that were not affected by race-based redistricting, large decreases in black population did not influence high quality, prospective challengers' decision to run for office. In states that did undergo race-based redistricting, the large loss in black population was the single most important factor driving a prospective candidate's decision to run for office.

In addition, the pseudo-R^2 in Table 4.3 increases substantially in those models which concentrate on the eight southern states, signifying these models' increased ability to explain quality candidate emergence. Generally, the models explain between 17 to 35 percent of the variance in the equation. As Bond et al. (1985) explain, the decision to run for office can be very idiosyncratic. Therefore, there are many factors that may influence whether a person runs for office that simply are not quantifiable. The fact that this model explains up to 35 percent of the variance in quality challenger emergence in the 1994 congressional elections is therefore interesting based on the difficulty in explaining and predicting candidate emergence.

Discussion of Results

This research uncovers several important findings. First it seems that prospective challengers from southern states that underwent race-based redistricting considered different factors than prospective challengers in other states when determining whether to challenge an incumbent. Prospective challengers in nonsouthern states and states not affected by the 1990s race-based redistricting were more likely to consider how popular the incumbent was in the previous election and whether the incumbent shared the same party as the president. On the other hand, prospective challengers in the eight southern states did not focus on any of the more traditional factors included in the model. Instead, the higher quality challengers seemed to target those incumbents whose districts experienced a change in their black population.

This leads to the second point, which is that the type of change in black population proved to be very important. It might be theorized that any change in black population, whether positive or negative, would make the incumbent House member more vulnerable because this would change the political makeup of the district. This research indicates, however, that in 1994 only those race-based redistricted southern districts that lost black population attracted strong challengers. In turn, this finding supports the claim that 1990s race-based redistricting created districts that would attract more experienced and quality challengers.

In the 1994 House elections, higher-quality candidates were more likely to be Republican. This is true, however, only when considering all House challenges. When focusing exclusively on the eight southern redistricted states, there does not seem to be a similar pattern. In these states, in fact, there is no

Table 4.3

Parameter Values for Logit Models of District Level Challenger Quality in 1994—Including Large Decreases in Black Population

	All		Redist		Nonredist		Redist/white	
	(a)		(b)		(c)		(d)	
	b	t	b	t	b	t	b	t
Incumbent Margin of Victory 1992	-0.023	-1.303*	0.427	1.368*	-0.044	-2.112**	0.041	1.304*
District Level Presidential Vote 1992	-0.144	-3.526***	-0.046	-0.392	-0.186	-3.553***	-0.030	-0.218
Challenger Party	-5.709	-3.395***	-1.969	-0.459	-7.612	-3.490***	-1.402	-0.283
Large Change in Black Population	-0.089	-1.865**	-0.287	-1.943**	-0.035	-0.570	-0.288	-1.965**
Constant	-1.189	-2.370**	-4.265	-2.620***	-0.531	-0.976	-4.291	-2.600***
Pseudo R2	0.189		0.350		0.244		0.341	
N=	213		38		175		36	

*** significant at .01 level; ** significant at .05 level; * significant at .10 level

Source: Calculated by the author from census and election data.

relationship between challenger party and the quality of the challenger himself or herself. Based on the Republican gain in the South, the point is not that Republicans did not win elections in these southern states, rather the successes were not due to the fact that they fielded very strong or experienced candidates. This finding counters the hypothesis that the Republican gains in the South were due to the emergence of high quality strategic challengers in states affected by race-based redistricting; rather, it appears to be the case that there were national forces (such as a Democratic president facing a midterm election) at work. Republicans experienced electoral success in the eight southern states regardless of quality, whereas in other states, the Republican candidates were more likely to be defined as the "high-quality" candidates. Prior political experience did not seem to count for much in these elections.

In the 1994 congressional elections, to summarize these findings, quality challengers were more likely to emerge in districts that lost large portions of their black population. However, these high quality challengers were no more likely to be Republican. Thus, the creation of majority-black districts (and the unintended consequence of creating substantially altered districts) did prove to make the incumbent House member more vulnerable to high- quality strategic challengers, but not necessarily *Republican* challengers. High quality challengers were more likely to emerge in the eight southern states. Strategic politicians of both political parties may have chosen to enter races in which the incumbent was vulnerable due to district boundary changes that resulted from the 1990s redistricting.

CONCLUSION

It is difficult to determine what part the creation of majority-black districts played in the conservatism that swept the nation in the 1990s. Were there more powerful forces at work? Did the timing of the court-ordered redistricting unjustly implicate the majority-black district? These questions are difficult to answer. However, two important factors must be considered. First, the creation of majority-black districts coincided with the election of the first Democratic president in 12 years. The significance of this relates to the argument over divided government and split-ticket voting. If we accept Fiorina's (1996) contention that voters purposely divide their vote, then it would follow that the election of a Democratic president would be accompanied by the election of a Republican Congress. Explaining why this effect was not immediate is outside the scope of this chapter. Although Republicans did not win control of the House in 1992, they have maintained control since their takeover in 1994. The fact that the increase in quality Republican candidate emergence was limited to those nonsouthern states, and states unaffected by the race-based redistricting lends credence to the proposition that the increased conservatism had less to do with the creation of majority-black districts and more to do with an unrelated national trend. It is also important to note that the Senate, unaffected by the race-based redistricting of the 1990s, also came under Republican control in 1994.

The second factor that must be considered is the issue of "realignment" in the South (see chapter 1 in this volume for a more in-depth discussion of the concept). The South remained a one-party system from shortly after Reconstruction to the 1990s. For over the last 100 years, the Democratic Party has dominated southern politics. Throughout the 1990s, observers began to witness a shift in the electoral base of the Republican Party in the South. Many conservative Democrats no longer accepted the stigma attached to the Republican Party from the Civil War and Reconstruction period; additionally, several conservative southern House members who identified with the Democratic Party largely for electoral purposes switched their affiliation to the Republican Party in the 1990s. Large portions of the southern white electorate that had identified with the Democratic Party also began to switch their party affiliation. It is important to recognize that both the public officials and the white voters did not change their political ideology or philosophy—they simply changed the party with which their ideology was becoming increasingly identified. As Kevin Hill (1995, 400) illustrates, Republicans in the South "gained seats in both districts losing blacks and those relatively unaffected by racial redistricting." It is difficult to determine what aspect of the increased Republicanism can be attributed directly and exclusively to the creation of majority-black districts. At this point, the indirect impact of the creation of these districts on increased Republicanism is also unclear.

In 1949, V.O. Key proclaimed that southern politics was dominated by race. The predominant role of race was due to the fact that the South was composed of a large black population and a prejudiced white population that continually constructed obstacles to black advancement and enfranchisement. However, it has become increasingly arguable among professional pundits whether race still dominates politics in the South in the modern day. In the 1990s, the most dramatic aspect of this alleged struggle was the redistricting process, which created substantial numbers of majority-minority districts. At the onset of the twenty-first century and better than fifty years after Key's proclamation, this research indicates that issues of race may well continue to dominate the debate over the redistricting process in the South for some time to come; to the extent that such redistricting directly plays into explanations of partisan control of the Congress, however, we still have many inquiries to undertake.

NOTES

1. Eight majority-Hispanic districts were created nationwide in 1992. These districts have also been challenged in Texas, Illinois, and New York. For the most part, however, the effects of the 1990s redistricting are focused on majority-black districts in the South.

2. In Katherine Tate's (1993) *From Protest to Politics: The New Black Voters in American Elections*, the author explores the political views of blacks by studying their response from the National Black Election Study (NBES). Tate finds that although African Americans have become more conservative in terms of ideology in the last 30 years,

they are still overwhelmingly liberal. An analysis of an National Election Study (NES) policy position table spanning 36 years shows that blacks have remained liberal across a wide range of policy issues.

5

The Contemporary South and the 1998 Elections

CHARLES S. BULLOCK III

Some elections display strong and consistent patterns of change. For example, 1994 rewarded Republicans while devastating Democrats. The last election of the twentieth century reveals no easily discernable trend. In the South, as in the rest of the nation, virtually nothing happened. A lobbyist who knew the members of the 105th Congress by sight had very few new faces to learn in 1999. What accounts for the absence of change? Have Republicans peaked so that with the new century they will begin to recede like glaciers at the end of an ice age, or was 1998 a brief moment of equilibrium that allows Republicans to catch their breath before completing the conversion of the Solid Democratic South into the Solid Republican South? Alternatively, is the stasis of 1998 likely to persist with both parties "winning some and losing some?"

PARTY FORTUNES IN THE 1990s

A brief review of the earlier elections of this decade will show how the 1998 election differs from its immediate predecessors. The decade dawned with Democrats still entrenched with majorities in the South's delegations in both houses of Congress. Democrats held a 15 to 7 advantage in the Senate, as they had after the 1988 election, and only a seat or two weaker than they had been throughout the 1970s. Memories of the first three elections of the 1980s, during which Republicans held about half the region's Senate seats, were rapidly fading. In the House, the partisan makeup in 1991 remained as it had been after the two previous elections with Democrats holding eight more seats than when Ronald Reagan became president. Democrats seemed likely to retain solid majorities in the South and in the House for the near future. Early each election year, Republicans naively boasted that this would be the year in which they broke out of their enclaves and became the region's majority, but once the votes were counted, Democratic dominance remained unshaken.[1]

The fortunes of southern Republicans running for Congress began improving in 1992, when they won three of the seven Senate seats at stake and added nine House seats. While this preview titillated Republican viewers, the main attraction proved captivating. In the next election, Republicans gained control of Congress, in part, because three Senate and 16 House seats in the South changed hands. For the first time in recent history, Republicans held majorities in the delegations sent to both congressional chambers from Dixie. The GOP momentum continued as Senator Richard Shelby (AL) switched parties immediately after the election and, in April, Nathan Deal (GA) became the first of five southern House Democrats to depart the party of their ancestors. The GOP pushed on to new heights two years later when they picked up a brace of Senate seats and a net of two more House seats. Since 1991 Republicans had increased from 32 to 68 percent of the Senate seats and from 30 to 57 percent of the southern House seats. Comparable GOP gains occurred in governor's mansions (with a majority of them held by Republicans after 1994) and state legislatures, where Republicans won control of three southern chambers in 1994.

GOP prospects for further congressional victories in 1998 paled because of their previous triumphs. In the past, Republicans could cast covetous glances at congressional districts represented by Democrats despite regularly voting for Ronald Reagan and George Bush (Bullock 1988a; Aistrup 1996; Bullock and Shafer 1997). Successes of presidential candidates registered as early as the Eisenhower elections in the Rim South and since Goldwater's 1964 campaign in the Deep South had softened the electorate up to the notion of voting Republican. If an attractive local could be recruited to carry the GOP banner, and especially if the dreaded "L" word (liberal) could be attached to the Democratic nominee, voters might be persuaded to bring their congressional choices into alignment with their presidential preferences (Black and Black 1987).[2]

In 1988 schizophrenia characterized southern congressional voting behavior as most districts supported George Bush along with a Democrat for Congress. By 1996, in well over 80 percent of the districts, voters favored nominees of the same party for president and Congress. Only fourteen districts persisted in voting Republican for president but Democratic for Congress. Instrumental in the new consistency were Republican advances made earlier in the decade. Of 54 House districts still in Democratic hands in 1996, 16 sent African Americans to Congress and five Texas districts elected Hispanics. Republicans running in these districts would confront a fierce head wind because of concentrations of minorities, so that perhaps no more than half of the Democratic House seats held much prospect for GOP success under any but the most extraordinary conditions.

On the Senate side, where Republicans held 15 of 22 seats, their majority status placed them on the defensive. Early in 1998, the GOP hold on seats in Georgia and North Carolina appeared tenuous while only Fritz Hollings (SC) looked vulnerable among Democrats. The Arkansas seat, being vacated by Dale

Bumpers (D), beckoned to both parties with Republican hopes inflamed by their 1996 successes, which saw them capture the governor's mansion for the first time since 1980 and win their first Senate seat since this office became popularly elected.

THE 1998 RESULTS

Although the numbers fluctuated between the primaries and November, pundits identified only a few dozen competitive congressional districts nationwide and these included but a handful in the South. The region continued to have more uncontested seats than the rest of the nation as it contained 58 of the 93 districts that offered a nominee of only one of the two dominant parties. Florida was the least competitive state with a dozen Republicans and five Democrats drawing a general election bye. As shown in Florida, the persistence of uncontested districts had ceased to be the result of Democratic dominance. The pattern first observed in 1994, when more Republicans than Democrats ran unopposed, reemerged in 1998 as Democrats in 35 southern districts went to the polls with no member of their party to support. Republicans did a more thorough job of recruiting and offered nominees in all but 23 districts.

While 67 of 125 districts had bipartisan competition, incumbent success rivaled that achieved when Republicans still struggled with the albatross of Reconstruction. Of the six sitting members of Congress rejected by the November electorate, none came from the South. Southern incumbents were bathed in such bountiful popularity that only three failed to secure at least 55 percent of the vote. Again, it is important to note that both parties now benefit from security while in the not too distant past invulnerability was a suit that fit only Democrats.

Even southern open seats displayed little variability as only two changed hands. In Mississippi's Fourth District, Ronnie Shows (D) replaced Mike Parker (R). The retiring incumbent won the seat in 1988 as a Democrat but along with four other southerners changed parties during the 104th Congress. With 41 percent of its population being African American, this had been the most heavily black district in the nation represented by a Republican. North Carolina's Eighth District moved in the opposite direction as one-time unsuccessful gubernatorial candidate Robin Hayes succeeded Bill Hefner (D). This was among the handful of districts in the region that voted for both Bush and Dole yet sent a Democrat to Congress and, as noted above, this kind of inconsistency has recently presaged GOP advances. Since Hefner had broken 60 percent of the vote only once in a 24-year career and had twice been held to 51 percent, the surprise surrounding this outcome was not that it went Republican but that Hayes managed only 51 percent.

Sitting southern senators were less immune to shifts in public attitudes as Lauch Faircloth (R-NC) fell to a political novice, wealthy trial lawyer John Edwards, 51–47 percent. In Georgia, where Paul Coverdell had been listed on endangered lists early in the season, the incumbent became the first holder of that seat to be reelected since Herman Talmadge won his fourth term in 1974. The most endangered Democrat, 76-year-old Fritz Hollings, took 53 percent of the vote against Representative Bob Inglis and thereby began his thirty-third year as junior senator from the state of South Carolina—a record period for being "number two" to venerable Republican Strom Thurmond. Incumbents Richard Shelby (R-AL), Bob Graham (D-FL), and John Breaux (D-LA) surged to additional terms with more than 60 percent vote shares.

Arkansas provided the region's one open Senate seat when Dale Bumpers (D) called it quits after four terms. In light of GOP successes in 1996, when Mike Huckabee won two remaining years of a term after replacing Jim Guy Tucker, who drowned in the Whitewater scandal, and Tim Hutchinson became senator, Republicans hoped to pick up the open Senate seat. Their nominee, religious conservative Fay Boozman, was slow to catch fire and then, when he began closing the gap, he made a sexist gaffe *a la* Clayton Williams (R-TX) from which he never recovered. Blanche Lambert Lincoln, who had left the House to tend to infant twins, came back from maternity leave and captured 55 percent of the vote.

The negligible changes in the partisan makeup on the South's congressional membership are but part of a broader picture of modest shifts up and down the ticket in the region. The most notable changes involved governors as GOP incumbents Fob James (AL) and David Beasley (SC) succumbed to lottery fever. Georgia's use of lottery revenues to pay college and vocational school tuition for in-state high school graduates who maintain B averages and to fund a voluntary pre-kindergarten for four-year-olds prompted covetous looks from neighbors. Democrats used promises of instituting a Georgia-style lottery to unseat incumbents who seemed to view this revenue source as evil.

Other Republican governors fared better as Mike Huckabee (AR), George W. Bush (TX), and Don Sundquist (TN) won four more years. Continuity also reigned in Georgia, where Democrats passed the baton from term-limited Zell Miller (creator of the lottery) to state legislator Roy Barnes and thereby kept the GOP zero for the century at the governor's mansion. The other open seat helped Republicans offset their losses in Alabama and South Carolina as Jeb Bush ran a smarter campaign than in 1994 and became Florida's governor.

As with the region's congressional membership and chief executives, only modest changes touched state legislative chambers. Across the eight states that elected legislators, Republicans netted 15 seats in lower houses while suffering a net loss of nine state senators. The biggest GOP gains came in state houses in Arkansas (nine), Florida (seven), and Tennessee (seven) while Democrats made their biggest inroads in the North Carolina House (six)—where they returned as the majority party after a four-year hiatus—and Senate (five) and the South Carolina House (four). Republicans registered a total of 26 new House seats and a net loss of one Senate seat in states in which they won the governorship, compared with Democratic gains of five House and four Senate seats in states where they won governorships. In North Carolina, which did not have a gubernatorial election in 1998, new Senator John Edwards may have provided the pull for the Democratic pickup of 11 legislative seats.

To summarize, the 1998 elections produced scant partisan change in the South. Net partisan shifts were zero in the House, one additional Democrat in the Senate and among governors, 15 more state house Republicans, and nine more Democratic state senators. These totals hardly sustain the interpretation urged by Democratic activists who claim that the last election of the century signaled a resurgence of the region's traditional majority party. Democratic gains pale in the harsh light of numbers of changed seats. They take on significance only when juxtaposed against Republican expectations for 1998 or the advances rung up earlier in the decade. Republican inroads have stalled, but it is premature to conclude that Democrats are on the way back. They must make additional gains in 2000 and 2002 to authenticate a claim that they have the Republicans on the run.

BEHIND THE RESULTS

Some of the more notable changes in 1998 stem from ticket splitting by white voters. Five states elected both a governor and a senator in 1998, and in all but South Carolina, each party claimed one of these offices. White split-ticket voting is, at a minimum, the difference between the share of the white vote going to the Republican nominees for these offices. As reported in Table 5. 1, in states producing a split decision, white voters were at least 11 percentage points more likely to vote for the winning Republican than for the loser, and in Alabama, Richard Shelby attracted 74 percent of the white vote in retaining his Senate seat while Fob James managed a bare 51 percent white majority in being turned out of the governorship.

Another perspective on split-ticket voting appears in Table 5.2, where defections from the losing candidate's party to the winner are presented for states with split-party results. These figures are not limited to whites but involve all voters although we expect that most of the fluctuation involves whites. As we see, Alabama Governor James lost 36 percent of the voters who had supported Senator Shelby and departed from the governor's mansion. In contrast, Shelby took 40 percent of the vote that had gone to Democratic gubernatorial nominee Don Siegelman. For Alabama, Arkansas, and Florida, about one-third of the electorate defected from the loser, indicating a sizable ebb and flow of voters across the partisan divide. Defections were fewer in Georgia, but Senator Paul Coverdell (R) and new Governor Roy Barnes (D) each attracted one voter among five who backed the other party's nominee for these top-of-the-ticket posts. Despite the reduction in the number of districts that produce different partisan results for congressional and presidential elections, a sizable component of the white electorate is not firmly committed to either party in high visibility contests.

Table 5.1
Percent White Support for Republicans in Southern Contests for Governor and U.S. Senator, 1998

State	*Governor*	*Senator*
Alabama	51	74*
Arkansas	61*	44
Florida	60*	42
Georgia	58	69*

*Republican nominee elected.
Source: Exit poll results from CNN.com/ELECTION/1998/states/.

Table 5.2
Total Defections from Losing Candidates in Southern States That Elected Governors and Senators, 1998

State	*Governor*	*Senator*
Alabama	36	40*
Arkansas	35*	33
Florida	32*	36
Georgia	20	20*

*Republican nominee elected.
Source: Exit poll results from CNN.com/ELECTION/1998/states/.

Postelection commentators suggested that 1998 may have witnessed two changes: heightened participation rates by African Americans and a lesser role for religious conservatives. Since black voters regularly give in excess of 80 percent of their votes to Democrats, if this component of the electorate increased then it should help Democrats. Whites who march under the banner of the Religious Right provide support to Republicans that often rivals black cohesion behind Democrats. For example, exit polls show that Senator Richard Shelby (AL), Governor Mike Huckabee (AR), Governor Jeb Bush (FL) and Senator Paul Coverdell (GA) each got the votes of more than 80 percent of the whites who identify with the Religious Right, and even unsuccessful Republican candidates typically amassed at least 70 percent support among these voters.

Comparing exit polls for 1998 with those for the previous midterm election provides convincing evidence of heightened black participation rates only in Georgia. In the Peach State, the exit polls indicate that blacks voted at higher rates than whites in 1998 as blacks constitute a quarter of Georgia's registered voters but cast 29 percent of the votes. This constitutes almost a 100 percent increase over the 1994 exit poll estimate that blacks cast one-sixth of the ballots. In Alabama, Florida, South Carolina, Tennessee, and Texas, however, blacks comprised about the same proportion of the vote in 1998 as in 1994, whereas in Arkansas they declined.

Defeats of Republicans associated with the Religious Right in contests for senator in Arkansas and North Carolina and for governor in Alabama, Georgia, and South Carolina suggested that conservative Christians may have become less significant. Among states for which 1994 and 1998 exit polls are available, only Georgia experienced a sizable decline in the share of the white electorate that reported identifying with the Religious Right. In Georgia a seven-point drop from 26 to 19 percent of white voters was reported. In contrast, Florida exit polls tapped a nine-point increase in religious right affiliates among white voters over the four-year period—and in Tennessee, a striking increase from 10 to 31 points occurred. Alabama and South Carolina had negligible changes.

While changes in the composition of the electorate seem not to hold the key to 1998 results, a more conventional explanator, incumbency, remains useful. Five of six sitting senators, three of five governors, and all House members seeking additional terms succeeded. In the most notable exception to the power of incumbency, two governors fell after opposing a state lottery despite it being favored by 56 percent of the Alabama electorate and 60 percent of South Carolina's voters. Exit polls show that lottery supporters cast 76 percent of their votes for the Democratic challenger in South Carolina and a remarkable 88 percent for the challenger in Alabama so that Siegelman ran almost as well among lottery lovers as among blacks.

PARTY PROSPECTS FOR THE FUTURE

Redistricting at the outset of the new century may pose stiff challenges for Democrats in some congressional and state legislative districts. After new districts were put in place at the beginning of the 1990s, Republicans gained a net of a dozen senate seats and almost five times as many house seats across the region. The GOP may be even better positioned to influence the process at the beginning of the century. They seem likely to hold at least five governorships with an intervening election still to be held in Louisiana and Mississippi. Regardless of the party holding the governorship of a state, the components of the coalitions that heavily influenced reapportionment decisions at the outset of the 1990s will be stronger at the beginning of the third millennium. As of January 1999, Republicans held 198 more house seats and 75 more senate seats across the South than eight years earlier. The ranks of African Americans also swelled by 62 in lower chambers and 28 in senates between 1991 and 1997 so that the coalition of blacks and Republicans constitute a majority in all of the region's legislative chambers except for Arkansas, the Louisiana House, and the North Carolina Senate. If Republicans and African-American legislators work together to promote their individual interests at the expense of white Democrats, as occurred in the 1980s and 1990s (Bullock 1983, 1987, 1995a), they will be even better positioned than in the past.

Democratic governors could veto such efforts, but would they dare do so if they enjoyed strong support in the black community in light of the importance of black votes to statewide Democratic candidates? Thus it seems reasonable to expect that reconfiguring congressional districts early in the new century will produce more heavily white suburban districts likely to elect Republicans and central city and black belt districts favorable to Democrats. Florida, Georgia, and Texas will gain seats as may North Carolina and Virginia. In each of these states, growth has been concentrated in the suburbs, and much of this growth has involved Republican voters. Absent new guidance from the Supreme Court countermanding *Shaw v. Reno* and *Miller v. Johnson,* the GOP black coalition will not promote the cartographic extremes witnessed in the affirmative action gerrymanders of the early 1990s. Nonetheless, the outcome may be compact, contiguous districts that follow political boundaries and promote the fortunes of Republican and African-American candidates.

CONCLUSIONS

The last election of the twentieth century gave no guidance as to political change in the South. If a different direction is about to be taken, it must await the new millennium. If there is to be a shift, the 1998 results suggest that the key to success for each party may remain unchanged. With the notable exception of Georgia, 1998 did not see increased levels of black participation nor decreased turnout among whites who identify with the Religious Right so that the presence of key components of the two parties' supporters underwent little change.

Since Republicans still struggle to get 10 percent of the black vote, they need more than 60 percent of the white vote to win statewide. Democrats win by assembling a biracial coalition of overwhelming black support and the votes of 40 percent or more of the whites who go to the polls. In congressional districts that are more heavily white, Republicans can win with less than a 60 percent share of the white vote while Democrats can survive with less than 40 percent of the white vote in districts that are at least 30 percent black. With most whites now often voting Republican, the GOP dominates congressional districts that are less than 10 percent black and have made inroads in other heavily white districts. Following the retirement of Mike Parker (MS), Democrats hold all districts at least 40 percent black. Moreover, all of the black legislators from the South won additional terms even though most of them ran in whiter districts in 1998 than prior to 1996 as a result of court-ordered redistricting pursuant to *Miller v. Johnson.*

Although 1996 saw lower levels of split ticket voting for presidential and congressional preferences in the South, four states rendered split decisions in selecting governors and senators in 1998. Given the constancy of black preferences for Democrats, the fluctuations stem from variations in white support.

Incumbents seeking reelection to high offices generally ran better among white voters, regardless of the officeholders' party. The exception involved the Republican governors of Alabama and South Carolina, whose defeats provide evidence that issues matter. These incumbents went into 1998 as favorites for second terms but managed to lose when they opposed a state lottery that would help fund education as done in neighboring Georgia. Whether these defeats stemmed from principle or stupidity, it seems more likely to have been an anomaly rather than a trend, especially if Republicans see in this a warning that extremity is not a winning hand.

The results of 1998 demonstrate that both parties have the potential to win statewide contests. To succeed, they must recruit attractive candidates. Furthermore, if a candidate stumbles into a widely unacceptable policy stance, even incumbency will not stave off defeat. To become secure as the South's majority party and extend its control to include most of the region's legislatures, Republicans will have to attract support from a larger component of the white electorate and will have to convince those voters to cast straight-party ballots. Alternatively, if the GOP could nail down even as little as 20 percent of the black vote that should permit consistent victories in statewide contests. To regain their dominance, Democrats either need to broaden their support among whites or coax higher levels of participation among minorities. A replication of Georgia's record levels of black voting in other states would produce results like those in the Peach State, where Democrats turned back GOP efforts to capture the posts of governor, lieutenant governor, secretary of state, attorney general, and labor commissioner—none of which had an elected incumbent. The strategies leading to success for the parties are far clearer than the likelihood that any of these scenarios will transpire in the next few elections.

NOTES

1. The GOP swept all of the region's electoral votes in 1984 and 1988 and failed to achieve that level of dominance in 1980 only when President Jimmy Carter managed to hold on to his home state.

2. On the dangers for Democrats associated with being labeled as "liberals," see Black and Black (1987).

PART II

IDEOLOGY AND OPERATIONS

6

Southern Party Leaders in the Postreform House

RONALD M. PETERS, JR.

HISTORICAL PATTERNS

In its lengthening history, the United States House of Representatives has often been led by members from the South.[1] During the antebellum period (which I have elsewhere called the House's "parliamentary" era), 13 of 22 House speakers were from southern or border states, including such influential speakers as Nathanial Macon of Virginia, Henry Clay of Kentucky, Andrew Stevenson of Virginia, and James Polk of Tennessee (Peters 1997).[2] After the Civil War, during the House's partisan era, the number of southern speakers decreased because the Republicans were more often in the majority. Still, two of the three Democratic speakers of that era were from southern or border states, John G. Carlisle of Kentucky and Charles T. Crisp of Georgia.

In the early decades of the twentieth century, as the House was in transition from its partisan to its feudal era, the Republicans were led uniformly by northerners and westerners, while the Democratic leadership was largely derived from southern and border states. During this period, the position of party floor leader was institutionalized, creating a larger pool of party leaders.[3] After the revolt against Speaker Joseph Cannon of Illinois in 1910, the Democrats were led by a border state member, Champ Clark of Missouri, who became speaker in 1911. His floor leader was Oscar Underwood of Alabama, who exercised effective political power in the Democratic caucus. Subsequently, Democratic leaders included John Nance Garner of Texas, Joseph Byrns of Tennessee, William Bankhead of Alabama, and Sam Rayburn of Texas, who died in 1961. During this long period, during which the Democrats were almost always in the majority, the Republican leadership was entirely northern; it could hardly have been otherwise because there was effectively no Republican Party in the South.

The main factor that shaped this historical pattern (Democratic leaders from the South; Republican leaders from the North) from 1789 through the mid-1960s was the politics of race. During the antebellum period, the southern Democratic speakers fended off northern abolitionists by exercising powers of committee assignments and floor recognition. Speakers from the North, Federalist and then Whig, were more receptive to antislavery sentiment. The great compromises of 1820 and 1850 corralled but could not contain the sectional split over slavery, and after the Great Compromiser, Henry Clay, passed from the scene in 1854, the Congress and the nation became deadlocked on the slavery question. So divisive was this issue that the House often found it difficult to organize by choosing a Speaker. On the eve of the Civil War, William Pennington of New Jersey was elected Speaker on his first day in office, a compromise choice that did not stave off the disaster to follow.

The Civil War settled the slavery question but did not end the race issue. The Republican Reconstruction led the South to become solidly Democratic, and in the 1870s and 1880s Republicans pushed "force bills" aimed at coercing the South to enforce the Civil War amendments to the Constitution. For a hundred years after the end of the Civil War, southern members of Congress were virtually all Democrats who opposed civil rights legislation. Even southerners who were progressive on other social and economic issues had to be "right" on race issues in order to survive. With no Republican opposition and very few black voters, southern Democratic members had little incentive to challenge the racial prejudices of the voting majorities that elected them. This fundamental political reality was reflected in the behavior of the southern congressional leaders. These men were selected for leadership within the Democratic caucus with the support of northern Democrats as well as southern Democrats; otherwise, they could not have attained majorities. Yet it was silently understood that their constituencies would prevent them from taking active leadership roles on civil rights issues.

Of course, race was not the only issue that defined the two parties and their leadership. During the nineteenth century, the two parties were regularly at odds over the tariff, and in the twentieth century they became divided over federal tax policy and the rise of the national government attendant to the New Deal. Up until the Smoot-Hawley Tariff disaster in 1930, the Republicans always stood for high tariffs, small government, and low taxes. After that they switched to become the party of free trade, small government, and low taxes. Progressive Republicans sought a more expansive role for the federal government than did stand-patters, but the Republican Party was nonetheless defined primarily by its support of pro-growth economic policies. As the Republicans became increasingly associated with the business class, the Democrats became more and more the party of the lower classes—farmers, factory workers, racial and ethnic minorities, and the urban unemployed. The Democratic constituencies demanded more government rather than less, and when the Great Depression threw a third of the labor force out of work, the center of the American electorate gravitated to the Democratic Party as the Roosevelt coalition was formed. That coalition was grounded in the desire for a helping federal government.

The role of the South in American national politics during the period from 1932 through the 1970s was, then, defined by two basic policy positions: resistance to civil rights legislation and support of federal spending programs. The practical political problem that the South faced lay in finding a means of attaining its policy goals given that it remained a politically isolated region that could not succeed in a majoritarian policy game. The solution to which the South came lay in manipulating and controlling political process. The game began in the courthouse rings of southern Democratic party politics and extended its reach into the Democratic cloakroom of the United States House of Representatives.

The domination of the South by the Democratic Party led to pathologies that characterize one-party political systems (Key 1949). Courthouse politics is grounded in power and personality, not in policy. When distributed benefits are the only goals, political competition centers on delivering the goods. With no viable two-party competition, elections become easily corrupted. Even when the political process is itself clean, politics becomes dominated by factionalism, and the dominant faction will control the instruments of governmental largess, thus reinforcing its power. In the southern states, county courthouse rings lay at the center of concentric circles of power that surrounded state legislatures, state executives, and congressional offices. This power structure resulted in the prolongation of congressional careers among southern representatives to the U.S. House (Polsby 1968; Polsby, Gallagher, and Rundquist 1969). A Democratic representative from a southern state, facing no Republican opposition, could be assured of a long congressional career provided only that he continued to deliver benefits to the state and continued to oppose civil rights legislation.

The longevity of service among southern House members assumed more importance because of the seniority norm. Given its internal divisions, between North and South, and between liberals and conservatives, it was in the interest of the House Democrats to find a method of internal governance that would minimize conflict. The seniority rule—which dictated that selection of committee assignments, committee chairmanships, and subcommittee chairmanships would be based on length of House service—becalmed decision-making processes that would otherwise have been quite turbulent. Seniority can also be justified on the grounds that it empowers members with long experience. But southern Democrats always understood that their minority status in the Democratic caucus as well as in the House as a whole demanded that they find means to offset their numerical disadvantage by procedural rules.

Thus, the Democratic Party has always been sectionally and ideologically divided, and this division has been reflected in its selection of House leaders. From the late 1930s until Tip O'Neill's retirement in 1987, the House Democrats always had one leader from Massachusetts and one leader from Texas or Oklahoma (Rayburn/John McCormack; McCormack/Carl Albert; Albert/O'Neill; O'Neill/Jim Wright). This "Austin-Boston" axis served the party's interest by ensuring that its leadership had roots in the Northeast and the South, including both "city boys" and "farm boys." The Republicans, by contrast, selected their leaders from among "small town boys" from the Northeast, Midwest, and West, including Joseph Martin of Massachusetts, Leslie Arends of Illinois, Charles Halleck of Indiana, Gerald Ford of Michigan, John Rhodes of Arizona, and Bob Michel of Illinois. The first entry of a southern Republican into the GOP leadership ranks was that of Trent Lott of Mississippi, who became whip in 1981, reflecting the rise of the Republican Party in the South.

Political scientists have suggested that the "style" of House leaders is largely determined by the "institutional context" in which they are called upon to lead (Cooper and Brady 1981). After they took control of the House in the 1930s, the Democrats imposed a regime in which power was largely held in the committee rooms by senior committee chairmen, who were disproportionately from the South. Democratic speakers, especially Sam Rayburn, adapted to this situation by developing an accommodating leadership style. I have called this period in the history of the House its "feudal" era because of the power that the committee chairmen wielded. Just as the English monarchs of old, Speaker Rayburn had to work with his committee barons because he could not command them. This system of dispersed power enabled the party to cope with the underlying divisions within the Democratic caucus that defined it. In the committee rooms deals were struck, compromises reached, and interests balanced. Rayburn's job was to preside over this process of mutual adjustment and accommodation. His style was suited to the task. Rayburn became not the characteristic speaker, but the characteristic Democratic speaker. Democratic House leaders, emulating Rayburn, were accommodators and compromisers, rather than being ideologues or policy makers. This description would apply, with stylistic variations, to speakers John McCormack, Carl Albert, Tip O'Neill, Jim Wright, and Tom Foley, as well as to other Democratic leaders of otherwise diverse background and description, such as party whips Hale Boggs of Louisiana, John Brademas of Indiana, Bill Gray of Pennsylvania, and Tony Coehlo of California. A Democratic leader was characteristically a pragmatic deal maker rather than an idealistic policy maker, as was appropriate to the coalitional nature of the party.[4]

The hegemony of the Democratic committee chairmen was challenged by the reform movement of the early 1970s. Plainly, the main impetus for reform came from within the Democratic caucus among liberals whose policy aims were frustrated by a power structure dominated by southern conservatives. Speakers John McCormack and Carl Albert were progressives who embraced liberal policy goals; but both speakers were dependent upon and deferential to the southern committee barons who sat astride the legislative process. McCormack and Albert understood that the preservation of the Democrats' majority depended upon reconciling the divergent views and interests of the party's southern and northern wings. Albert, in particular, sought to preside over the reform process in a manner to hold the caucus together. The liberal reformers sought to strengthen the party leadership, on the one hand, and to undermine the power of the committee barons, on the other hand. The decentralizing pressures were more powerful, and after 1975 power in the House was largely grounded in its subcommittees. With over half of the Democratic caucus holding subcommittee chairmanships, the southern influence was diluted (Sheppard 1985; Peters 1997).

Another manifestation of the southern influence in the Democratic Party was its reliance on the leadership ladder. In 1932 the Democrats had a contested election for the Speakership in which Henry Rainey of Illinois defeated Joseph Byrns of Tennessee, who became the Democratic floor leader. With Rainey's death in 1934, Byrns became Speaker in 1935. This began a string of eight Democratic majority leaders who were initially elevated to the Speakership without contest in the Democratic caucus. In this sequence there occurred only three instances of a contested Speakership election. Congressman Morris Udall of Arizona mounted a symbolic challenge to Speaker McCormack in 1969, and Congressman John Conyers of Michigan twice challenged Speaker Albert, on each occasion winning only a handful of votes. Further, from 1937, when Rayburn was elected Democratic majority leader, until 1971, when Hale Boggs won that post over four other candidates, there was no contested election for that position either.[5] In 1976 a contested majority leader election took place in which Jim Wright won a narrow victory over Richard Bolling of Missouri and Phillip Burton of California. But in 1986, when Jim Wright became Speaker, party whip Tom Foley was elected majority leader without opposition.[6]

This pattern of stability in leadership succession among the Democrats has been thoroughly chronicled by Robert Peabody and Lynne Brown (Peabody 1976; Brown and Peabody 1990). They attribute it primarily to the Democrats' need to provide for orderly transfers of power in a divided caucus. The fault line within the Democratic caucus was, however, that between southern conservatives and northern liberals. In order to maintain harmony, the Democrats avoided fights over the Speakership and sought to provide regional balance across the several party leadership positions. It was the concern for regional balance that led to the "Austin-Boston" axis. The evolution of this pattern was usually due to choices made by Speakers as, for example, when Rayburn put Carl Albert on the leadership ladder by appointing him whip in 1955, and on occasion due to choices made by the caucus in contested elections as, for example, in 1976 when Jim Wright won a contested election for the position of floor leader. But underlying these particular choices was the Democrats' need to balance the interests of its southern and northern wings.

DYNAMICS OF SOUTHERN DEMOCRATIC LEADERSHIP

House leadership during the long period of Democratic control was a balancing act in structure and execution. The party balanced its leadership team, and its leaders sought to promote harmony by maintaining the balance. They imposed a decentralized regime that facilitated logrolling, they structured committee appointments so as ensure that important regional interests were protected, they used control of the floor to fend off divisive legislative proposals, and they focused the party agenda on core economic interests around which consensus could be built. They wrapped this panoply of devices in a set of norms that included reciprocity, specialization, and logrolling by which new members were socialized into an old regime. Sam Rayburn taught new members "to get along, go along" to prevent them from disturbing the balance upon which he precariously perched.

The dynamics of the Democratic caucus can be seen in any number of policy areas. One well-known policy accord was the city/farm bargain by which agricultural price supports and urban spending programs were logrolled to enactment every year. Another lay in the way that federal welfare programs were structured to provide for rural and urban poor. Food stamps, among the larger federal welfare programs, is actually administered by the Department of Agriculture, long a bastion of southern influence, making explicit the Democrats' reliance on federal largess to bind a majority coalition spanning northern cities and southern farms. For many years, national defense was another policy domain that bound northern and southern Democrats. Under the umbrella of a bipartisan, Cold War foreign policy and a strong commitment to national defense, Democrats were happy to sustain a large military-industrial complex that serviced many factories and shipyards in the North and many military installations in the South. Until the Vietnam War rent the party, Democrats were united in support of a substantial defense budget.

Of course, not all issues united the Democrats, and one issue, civil rights, split the party all along. One might say that the sine qua non for Democratic leaders in the House was to negotiate the civil rights fault line within the caucus. Sam Rayburn deferred to the committee chairs in part because he knew that civil rights bills would die in either the Judiciary or Rules Committees. In the 1950s liberal Democrats pressed for civil rights legislation, but Rayburn never made it a party priority. When, in 1957, a substantial civil rights bill made it to the House floor, Rayburn kept as low a profile as possible, relying on the Senate (where southerners could utilize their institutional positions of power and the filibuster) to cripple the bill. Rayburn's supporters debate the extent of his commitment to civil rights (Hardeman and Bacon 1987). As a national Democrat, he was certainly supportive of civil rights in principal; but as a Texas Democrat he had to heed his district, in which there was strong opposition to civil rights legislation (Champagne 1984). This kind of balancing act characterized other Democratic Speakers on other issues. John McCormack carried the flag on civil rights, but he was isolated on the issue of federal support for parochial schools. Carl Albert walked the same tightrope as had Rayburn on civil rights and relied upon McCormack to take the lead during the enactment of the civil rights bills of the 1960s. Albert also had to walk a fine line on gun control legislation because of the strength of the National Rifle Association in his district. Speaker Jim Wright became enmeshed in immigration legislation as majority leader and then as Speaker because this was a hot issue in Texas. This put him at odds with Democrats from other parts of the country (Vega and Peters 1996).

The basic underlying strategy of Democratic speakers in coping with their divided caucus was to do everything possible to localize politics. "All politics is local" was Tip O'Neill's great aphorism. It defined a strategy for Democrats to maintain their House majority. In a larger representational sense, all politics should be local because members represent local district interests. That is the way in which the system is supposed to work. Viewed strategically, localizing national politics enhances the prospects of incumbents by enabling them to "work" their districts, to provide benefits, and to define issue agendas. When the Republicans "nationalized" the 1994 election, it was precisely to change the political agenda in order to deny Democratic incumbents their natural advantage. A localizing strategy requires members to define a district persona that enables them to withstand national gales in public mood. Richard Fenno sought to explain why citizens love their representatives but hate the House and found an answer in the "home style" that members adopt (Fenno 1978). It also enables members from different parts of the country to adopt home styles consistent with local political culture and values.

Thus, localizing politics also regionalizes politics. Southern and northern Democrats were able to adopt divergent home styles to reflect the values, interests, and culture of their respective regions. Northern Democrats could support civil rights legislation while southern Democrats opposed it. The former could be "doves" while the later were "hawks." As the older politics of race gave way to a new politics grounded in economic interests, northerners formed the Northeast-Midwest Coalition and Southerners joined the Sunbelt Caucus. This balancing of regional interests could only work, however, within a stable institutional framework in which all interests were protected. The "institutionalization" of the House of Representatives that began about the turn of the twentieth century and was deeply ingrained by midcentury served the organizational needs of a legislative body and the political needs of its majority party; but it also served the particular need of the Democratic Party to balance its regional interests (Polsby 1968; Cox and McCubbins 1993; Krehbiel 1991).

SOUTHERN DEMOCRATIC LEADERS IN THE POSTREFORM HOUSE

The reform movement began with the adoption of the Legislative Reform Act of 1970 and ended with the organization of the 95th Congress in 1975. It was in effect an attack on the southern regime by northern liberal reformers. The reformers stripped the committee barons of power and granted to the party leadership only enough power to ensure minimal discipline. The liberal majority in the Democratic caucus assumed that the leadership would be responsive to it.

The Speaker who presided over the reform movement was Carl Albert of Oklahoma, a border state member whose district had strong southern roots. Albert had been appointed Democratic whip by Speaker Rayburn in 1955 and had risen on the leadership ladder to become Speaker in 1971 without having faced a contested election. Albert's inner circle of advisers included senior colleagues in the Oklahoma delegation and senior committee chairs most of whom were from the South. Yet due to his long period in the leadership, Albert had forged strong friendships with influential northerners such as Richard Bolling of Missouri. Speaker Albert served on the Agriculture Committee for many years, but he never played a major role in legislation. Instead, like his predecessor John McCormack, Albert defined his role in the party leadership as that of a loyal lieutenant to Speakers Rayburn and McCormack. As Speaker, he played a mediating role among the committee barons and between them and the restive caucus majority that demanded institutional reform.

Albert was sometimes criticized for lacking assertiveness, but his critics (mostly northern liberals) seem to have had little appreciation of his strategic situation. In the early 1970s, the House and its committee system were still dominated by senior members, many from the South, and the Speaker needed to work through the committee system to develop a party legislative program. Albert was the first Democratic Speaker to develop a party legislative agenda, and he needed the cooperation of the committee barons to enact it. At the same time, the pressure for reform from among newer and more liberal members was incessant, and it was necessary to accommodate it. Albert's speakership was marked by greater institutional change than any since the revolt against Speaker Cannon, as well as such major governmental reforms as the Budget and Impoundment Control Act of 1974 and the War Powers Act of 1973. Some reformers sought more extensive change than either Speaker Albert or a majority of the Democratic caucus would accept. For example, Albert resisted attempts to provide to the Speaker the power to overrule the House Rules Committee, and when in 1975 the caucus voted to oust three senior, southern committee chairmen, Albert sided with the chairmen against the caucus majority.[7]

While another Speaker might have chosen to be more aggressive than Speaker Albert, it is clear that he was caught in a crossfire between the Democratic Party's past and its future. The southern wing of the party was empowered by the committee system, and the younger, more liberal northern members wanted to unseat the committee barons. Albert governed with the southerners and reformed with the northerners. He adopted, somewhat tentatively, strategies that would be refined by his Democratic successors. For example, Albert was the first Speaker to employ a press secretary, the first to use task forces to develop and enact legislation, the first to expand the party's Steering and Policy Committee, the first to wrest control of committee assignments away from the Ways and Means Committee, and the first to establish effective leadership control over the Rules Committee. By the time that Tip O'Neill became Speaker in 1977, he had at his disposal a panoply of powers and practices that would define Democratic Party leadership in the postreform House (Sinclair 1983).

Yet one cannot fully understand Albert's Speakership without realizing how firmly grounded it was in the South. In the end, party leadership is measured by legislation and not by institutional reform. During Albert's tenure, control over legislation remained firmly grounded in the committee rooms. Committee chairmen such as Wright Patman of Texas at Commerce, F. Edward Hebert of Louisiana at Armed Services, W.R. Poage of Texas at Agriculture, Wilbur Mills of Arkansas at Ways and Means, and George Mahon of Texas at Appropriations ran the House when it came to substantive legislation. The circumstances demanded that the Speaker work with these committee chairmen in the development of a party legislative program. This aspect of Carl Albert's Speakership was the last echo of the old regime in which the South had so much institutional influence. Democratic policy became the lowest common denominator of what southern conservatives and northern liberals could accept, and the committee barons were the brokers of the deals. The party leadership had the job of building floor majorities for the bills the committees produced. The old norms of seniority, reciprocity, specialization, and logrolling still regulated legislative behavior until the reform movement ran its course. Thus, Speaker Albert was both the last prereform Speaker and the first postreform Speaker; and he was also the last southern Speaker to govern according to the old rules of the game.

The story of southern Democratic leaders in the postreform House would have been very differently written had not majority leader Hale Boggs been killed in an airplane accident in 1972 (Maney 1998). Boggs would have been elevated to the Speakership in 1977, and Tip O'Neill would have served as his majority leader. As it happened, O'Neill served as Speaker for ten years, governing the House from the left side of the Democratic caucus. And Jim Wright would in all likelihood not have been elected majority leader and then become Speaker. Boggs, like Albert, was a protege of Rayburn. Indeed, had not Boggs been a Roman Catholic, he might have been selected as whip in 1955 in preference to Albert. Since John McCormack was Roman Catholic, Rayburn decided that the party whip must be Protestant, and so Albert became whip and a new position of chief deputy whip was created for Boggs. Boggs was even more firmly rooted in the politics and culture of the South than was Albert; however, had he become Speaker in the postreform House he would have had to adapt his style to the new institutional circumstances that Tip O'Neill faced, perhaps without the benefit of the solid, northern liberal caucus majority that O'Neill enjoyed. Hale Boggs's majority coalition would have been very different from Tip O'Neill's, being anchored in the southern and border states.

In fact, Bogg's coalition might have looked somewhat like that which brought Jim Wright to power in 1976. A Speaker's core coalition may be defined as those members of the caucus who would certainly vote for him in a secret and contested leadership election. Such elections usually have a regional cast to them. Jim Wright won a four-way race with John McFall, Richard

Bolling, and Phillip Burton in 1976 because he was the "swing" candidate and had a solid core of support among southern members. After Bolling and McFall were eliminated, enough of their backers swung to Wright to bring him a very narrow victory over Burton. Wright started on the right, secured the middle, and won against the left. He served to balance the Democratic leadership under Speaker O'Neill, but his core coalition was different from O'Neill's.

During his decade as majority leader, Jim Wright played three important roles. He was a dutiful majority leader, working to build majority floor coalitions on behalf of party bills. He was a bridge from the leadership to the southern wing of the party. And he was an outspoken advocate for a strong party leadership and for party responsibility. In this respect he was at a far remove from the last Texas Speaker, Sam Rayburn, and was in front of the old Democratic ward-heeler, Speaker Tip O'Neill. In the mid-1980s, Wright became the first Democratic Party leader to propose sanctions for members who strayed too often from the party line. The concept of sanctions was alien to the tradition and culture of the party, which had thrived for so long by allowing members to vote their districts rather than the party position. That it was Jim Wright, the southerner, and not Tip O'Neill, the northern liberal, who pressed for a sanctions policy, indicated the changing role of the South in Democratic caucus politics. Wright's more hard-nosed approach to party leadership was in part a reflection of his personality; but it also indicated the changing circumstances of the Democratic majority. In 1976, when Wright was elected majority leader in preference to Bolling and Burton, two liberals with a reputation for assertive leadership, it was in part due to the preference of southerners for a more conciliating leader, one who would be sensitive to their concerns. By the time that Wright became Speaker in 1987, the hold of the Democrats on power had come to rely more and more on tight agenda control by the party leadership (Sinclair 1992). Wright's own insistence on party discipline reflected this change. It was ironic that the changing demands on the Speaker led Wright to adopt policies within the Democratic caucus that in the end penalized southern Democrats the most.

Speaker Jim Wright could not manage the House in the same manner that other southern Democratic Speakers had (Peters 1997; Barry 1989). His relationship with the committees and their chairmen was important, but not as central to his Speakership as had been the case for Albert and Rayburn. They had been able to rely upon the committee system to contain and resolve conflict, whereas Wright had to deal with conflict in the Democratic caucus and on the House floor. The techniques for majority coalition building and floor management that had evolved during the postreform period (with Wright playing a major role in the process) now supplanted the older game in which the committees were the fulcrum of the legislative process. In consequence, Jim Wright built his legislative majorities step-by-step, beginning with the liberal Democratic caucus majority, then adding the southern Democrats, then picking up moderate Republicans. Republican efforts to pull the southern Democrats away were frustrated by the Democrats' control over floor procedure and undermined by the widely shared perception (among Democrats and Republicans alike) that the Democrats were likely to retain their majority for the foreseeable future. In the 100th Congress, Wright drove the legislative agenda and public policy. He brought the committee system to heel and passed several substantial measures with bipartisan majorities. If Carl Albert had been the first Democratic Speaker to offer a legislative program, Jim Wright was the first to drive one to enactment. In doing so he deviated from the accommodating practices of previous Speakers and put in place mechanisms that enabled the liberal majority in the Democratic caucus to have greater control over the legislative process.

In the tight control that the Democratic leadership exercised, however, lay the seed of its own destruction, for the southern Democrats became increasingly marginalized in the 1980s and 1990s. This was in part due to their declining numbers. In the 98th Congress (1981–82) a group of around forty southern Democrats organized themselves into the Conservative Democratic Forum. The CDF sought to hold the balance of power in a House in which the Democrats held a tenuous 26-seat majority, and they had enough members to have clout. In the 103rd Congress (1993–94), the southern Democrats called themselves the "blue dog" coalition, and there were only 24 of them. With the Democrats holding a substantial majority, they did not have enough votes to threaten the party leaders. Knowing this, the liberal Democratic majority, led by Tom Foley from Washington, Richard Gephardt of Missouri, and David Bonior of Michigan, chose to ignore the southerners in pressing for the liberal agenda of the Clinton administration.[8] In effect, the old North-South coalition had broken down within the Democratic caucus. The traditional logroll on pork barrel spending had become less important because of the budget deficit. Republicans pushed an ideological agenda on the so-called "social" issues (abortion, prayer in schools, school vouchers, crime, gun control) that divided southern from northern Democrats. One main goal of Speaker Wright had been to keep the social agenda at bay so that the caucus would not become divided over it. This led the leadership to exercise tight controls on the House floor, further centralizing power in the party leadership.

In 1989 Speaker Wright was forced to resign in the face of ethics charges brought by Republican Newt Gingrich, the GOP whip. Wright did not lose his Speakership because the Republicans were out to get him; he lost it because he did not have enough support in the Democratic caucus. The coalition that had elected him majority leader in 1976 no longer existed. It was this vestigal group of southerners that was most threatened by the Republican surge in the South. Jim Wright, perhaps the last southern Democratic Speaker, became a political liability to southern Democrats. Ironically, Wright turned over the more centralized regime that he had helped put in place to northern liberals, who were less sensitive to the needs of southern members. The stage was set for the Republican takeover of the House.

REPUBLICANS IN CONTROL

The election of a Republican House majority in 1994 was an historic event. Led by party whip Newt Gingrich of Georgia, the Republicans swept to a 236-seat majority, their first in 40 years. Gingrich became the first Republican Speaker since Joe Martin of Massachusetts had presided in 1954–55 and the first southern Republican ever to sit in the Speaker's chair. Alongside Gingrich, the Republicans elected Richard Armey and Tom DeLay of Texas as their majority leader and whip. For the first time since before the Civil War, the entire majority leadership was from the South, and they were Republicans. This astonishing development tells us a great deal about the transformation of American politics that has been under way since the adoption of the Voting Rights Act of 1965 and opens a new chapter on southern House leadership.

Although Republican Speakers had predominated from 1860 until 1930, the only Republican Speaker between 1931 and 1995 was Joseph Martin of Massachusetts, one of several Republican Speakers from New England.[9] In fact, with the exception of John McCormack and Tip O'Neill, all Speakers from New England have been Federalist, Whig, or Republican. Since the Republican Party effectively did not exist in the South until the 1970s, it is not surprising that Republicans did not select southern leaders from the inception of the party in 1854 until 1981, when Trent Lott became whip. Joseph Martin appeared as a link in the "Austin-Boston" axis for reasons that had little to do with the politics that drove leadership selection in the Democratic caucus. Instead, Martin reflected the long domination of the Republican Party in New England, a domination that was brought to an end in Massachusetts in 1946 when Tip O'Neill became the first Democratic Speaker of the Massachusetts General Court (as the legislature is there known).

The difference in regional cast of the Republican leadership lineup was one important distinction between the two parties with respect to leadership selection. In the twentieth century, the Republican House Speakers and minority leaders have included David Henderson of Iowa, Joseph Cannon of Illinois, James R. Mann of Illinois, Frederick Gillett of Massachusetts, Nicholas Longworth of Ohio, Bertrand Snell of New York, Martin, Charles Halleck of Indiana, Gerald Ford of Michigan, John Rhodes of Arizona, Robert Michel of Illinois, and Newt Gingrich of Georgia. Obviously, all except Gingrich were from the North or West, and each leader came from a section of the country that was strongly Republican at the time of his election as leader.

Another important difference has been the greater propensity among Republicans to challenge incumbent leaders (Altemus 1977). For example, in 1956 Charles Halleck challenged incumbent leader Joseph Martin, charging that Martin was too close to Rayburn to vigorously assert the party's positions or interests. A decade later, Gerald Ford challenged Halleck, claiming that under Halleck the Republicans had not offered a positive legislative agenda to counter the Great Society. While John Rhodes was not challenged, Robert Michel was challenged by Guy Vander Jagt of Michigan in 1980. In 1994 Newt Gingrich had made it clear that he was contemplating a challenge to Michel when Michel decided to retire.[10] These contested party leadership elections were in marked contrast to the largely symbolic challenges posed by Udall and Conyers to John McCormack and Carl Albert. They suggest a different dynamic in the Republican conference. It appears that the GOP fault lines are more often grounded in tactics and strategies and less tied to enduring regional differences. Consequently, they have been able to have contested leadership elections without fear that the conference would be rent asunder. While Democrats always had to worry that disaffected southern conservatives might bolt the party, Republicans appear to have been less concerned that party moderates might take their departure.

The Democrats had localized politics because this was the secret to maintaining their House majority. If each member could tailor his or her message to appeal to local constituencies, then the Democrats could use the power of incumbency to retain their majority. This strategy worked for a very long period of time, enabling even southern Democrats to stave off challenges from the burgeoning Republican Party. Beginning with the Civil Rights Act of 1964 and the Voting Rights Act of 1965, southern politics underwent a transformation that would eventually undermine the Democrats' control and bring the Republican Party into ascendency in the South and to a majority in the House of Representatives. The rise of the Republican Party in the South was due to two principal factors: one was the shift of white, middle-class southeners to the GOP; the other was the shift in population from the North to the South. The former trend brought converts to the GOP; the latter trend brought new Republicans to the South (Black and Black 1987; Steed, Moreland, and Baker 1997; Lamis 1988). The Republicans increased their share of House seats even as the number of House seats in the region was increasing. In 1970, on the eve of the reform movement, there were 108 House seats in the eleven southern states; by 1990 that number had increased to 125. In 1960 the Democrats held 94.2 percent of southern congressional seats, but by 1996, their percentage had fallen to 43.2 percent. Obviously, as the percentage of southern seats held by Republicans rose and by Democrats declined, the share of southern seats in each party's caucus changed accordingly. Thus, in 1972 the South held 30.3 percent of Democratic seats and 17.7 percent of Republican seats; by 1996, southern Democrats held 26.1 percent of their party's seats, while southern Republicans held 31.3 percent of the seats in the GOP conference (Ornstein, Mann, and Malbin 1998).

Perhaps surprisingly, from 1970 to 1990 the southern House delegation became more liberal rather than more conservative (Hoppe 1997; also, see chapter 8 in the present volume). During this period a generation of conservative southern Democrats was replaced by a cohort of more liberal southern Democrats. The Republican delegation increased in number and became slightly more liberal although remaining substantially more conservative than the southern Democrats. This was probably due to the nature of Democratic control over the congressional agenda, which offered incentives for southern Republicans to vote their districts rather than their ideology when presented with restricted choices (for example, in those cases where constituents were somewhat more moderate than the personal ideological preferences of the Republican representatives). The Republican takeover of the House should have the reverse effect, encouraging more conservatism among southern Republicans and among Democrats elected in swing districts who either switched parties or turned to the right in order to hang onto their seats.[11]

Under the Democratic regime, the southern strength had expressed itself in the committee system, where senior southern barons sat astride autonomous fiefdoms, and in the party leadership, which was usually balanced between southern/border and northern/western members. The pattern that emerged on the Republican side of the aisle was different. The more senior Republicans were typically from the North. Under Democratic control, they rose to the top of the committee lists. Southern Republicans, such as Trent Lott, could access the party leadership more quickly than they could rise on the seniority lists. After Lott, the next southern Republican party leader was Newt Gingrich of Georgia, who was elected whip in 1989. The first two southern GOP congressional leaders represented the two trends that brought the GOP to power in the South. Lott, a former Democrat who had apprenticed under former Democratic Rules Committee chairman William Colmer of Mississippi, reflected the new southern Republicans who had converted from the Democratic Party but who still reflected its cultural roots in many ways. Gingrich, a transplanted northerner, reflected those new Republicans who had migrated to the South since the 1960s. While the southern delegation had power within the Democratic majority due to longevity of service, party norms, and House rules, the southern delegation under the Republican regime attained power through majoritarian politics within the GOP conference.

Thus, the role of the South and of southern party leaders was different for the Republicans than it had been for their Democratic counterparts. Under the Democrats, the region and its power barons stood against the northern liberal majority in their own party caucus and used the levers of institutional power and the power of their votes to pull the party towards the center. Under the Republicans, the southern delegation was as or more conservative than were other Republicans.[12] As mentioned above, Republicans have more often had contested leadership elections than Democrats. They have had more elected party leadership positions. They have shown less deference to seniority. They have adopted rule changes (such as the elimination of proxy voting in committees) that enhance the power of voting majorities. They have granted less autonomy to committees and have thus diminished the power of their chairmen. And they have resorted to nonformal arrangements such as task forces to shape legislation and build majority coalitions in support of it. Due to these factors and others that might be mentioned, the nature and role of the Republican leadership has been different in many respects than that of the Democratic Party.

That the first Republican speaker, majority leader, and whip in forty years were from the South reflects to some extent the strength of the southern delegation in the GOP conference, but it also reflects the nature of Republican politics. Speaker Newt Gingrich of Georgia, majority leader Dick Armey of Texas, and majority whip Tom DeLay of Texas, all came to power in contested conference elections in which they had to build majority coalitions. While the southern delegation no doubt comprised an important component of their respective majority coalitions, in each case the winning coalition cut across regional lines and was grounded in ideology, personal relationships, and political favors. An additional factor in each case was the kind of leadership offered to the conference, consistent with member expectations and the party culture. The Republicans wanted a different kind of party leader than the Democrats had preferred, and that is what they got.

THE SOUTHERN REPUBLICAN LEADERS

The Republican House leaders in the 104th and 105th Congresses reflected the party's culture and constituencies. They were as a group more conservative than their brethren, yet they fought amongst each other like spoiled siblings.[13] They came from suburban districts that have come to define the Republican Party, districts loaded with money and weighted down by chain stores and restaurants. Just as these businesses have trampled down the indigenous cultures of these southern districts, so too have the new Republicans supplanted the ancient pattern of Democratic Party politics with a new regime grounded in a different combination of interests and ideology.

The three top House leaders, Newt Gingrich, Dick Armey, and Tom DeLay, were all southerners, as we have noted. Gingrich and Armey, however, were northern transplants who had no southern accent and no southern roots. DeLay, by contrast, was identifiably southern in accent and upbringing, his background that of a small businessman whose initial attraction to politics lay in a revulsion against federal environmental regulation. DeLay listed himself as a "pest control executive," and he came to the Congress to destroy the pests in the federal bureaucracy that were driving up the costs of his business. While the three top Republicans were all conservative and each was ideological in his own way, their ideological roots were quite different. Gingrich, holder of a Ph.D. in history from Tulane, was the historical visionary whose conception of conservatism was grounded in nineteenth-century British Toryism. Armey, holder of a Ph.D. in economics from the University of Oklahoma, assimilated the economic theories of the Chicago school as a graduate student, and wanted to apply them to public policy (Starobin 1995). Both Gingrich and Armey authored books articulating their vision for America (Gingrich 1995; Armey 1995). DeLay's ideology was of less lofty origin, but more viscerally felt.

These differences in their ideological underpinnings were reflected in the roles that they played. Gingrich was the grand visionary and strategist. Armey was the stolid conservative, who anchored the conservatives in intraparty debate. DeLay was the exterminator, the point man in challenging the K Street lobbyists and the corporate political action committees (Rosin 1996). The GOP leadership team thus offered a balance of a sort, but one much in contrast to the kind of balance sought by the Democrats. The Democrats wanted to balance their liberal and conservative wings, their northern and southern delegations. The Republicans had no geographical and little ideological balance in their leadership team and instead defined "roles" for their leaders. Perhaps surprisingly, the apparently more homogenous Republican leadership team experienced far more conflict than its Democratic counterpart.

The most obvious manifestation of this phenomenon occurred in June and July 1997, when a rift in the leadership ranks on a disaster relief bill presaged an attempt to oust Speaker Gingrich from the chair. At the outset of the 105th Congress, Gingrich had plea-bargained ethics violations and narrowly won reelection as Speaker. During the first half of 1997, he had diluted the leadership regime by creating a 23-member steering committee and had distanced himself from legislative strategy (Eilperin and Vande Hei 1997a). This proved to be a mistake because it unleashed the leadership team to compete for the favor of the party's more extreme members on a variety of issues. Emboldened by their reelected majority and unrestrained by more temperate leadership, House Republicans rushed into confrontation with President Clinton on a variety of issues that were attached to a supplemental appropriations bill that also provided disaster relief for flood victims in the upper Midwest. When it became apparent that Clinton would veto the bill and once again blame the Republicans for denying government services to those in need, Gingrich stepped in to engineer a compromise that stripped the extraneous provisions, in effect capitulating to Clinton (Bradley and Vande Hei 1997; Cook 1997). This was the correct strategy but it rankled hard-line conservatives who charged that Gingrich had surrendered to Clinton. Faced with the choice of supporting Gingrich or pandering to the hard-right in the conference, every member of the leadership team voted against Gingrich, who ultimately passed the bill with a majority built largely on the votes of Democrats.

The coup was initiated by a dozen archconservatives who felt that in the wake of his ethics mea culpa the Speaker had become too accommodating to the Democrats. The members of the leadership team, including Armey, DeLay, conference chair John Boehner of Ohio, and campaign committee chair Bill Paxon of New York, were approached by the renegades and met with them. Accounts of what happened next vary, but it is clear that to a greater or lesser degree each of these leaders was positioning himself for Gingrich's fall. Armey was the first to get cold feet and told the speaker about the coup, which was quickly quelled in conference. Paxon took the fall, resigning from the leadership. DeLay seems to have gone the furthest in encouraging the renegades, yet he later apologized to the conference and somehow managed to escape with his core support intact.[14]

This kind of thing would never have happened under the Democrats, in part because southern Democrats would never have supported insurrection. Southern Democratic committee chairmen were sometimes mavericks who charted their own course, but none ever contemplated an ouster of a sitting Speaker.[15] Southern Democratic floor leaders and whips were always loyal to their Speaker, even when the Speaker was under criticism, as was Albert during much of his tenure, O'Neill after the 1984 election, and Wright during his last year. Here, we observe the coup itself to have been instigated by a southerner, Lindsey Graham of South Carolina, and southern leaders Dick Armey and Tom DeLay offering at least implied support to it. Their motive was apparent; each wanted to become Speaker and each wanted to be correctly positioned in case Gingrich was ousted. Paxon, the only leader to resign, explored a candidacy for the Speakership and when he concluded that he could not win it, decided to retire from the House. Armey made amends with Gingrich on the theory that his best path to the Speakership was to restore stability in hopes that the leadership ladder might boost him to the top. DeLay remained a maverick, occasionally opposing Gingrich on the House floor and in campaign strategy (Vande Hei 1998; Rosin 1997).

Party leaders have core constituencies upon which their leadership careers are built. Speaker Gingrich had built a core constituency among new and more conservative members during the 1980s, leading to his narrow election as whip in 1989. The 1992 and 1994 election cycles had swept into office 119 new Republicans who identified with Gingrich as the messiah who had brought the party to the promised land. This gave Gingrich a commanding but deceptive plinth inside the Republican conference. His support was wide but not deep because he had not built relationships with most members over a long period of time, as would have been characteristic for the Democrats. Armey and DeLay are both from Texas. The Texas delegation is ordinarily good footing for a party leader because it is large and under the Democrats was usually quite cohesive, lunching together every week. There was no doubt that southern votes helped put both Armey and DeLay into their leadership positions, but they then found themselves sharing the same core constituency. Since both aspired to the Speakership, they then had to compete to build the core constituency that could carry the winner to a majority in the conference. Thus, when Gingrich appeared endangered, Armey and DeLay each had to calculate how to turn the coup to advantage. As majority leader, Armey had built links to the committee and subcommittee chairs with whom he worked regularly on floor scheduling; as whip, DeLay built links through the whip organization, largely comprised of members who were not chairs.

One legacy of the coup attempt was to make it clear that neither Armey nor DeLay could count on winning the Speakership in a contested election. Paxon appeared to be the candidate of choice among the rebels, and other members such as Appropriations Committee chairman Bob Livingston of Louisiana, another southerner, had support. Livingston's network ran through the

Appropriations Committee to all House Republicans. Thus, Speaker Gingrich presided over a rambunctious conference salted with revolutionaries and guided by a recalcitrant leadership team. The Democrats had not witnessed this kind of instability since the early 1930s. Then, however, the divisions within the Democratic caucus were regional and ideological. Today, the divisions in the Republican conference are personal and political. These were the conditions that defined Speaker Gingrich's leadership challenge.

Speaker Newt Gingrich was, in his own words, "sui generis," like no other. In this he was correct. His Speakership was unique in many respects, stamped by the unusual circumstances in which he came to power and by his many idiosyncracies. Perhaps the most unusual aspect of his role as a *southern* Speaker was indicated by the fact that it did not make much difference that he was from the South. Gingrich's congressional district (Georgia, 6) was on the north side of Atlanta, centered in Marietta, and dominated by Martin Marietta. The district has changed considerably due to redistricting, and has never been a traditionally safe seat. Yet it is sufficiently Republican and sensible to know better than to evict a sitting Speaker of the House. And while it is a southern district, its constituents include many people who, like Gingrich himself, have migrated from the North. Gingrich is a nonsouthern man, with a distinctly Pennsylvania accent ("Worshington") and a definitely nonsouthern name. He likes to be called "Newt" in part because there are more Newts in the South than there are Gingriches.

A nonsouthern southerner, Gingrich differed from his southern Democratic counterparts in other ways. He did not grow up in the district he represented, and his closest political associations are not in the district or even in Georgia. From his early days in the House in the late 1970s, Gingrich formed close ties with other Republican members who shared his ideological and political commitments, and most of these members were perforce northern—there were not many southern Republicans in those days. The "five amigos" who launched the conservative movement in the House included southerners Gingrich and Lott and northerners Jack Kemp of New York, Vin Weber of Minnesota, and Bob Walker of Pennsylvania. By the time that Gingrich organized the Conservative Opportunity Society in 1983, Lott had moved to the Senate, and Gingrich worked with an essentially northern crew.

Thus there was nothing distinctively southern in the political movement upon which Gingrich rode to power. While the increasing number of southern Republicans was no doubt a necessary precondition of the GOP capturing a House majority, Gingrich did not pursue a "southern" strategy. Instead, he sought to nationalize House elections, turning them into a contest between outsiders and insiders, challengers and incumbents, Republicans and Democrats. He wanted to sharpen these distinctions and to blur geographic distinctions. The Solid South upon which Democratic majorities had rested was a regional phenomenon; the Republican South was a part of a national movement.

It was for this reason that the Republicans could accept a geographically unbalanced leadership team. If region had mattered to the Republicans, they would not have ended up with their three top leaders from the South. This phenomenon did not reflect the dominance of southern Republicans; it suggested the irrelevancy of region. For what bound Republicans together was the homogeneity of their constituencies and the ideological consistency of their beliefs. Republicans would come to strong intraparty disagreements, but those disagreements were usually on strategy and tactics, rather than on ultimate policy objectives. Of course, regionalism still played a role. But in this case it was not because the South was distinctive but rather because the Northeast was. Southern Republicans did not differ much from their midwestern and western brethren; but a substantial number of northeastern Republicans were more moderate, in part reflecting the districts that they represented.

Speaker Gingrich was called to lead a GOP conference that was at one and the same time strongly homogenous and deeply fractious. His preferred method—listen, learn, help, and lead—derived from his devotion to contemporary management and military command theories. In form, this credo did not differ greatly from the style of southern Democratic Speakers such as Sam Rayburn, who often listened, learned, helped, and led. But Rayburn's political instincts were honed in the culture of southern politics, and his nondirective style was an adaptation to his situation (Cooper and Brady 1981). Gingrich, by contrast, sought to impose his management style on the House and to transform its culture (Peters 1999). He wanted to develop a "doctrine" of conflict resolution that would accommodate open dialogue in the conference—free speech—but would also enable the party to coalesce behind leadership-driven strategies and tactics. Like Jim Wright before him, Gingrich wanted to shape the legislative agenda; and like Wright, he encountered resistance from among the party rank-in-file.

This is not the place for a full exploration of Newt Gingrich's Speakership. Our focus is on Speaker Gingrich as a species of southern *homo politicus*. And our point is that, in the end, he was not. Whether one considers his national organizations, his closest associates, the sources of his campaign contributions, or his strategies and tactics, Gingrich did not govern the House as a southerner in the manner of Democratic Speakers such as Sam Rayburn and Carl Albert (McAllister 1998; Jacobsin, 1998).[16] Instead he governed as a national politician seeking to build a national Republican majority. Furthermore, in doing so he was able to carry a single political persona from his Georgia district to Washington. Sam Rayburn always had two personas, one for home consumption and the other for Washington. At home, Rayburn was the Texas farmer; in Washington, he was a "national" Democrat (Champagne 1984). Gingrich was a conservative Republican at home and abroad. His political message fluctuated from day to day, but not from place to place.

SOUTHERN HOUSE LEADERSHIP AFTER NEWT GINGRICH

In the aftermath of the 1998 House elections, Newt Gingrich resigned his seat in the House of Representatives, relinquishing the Speakership that he had sought to attain during his entire political career. Facing a challenge from House Appropriations Committee chairman Bob Livingston of Louisiana, Gingrich decided to not fight to retain the Speakership, and instead to leave the House altogether. This decision was in keeping with Gingrich's character: it was radical, abrupt, realistic, and in the best interest of the Republican Party. Livingston's challenge to Gingrich was the leading edge of a general upheaval among House Republicans, who blamed their relatively poor showing in the election (with the loss of five seats to the Democrats) on the leadership. Not only did Livingston choose to run against Gingrich for Speaker, but majority leader Dick Armey was challenged by Steve Largent of Oklahoma and Jennifer Dunn of Washington, while conference chair John Boehner faced competition from J.C. Watts of Oklahoma. Only Republican whip Tom DeLay continued without opposition.

Commentary surrounding these contested leadership elections stressed the "southern, white male" composition of the incumbent leadership team (Chen 1998). Supporters of Jennifer Dunn and J.C. Watts argued that the party needed to present a new and more diversified face to the voters. Analysts saw this as an opportunity for the Republicans to break the mold in which their party's image had been shaped. Interestingly, no one representing northeastern moderates chose to run for a leadership position. In the public discussion surrounding the leadership races, it appeared necessary for all viable candidates to affirm their conservative credentials. The Republican conference seemed uninterested in ideological or regional balance. House leadershp races are intensely personal. Incumbent leaders build constituencies over time by doing favors for members, by raising money and making campaign appearances on their behalf, and by facilitating legislation that is important to constituents. Challengers draw upon natural networks of support among their state delegations, committee cohorts, and friendships forged in informal groups or other informal settings. Candidates ask for votes, and commitments are highly personal. This is not to say that all commitments are honored. The party memberships vote by secret ballots and sometimes the results are surprising. Even though these races take place in a surround-sound of rhetoric and reasoning, they are inevitably personal and idiosyncratic.

Thus, it came as no surprise that Bob Livingston quickly emerged as an uncontested candidate for Speaker. Congressman Chistopher Cox of California spent a weekend canvassing for votes before withdrawing. Livingston owed his candidacy to Speaker Gingrich in several ways. First, Gingrich had vaulted him over several more senior members to chair the Appropriations Committee. Second, Gingrich had persuaded him to remain in the House when he contemplated retirement in 1996. Third, Gingrich botched the 1998 election campaign, thus opening the door for Livingston to challenge him. Livingston was, in a sense, a Newt Gingrich protégée, and the two remained friends. What was surprising about Livingston's elevation to the Speakership was not that he challenged Gingrich; Republican House leaders have often been challenged. What was surprising was that he so easily surpassed Dick Armey. On the Democratic side, party floor leaders had succeeded to the Speakership in an unbroken line of succession from 1934 forward. The last Democratic committee chair to seek the Speakership was Sam Rayburn in 1937; he failed, and became floor leader instead.[17] Livingston and Armey are, of course, both southerners. By seeking to retain his position as majority leader Armey ensured that he would not fight with Livingston for southern support. Livingston and Gingrich are also southerners and would have competed for support in the region. Yet Livingston's core constituency appeared less grounded regionally than through the network of support he had built on and through the Appropriations Committee.

Armey faced a candidate from the West (Dunn), from a neighboring and border South state (Largent), and from the Midwest (Hastert). But the divisions within the conference in this contest appeared less geographic than ideological. Largent had his core support among the more radical conservatives with whom he had been associated in, among other things, the attempt to oust Gingrich. Dunn drew her support from among moderates and conservatives who thought that Armey portrayed the wrong image for the party, but who feared that Largent was too strident. Largent would draw from among his peers in the class of 1994, Dunn from among her peers in the class of 1996. Hastert, who reluctantly permitted his name to be placed in nomination, did not actively seek votes and drew little support. When Largent ran ahead of Dunn on the second ballot and obtained the runoff with Armey, Armey's victory was assured because Dunn's moderate supporters perceived Armey to be more flexible than Largent. Thus, while there may have been some regional cast to the voting, region was not the defining characteristic of the election.

A similar point can be made about Watts's defeat of Boehner. Boehner was in the weakest position to defend his hold on office in part because the conference chair has fewer levers of influence than the majority leader or whip. In challenging him, Watts stressed his ability as an effective communicator who could expand the party's appeal beyond its base. As the only African-American Republican in the House, Watts could offer a different image for the party; however, Republicans would not have chosen him for this reason alone. During his four-year career, he had forged many friendships among members and had appeared on behalf of members all around the country. He had also taken an active interest in intraparty communication and had pressed Speaker Gingrich to improve it. Whatever factors affected Watts's rapid rise to power, unprecedented in the modern House, region did not appear to be among them.

The final result was a prospective Republican leadership team that is more southern than the one it replaced. The top three positions would be held by southerners and the fourth position by a border state member. The chairman of the Campaign Committee would be Tom Davis from Virginia, and the vice chair of the conference would be Tillie Fowler from Florida. Only the conference secretary, Debra Price of Ohio, would be a northerner (Chen 1998). Yet there was little sense that the southern profile of the House Republican leadership was of particular concern or importance to the Republican members. If it had been, they would have made sure that one of their leaders was from the North. As the new GOP leadership team gathered itself under Speaker Livingston's direction, it faced the challenge of pulling the fractious Republican conference back together into a working unit. With a thin 223–212 majority, every vote would be needed. Livingston offered himself as a different kind of leader from Gingrich, more a manager and less a national spokesman. After Speaker Gingrich's sometimes erratic approach, Livingston offered stability and managerial competence. Yet he made no particular appeal to region in winning the Speakership or in articulating his purposes as Speaker. As the Republicans were selecting their southern slate of leaders, the Democrats chose only one southerner, Martin Frost of Texas, their caucus chair, for their leadership team (Alvarez 1998). It was not apparent that region played a major role in the Democratic caucus elections either. Thus, we encounter the irony that the two parties' leadership teams are more regionally distinct than ever before, just at the moment when regional affiliations seem least important to members.

The southern-dominated House GOP leadership slate was transformed in mid-December of 1998 when in the midst of the House debate over the impeachment of President Clinton, Speaker-designate Livingston took the floor to announce his withdrawal from the Speakership and his prospective resignation from the House. Allegations of marital infidelity were to be made public, and Livingston took the honorable path of resignation. Within hours of his announcement, Representative Dennis Hastert of Illinois, the party's chief deputy whip, emerged as a consensus candidate for speaker. Hastert had at one point contemplated a challenge to Dick Armey; however, he had previously committed his support to Armey, and Armey refused to release him from the commitment. Even so, at the last minute Hastert's name had been placed in nomination for majority leader, and he gathered a handful of votes. Now, he leaped ahead of all the other party leaders to claim the Speakership.

What explains Hastert's selection by House Republicans and what does it imply about the southern cast of the GOP leadership team? Hastert was chosen because he was widely liked and respected among Republican members and because he was as different from Newt Gingrich as could be imagined. Gingrich was the visionary of large ideas; Hastert was the back-bench operater who put together the deals. Gingrich was bombastic, Hastert modest. Gingrich was a national leader; Hastert was a man of the House. But why Hastert and not Dick Armey or Tom DeLay? Hastert offered the fresh face that the Republicans thought the circumstances demanded, and if he had not done as many favors as Armey or DeLay, he had not antagonized anybody either. A former high school wrestling coach (fondly known as "the coach" among GOP members), Hastert was seen as a leader who could bring House Republicans together.

The strongest force pushing for Hastert's selection was Whip Tom DeLay. "The Hammer," as he was sometimes called, pushed forcefully for Hastert to become Speaker. Hastert and DeLay had been aligned since 1989, when they joined forces to support Edward Madigan of Illinois in his unsuccessful race against Newt Gingrich for whip. Hastert supported DeLay in his race for whip against Gingrich loyalist Robert Walker of Pennsylvania in 1994, and DeLay named Hastert chief deputy whip. So close were DeLay and Hastert, and so forceful was DeLay in supporting his candidacy for Speaker, that many wondered if DeLay would become the power behind the Speakership. Yet Hastert claimed to be his own man and announced that as Speaker he intended to put the House back to its legislative mission.

Dennis Hastert is from the North, not the South, and the GOP conference jumped him over five southerners who had already been elected to the leadership. They chose him, however, not because he was from the North, but because he offered a style of leadership that suited the current circumstances of the House Republican party. In jumping a relative back-bencher to the Speakership, House Republicans once again demonstrated how very different they are from House Democrats, who have not skipped the order of their leadership ladder since Henry Rainey of Illinois won in the Democrats' last seriously contested Speakership election in 1933. But they also demonstrated just how inconsequential region has become as a criteria for party leadership and how deceptive the southern complexion of the House GOP leadership is.

CONCLUSION

"Southern Politics" has been the only geographically defined area of specialization among political scientists who study the American political system. From the time of the American founding, the South has been a distinctive political, economic, and cultural region and has played a distinctive role in the political life of the nation. This has been especially true in the U.S. House of Representatives. One manifestation of this is that the Democratic and Republican legislative parties in the House have so consistently been characterized by such stark regional variation in leadership selection. The Democratic and Republican leadership teams now being as geographically distinct as at any time in our history is an indication that region still plays some role in our politics. Yet it is not clear that southern Republicans are as different from their northern counterparts as the southern Democrats used to be. While the southern Democrats used to be substantially more conservative than their northern colleages, southern Republicans are just about the same as northern Republicans on the ideological scales. The southern economy is now integrated into the national economy. Federal programs and policies no longer single out the South as they did in the past. And southern culture is becoming increasingly homogenized with that of the nation as well.

The result is that the South is now unquestionably a critical component of the Republican Party's national constituency, but the appeal that southern Republicans make to their constituents is not greatly different than that which most nonsouthern Republicans make to theirs. In the GOP, it is the northeastern members who are the outliers, although even they are closer to the party mainstream than were southern Democrats a generation ago. Similarly, southern Democrats today have a greater ideological affinity with northern Democrats than was the case in the past. Thus, the two national parties are more distinct from each other and each party is more internally cohesive.

These facts suggest that while the Republican party is likely to continue to more often select southerners for leadership posts in the House while the Democrats more often will chose northerners, the dynamics of party leadership are such that the geographic differences are not as significant as was the case in the past. Bob Livingston would not have governed as a southerner, and Dennis Hastert will not govern as a northerner, but Republican Speakers will govern as Republicans. The divisions in the Republican conference will not be geographic; they will be ideological, strategic, generational, and personal. It is critical to recognize that the slate of southern Republican House leaders was elected by a conference in which the southern states held only a third of the Republican seats. The southerners were chosen by nonsoutherners. Speaker Hastert, a northerner, had unanimous support among southerners. If northeastern Republicans feel marginalized, it will not be due to the regional cast of the leadership; it will be due to their policy differences with the conservative conference majority. The liberalism of the Democratic caucus will be moderated by the need to maintain the viability of the congressional party in the South, but this will not lead the Democrats to ration leadership positions as they did during the era of the "Austin-Boston" axis. Thus, the study of southern House leaders will merge into the topic of House leadership in general, and attention will be focused on southerners who are leaders rather than on the southern leadership of the House.

NOTES

1. I would like to thank Jason Reese for his able research assistance and Keith Gaddie for his comments.

2. This historical discussion draws on Peters (1997). There, I divide the history of the Speakership into four eras: the parliamentary era, from 1789 to 1860; the partisan era from 1861 to 1911; the feudal era, from 1912 to 1961; and the democratic era, from 1962 to the present. Traditionally, the South denotes Alabama, Arkansas, Florida, Georgia, Louisiana, Mississippi, North Carolina, South Carolina, Tennessee, Texas, and Virginia, the states of the Confederacy. However, border states that include Kentucky, Maryland, Missouri, Oklahoma, and West Virginia have strong southern roots and members from these states often voted with the conservative coalition during its heyday, along with southern members. In this chapter, when I cite statistics regarding the South, the statistics refer to the eleven states of the Confederacy; however, in discussing southern leaders I take the liberty of including border state representatives such as Henry Clay of Kentucky,

Champ Clark of Missouri, and Carl Albert of Oklahoma. Albert, for example, comes from the southeastern part of Oklahoma, an area known in the state as "Little Dixie." The area has strong southern roots and these played a role in Albert's political career.

3. From 1900 until 1995, Republican floor leaders (majority leader or minority leader) have included Sereno Payne of New York, Frank Mondell of Wyoming, John Q. Tilson of Ohio, James R. Mann of Illinois, Nicholas Longworth of Ohio, Bertrand Snell of New York, Joseph Martin of Massachusetts, Charles Halleck of Indiana, Gerald Ford of Michigan, John Rhodes of Arizona, and Robert Michel of Illinois. Twentieth-century Democratic floor leaders have included James Richardson of Tennessee, John Sharp Williams of Mississippi, Oscar Underwood of Alabama, Claude Kitchen of North Carolina, Champ Clark of Missouri, Finis Garrett of Tennessee, John Nance Garner of Texas, Henry T. Rainey of Illinois, Joseph Byrns of Tennessee, William Bankhead of Alabama, Sam Rayburn of Texas, John W. McCormack of Massachusetts, Carl Albert of Oklahoma, Hale Boggs of Louisiana, Tip O'Neill of Massachusetts, Jim Wright of Texas, Tom Foley of Washington, and Richard Gephardt of Missouri. The score for the Republicans is 11 North and 0 South; the score for the Democrats is 11 South, 2 Border, and 2 North (Schamel et al. 1989).

4. Jim Wright is in some ways an exception to this rule, as discussed below.

5. Richard Bolling announced a candidacy for majority leader in 1962 but withdrew it before the caucus meeting because he did not have enough support.

6. The Democrats began electing their whip in 1986. Bill Gray, Tony Coehlo, and David Bonior were all chosen in contested elections, making the whip position the point of initial selection for the leadership ladder.

7. The three chairmen were Wright Patman of Texas of the Banking Committee, W.R. Poage of Texas of the Agricultural Committee, and H. Edward Hebert of Louisiana of Armed Services.

8. Centerpieces of the Clinton agenda in the 103rd Congress were a major tax increase to help balance the federal budget and a major health care proposal that would have in effect nationalized the health care system. These proposals were not popular in the South.

9. Others included Theodore Sedgwick (1799–1801), Joseph B. Varnum (1807–11), Robert C. Winthrop (1847–49), Nathanial P. Banks (1856–57), and Frederick Gillett of Massachusetts (1919–25) all of Massachusetts, and James G. Blaine (1869–75) and Thomas B. Reed (1889–91; 1895–99) of Maine.

10. On the 1998 upheaval, see below.

11. An indication of the pull of party on member behavior is the altered voting patterns of those southern Democrats who switched to the Republican Party. Taking ACU scores for (1996), 1995, 1994, and 1993, we find the following pattern: Tauzin (90), 83, 76, 78; Deal (90), 80, 67, 61; Parker (100), 63, 67, 67. *Source* (Duncan, P.D., and Lawrence, C.C., *Politics in America*, 1998: *The 105th Congress*, 1997). The discussion by Stanley P. Berard and David W. Rhode in chapter 2 of this volume also offers relevant material on this point. Also, see James M. Glaser's discussion of party switching in chapter 3 of this volume.

12. In 1997 the average ACU scores of Republican House members by region were: Northeast - 69.2; South - 95; Border - 91.4; Midwest - 89.9, Mountain West - 94.1; Pacific - 93. The Republican average was 89.1 (Duncan and Lawrence 1997). Thus, southern leadership aspirants were in the mainstream of the party and by a small margin the most conservative. Unlike the Democrats, who balanced their leadership teams to

incorporate northern liberals and southern conservatives, the Republicans included no northeastern moderates in their leadership team.

13. According to data reported in *Politics in America, 1996*, the average ACU score of Republican members was 85.7 in 1995; the average ACU score of the party leaders was 100 (Duncan, P.D., and Lawrence, C.C., *Politics in America, 1996*, 1996).

14. Among many accounts of the coup attempt see Yang 1997, Balz and Connolly 1997, Dionne 1997, Eilperin and Vande Hei 1997d, Eilperin and Vande Hei 1997b, and Eilperin and Vande Hei 1997c.

15. Wilbur Mills of Arkansas, the powerful Democratic chairman of the House Ways and Means Committee, often thought that he should be Speaker, but he never challenged either Speaker McCormack or Speaker Albert.

16. The comparison to President Clinton is useful. Clinton's political persona is that of a southern-fried John F. Kennedy. Yet if one considers the geography of his political coalition, he is weaker in the South than in most other parts of the country. In fact, Clinton's strongest support is bicoastal. Clinton violated a common rule of presidential politics when he put fellow southerner Al Gore on the ticket in 1992. Yet he was twice elected president anyway. Thus, in both presidential and congressional politics, the role of the South has become less distinctive and is now nondeterminative.

17. Rayburn was opposed in part because Texas Democrats chaired several of the major committees and the Democratic caucus feared its power. He lost to another southerner, William Bankhead of Alabama, who was the incumbent majority leader. Therefore Livingston, in leaping over Armey, accomplished something that Rayburn could not.

7

The Conscience of the Revolution: Southern Influence in the House Republican "Class of 1994"

NICOL C. RAE

The completion of the congressional realignment in the South in favor of the Republican party was one of the most distinctive features of American politics during the 1990s. As shown in Table 7.1, Republican growth in the region began following the 1990 redistricting in 1992, took the Republicans to majority status among U.S. House members from the region in 1994, and continued in 1996. Even in the relatively poor Republican electoral year of 1998, the Republicans held onto their margin of superiority in the South.[1]

The substantial gains made by the GOP in the southern states were crucial to the Republican takeover of the House of Representatives for the first time in 40 years in 1994. The greater conservative militancy of those new southern Republican members, moreover, played a major role in defining the 1994 freshman class and the 104th Congress as a whole. While the 105th Congress witnessed something of a move toward the political center by the House Republican leadership, the "class of 1994" remained a significant bloc in the House Republican caucus. Furthermore, several of the southern members of the class were consistently at odds with the leadership and figured prominently in the effort to depose Speaker Gingrich in the summer of 1997 (see the discussion in the preceding chapter by Peters). These same militants also were critical in forcing the resignation of the Speaker following the disappointing five-seat Republican loss in the 1998 midterm elections.

This chapter will examine the reasons for the strong Republican gains in the South in 1994, the impact of the southern members within the freshman class during the "revolutionary" 104th Congress, the elections of 1996, the continuing tensions between the sophomores of the class of 1994 and the leadership during the 105th Congress, and, finally, the 1998 election and its aftermath. Through all these events the southern members of the Republican class of 1994 have acted as the "conscience" or "keepers of the flame" of this Republican revolution.

Table 7.1
Republican Share of Southern U.S. House Seats: 1990–98[a]

Year	*Number of Republican Seats*	*Percent*
1990	44	34[b]
1992	52	38[c]
1994	73	53
1996	82	60
1998	82	60

Notes: [a]South includes Oklahoma and Kentucky.
[b]Prior to 1992 reapportionment the total number of southern House seats = 128.
[c]After 1992 reapportionment the total number of southern House seats = 137.
Source: Norman J. Ornstein, Thomas E. Mann, and Michael J. Malbin, *Vital Statistics on Congress: 1997–1998* (Washington, D.C.: Congressional Quarterly Inc., 1998).

THE 1994 ELECTION IN THE SOUTH

There is no question that the South was integral to the Republican triumph in 1994. Nineteen (or 36 percent) of the 52 Republican net gains were in southern states—significantly more than any other region—and a third of the huge 73-member Republican freshman class were southerners. According to exit polls, Republican House candidates' share of the vote among southern whites increased from 53 to 65 percent between 1992 and 1994 (Rae 1998, 60). Why did the Republicans do so well in the South in 1994? The answer can be put down to the three "R's": redistricting, retirements, and realignment. Court challenges based on the Voting Rights Act added to the number of overwhelmingly Democratic minority districts, while simultaneously reducing the core Democratic vote in the surrounding "lily-white" districts (on the impact of redistricting, see Hill 1995). Faced with the unappetizing choice of a tough primary against a minority candidate or a tough general election against a Republican, many white Democratic incumbents decided it was time to retire thus leaving a large number of open seats—which were much easier for Republicans to win—throughout the region (Rae 1998, 44–50). These developments combined with the ostensibly "liberal" tilt of the Clinton administration in its early days to greatly accelerate the gradual realignment toward the GOP in the South, with Republican tallies in congressional races now matching their long-standing presidential supremacy. In short, while the whole nation swung Republican in November 1994, the South swung more Republican.

Who were the southern Republican freshmen of 1994 and what inspired them to run for Congress? Although the freshman class was widely defined in the news media as being composed of "outsiders" or "political newcomers" with a passionate commitment to congressional reform and even revolution, not all of its members fitted this profile. As the 1995 class president (and former state senator) Roger Wicker of Mississippi put it, "I didn't come to Washington to burn all the buildings down" (Doherty and Katz 1998, 159). In fact, the southern Republican freshmen were a mixture of political newcomers and Republicans with political experience like Wicker who had "paid their dues" by serving in lower-level offices.

Among the political neophytes were Mark Sanford of South Carolina and Joe Scarborough of Florida. In fact, Sanford and Scarborough had not even been Republicans in 1994, and neither had deep ties to the party:

> I don't define myself as a Republican or Democrat. If I had to define myself, I would define myself first, as an American; second, as a South Carolinian; and third, as conservative or liberal. Most Americans would define themselves as conservative or liberal rather than Republican or Democrat. I don't view myself as hung-up on party labels. (Rae 1996f)

> I was a Democrat through November 1992. After Bill Clinton was elected, I switched to the Republicans. If you look at the freshmen in the House, you'll see that there's not as much identification with the Republican party, or with the traditional party stances, as is the case with those elected before 1994. On the House side, we were very influenced by the Independents who found Ross Perot as a vehicle to channel their anger in 1992. A lot of his positions in 1992, were our positions in 1994. (Rae 1996e)

Several other freshman southerners came from an even deeper Democratic background than Joe Scarborough. The story of Walter B. Jones, Jr., of North Carolina, pretty much encapsulates the Republican realignment in the South in the early 1990s. Jones's father, Walter B. Jones, Sr., was a long-serving Democratic congressman from North Carolina's First Congressional District who finally retired after the 1992 redistricting. The younger Jones ran in the new majority-black first district in 1993 and lost in the Democratic primary to African-American congresswoman Eva Clayton. In 1994 Jones ran in the adjacent, overwhelmingly white, Third District as a Republican and defeated white Democratic incumbent Martin Lancaster (Rae 1998, 48–49). Another North Carolina Republican freshman, David Funderburk, was also assisted by redistricting and the strong resentment against President Clinton in much of the South in 1994:

> There were four main reasons why I won so comfortably in 1994. Redistricting changed the district and made it more conservative. (The seat had been Democratic for more than one hundred years.) Clinton was unpopular and the policies of the Democratic Congress and President were anathema to most of the people in my district. My district is the second largest tobacco-growing district in the U.S., and the Clinton administration was clearly anti-tobacco. Most tobacco farmers had been Democrats, but they saw their livelihoods being threatened by Liberal Democrats. Finally, the first act of the Clinton administration was to end the ban on homosexuals in the military, which was very unpopular. Voters were also worried about threats to the Second Amendment. All this contributed to a GOP sweep through North Carolina in 1994. (Rae 1996a)

Interestingly, Congressman Funderburk and most of his southern colleagues attributed very little of the Republican success in the region to the Contract with America—the much vaunted program drawn up by Minority Whip Newt Gingrich on which the national Republican campaign was based, and which was to be treated as a Republican legislative agenda after the election.

Lindsey Graham of South Carolina and Zach Wamp of Tennessee had much less of a political pedigree than Walter Jones or David Funderburk, but both were conservative white southerners from Democratic backgrounds who no longer felt that there was any place for them in the 1990s Democratic party:

In my political career I've always been a Republican, but I haven't made a career as a party politician. When I got out of the air force in 1988, and I was looking around to scratch my itch, it was obvious that the agenda of the Republicans was closer to who I was and to what most people in the South think. The Democratic party left them some years ago. I wasn't born and bred a Republican by any means. (Rae 1996h)

I grew up in a southern conservative Democratic family, and my mother's relatives in Alabama served in the Alabama legislature, which was totally Democratic. Both my parents were from Alabama, but they later moved to Tennessee. I voted for Jimmy Carter in 1976, and my parents attended his inaugural because they knew some big Democratic operators in Tennessee. I became a Republican during the 1980 presidential election. I was motivated by Ronald Reagan and George Bush, who both inspired me at different times and produced the Reagan revolution. I'm a typical southern conservative: the Democratic party ran off and left us, we didn't leave the Democratic party. (Rae 1996i)

While these members were native southern white conservative Democrats who converted to the GOP, the freshman Republicans of the 104th Congress also included conservative Republicans who had moved into the economically booming areas of the South and brought their beliefs with them. (On the impact of population movement into the South, see Black and Black 1987, 15–22.) This group has been a key element in the growth of the southern GOP since the 1950s, and Congressman Bob Barr from suburban Atlanta was a clear example of a "migrant" Republican in the class of 1994:

My upbringing laid the basic ground work. Books that I read in college, particularly by Ayn Rand, had an impact, and if not strictly conservative, they were certainly antithetical to Democratic politics. In the 1970s while I was working here in Washington for the CIA, I couldn't become involved in politics because of the *Hatch Act*, but I felt more compatible with the Republicans' philosophy than the Democrats. When I moved to Georgia in the later 1970s, my philosophy was Republican. There was no doubt about that in my mind. The basis for that is a distrust of big government and my belief that people can handle problems much better than the government can. (Rae 1996g)

Of the southern members of the Republican freshman class of 1994 I interviewed in 1996 only Joe Scarborough, Mark Sanford, and Van Hilleary of Tennessee were complete political newcomers. Lindsey Graham had served for a term in the South Carolina state legislature; Zach Wamp had run for Congress and lost narrowly in 1992; Tom Davis of Virginia had been a local government officeholder in the Virginia suburbs of Washington, D.C.; Mark Foley had been in the Florida State Senate, David Funderburk of North Carolina had been U.S. ambassador to Romania and a former U.S. Senate candidate for the GOP; Bob Barr had been a federal prosecutor in Atlanta; and Oklahoma's J.C. Watts had served as a statewide elected official. Ed Whitfield of Kentucky's First District was another seasoned political operator (and former Democrat!) who decided to run for Congress as a Republican in 1994. His motivations were typical of the freshman class as a whole:

I was President of the Young Democrats of Kentucky, and the best man at my wedding was a former Democratic governor. I hadn't lived in Kentucky for 12 years before I went back to run for Congress. I worked for CSX railroads and spent time in Washington as a lobbyist on regulatory and legislative issues. I studied Congress up-close and began to feel strongly that one-party control of Congress was taking the whole country in the wrong direction. If the Republicans could not win a district like the First District of Kentucky, they would never win the House. So even though the district is 78 percent Democratic in registration, I decided I would run as a Republican to change control of Congress. (Rae 1996k)

THE IMPACT OF THE SOUTHERN REPUBLICAN FRESHMEN

The freshman Republican class in the 104th Congress acquired a national political profile very quickly. Despite the fact that a majority of the class did have some governmental experience, the freshmen were defined early on as "outsiders" eager to reform the political system and as the vanguard of a Republican conservative ideological revolution that sought to change the direction of American politics (Rae 1998, 65–66). Although the southern Republican freshmen constituted only a third of the freshman class (the same percentage of southerners as the entire House GOP), the fact that some of the loudest and most conservative voices and the most obvious outsiders in the class—such as Joe Scarborough, former pro football star Steve Largent of Oklahoma, and Steve Stockman of Texas—were southerners did give the class of 1994 a highly southern conservative cast. According to Tennessee freshman Congressman Zach Wamp, interviewed in the summer of 1996,

The South is still different, and values are the main reason that Bill Clinton is still unpopular. Southerners see right through his positions on issues, and southern values are returning, and the South is continuing an ideological shift to the right. It is of the same fiber as the trend of boll weevil Democrats leading to the Republicans. The South is to the right of the country, and the greatest Republican gains in the future are still going to be in the South. (Rae 1996i)

Regional tensions did not erupt within the freshman class during the early months of the 104th Congress, however. In fact that period, when the House Republicans were systematically passing the various items of the Contract with

America and the Republican budget package through the House, was characterized by remarkable Republican and freshman class cohesiveness. Ever since the original drafting of the contract in the spring of 1994, Speaker Newt Gingrich and the rest of the Republican leadership had concentrated on the fiscal and economic issues on which Republicans were broadly united, rather than the social issues such as abortion, church/state relations, and gay rights, where the southern members took much more strongly conservative positions than their copartisans in the North and West (see Rae 1998, 37–44; Gimpel 1996, 4–8, 16–21; and Bader 1996, 171–206). South Carolinian Lindsey Graham referred to the unusually close bonds between the members of the class: "The pleasant surprise has been the closeness of the freshmen. We ran on the same agenda regardless of region: an institutional reform agenda for Congress and a fiscal reform agenda" (Rae 1996h). Tennessean Zach Wamp also emphasized the congressional reform agenda (and the overplayed "outsider" factor) as a bonding element for the freshman Republican class:

> Our goal is to restore public trust, and that has bonded me with the freshman reformers. Many of the freshmen have not served as elected officials. I came from a small business background, but my roommates, Steve Largent (OK) and Tom Coburn (OK), come from the worlds of medicine and professional sports. The freshmen are different: the percentage of lawyers is lower, and that bonds me to certain members of the class. (Rae 1996i)

In addition to their high degree of unity, the freshman class also enjoyed an unusually intimate relationship with the Republican Party leadership. Again, southerners featured prominently in this relationship: The president of the freshman class for the first session of the 104th Congress was a southerner, Roger Wicker of Mississippi, and freshwoman Sue Myrick of North Carolina was one of two freshman "liaisons" (the other was David McIntosh of Indiana) named to Speaker Gingrich's leadership group. Of course the fact that the three major leadership positions in the new Republican House were held by members from southern districts—Speaker Gingrich (GA), majority leader Dick Armey (TX), and majority whip Tom DeLay (TX)—meant that the southern freshmen should have been able to enjoy a special rapport with the leadership.

During the initial "honeymoon" period involving the passage of most of the contract items through the House in the first 100 days of the 104th Congress, this was very much the case (Gimpel 1996). The relationship between the freshmen and the leadership became increasingly problematic, however, as the "showdown" with the Clinton administration over the 1996 budget got under way. As mentioned earlier, the budget was the glue that held the 1994 freshman class and the House Republican Conference together. The overwhelming Republican consensus on serious action to balance the budget and the priority given to that issue by the House party leadership succeeded in suppressing intra-Republican disagreements on more contentious social issues and was the driving force behind the entire policy agenda of the 104th Congress. After the failure of the balanced budget constitutional amendment to pass the Senate in March 1995, the

House Republicans tried to deal with the budget issue by means of omnibus legislation intended to produce a balanced federal budget by 2002. This budget package included cuts in domestic spending, welfare reform, and reductions in the projected rate of increase in key entitlement programs—principally Medicare and Medicaid—and a $245 billion tax cut for the "middle class" (Sinclair 1997). While the budget passed both House and Senate, the reconciliation bill (translating the Republican targets into real spending reductions) and most of the 13 annual appropriations bills necessary to keep the government going, were vetoed by President Clinton, resulting in two "shutdowns" of the federal government, in November 1995, and again over Christmas and New Year 1995–96.

At the time, most of the southern freshman members were among the most militant supporters of the shutdown, but as the struggle progressed and it became clear that public opinion held the Republicans more responsible for the budget impasse than the Clinton White House, even they began to have doubts about the strategy being pursued by the Republican leadership (Rae 1998, 96–130). In fact, the shutdown marks the point where the critical bond forged between the freshmen and Speaker Newt Gingrich was decisively broken. Florida's Joe Scarborough was unrepentant and believed that the Republican leadership had given up too soon:

> We didn't push hard enough! We had gone through two government shutdowns and by the end of the second the President finally came to the table and offered a seven-year CBO [Congressional Budget Office] budget. At that point we folded immediately because of the tremendous outcry against everything being closed. The polls showed Clinton's approval rating falling from 50 to 42 percent, and we should have gone ahead and closed the deal then, and stuck it out for another week or two. It was a horrendous time and we had a siege mentality, but unlike everybody else I think that we should have gone the extra mile and secured a seven-year deal. (Rae 1996e)

After the Republican leadership finally capitulated and submitted a resolution without conditions to reopen the government in January 1997, 12 freshman Republicans, including southerners Bob Barr, Lindsay Graham, Steve Largent, and Mark Sanford, voted against it on the House floor.[2] Representing very conservative southern districts, neither Barr nor Graham felt anything like the political pressure that their nonsouthern freshman colleagues (many of them reeling after an advertising assault by organized Labor) faced to reopen the government:

> In my district, constituents kept telling me to "hold the line" or "go further." In Georgia, citizens told me that they sent me to the federal government to shake things up and finally give some attention to serious national problems. I even had letters from federal employees supporting a hardline approach. It's a matter of principle and setting the tone. The overall response in my district was "hang in there." Most people understood that this was not politics as usual and that if America was going to change, conflict had to occur. (Quoted in Rae 1998, 126)

With the budget issue—the centerpiece of their policy agenda—neutralized, congressional debate now focused on an agenda set by the resurgent Clinton White House on issues such as health insurance and the minimum wage. Compromises on these issues were struck in the Senate while the House Republicans completely lost the initiative in the run-up to the 1996 elections. One southern conservative freshman member, David Funderburk of North Carolina, believed the overwhelming focus on the budget had detracted from the "values issues" that had also been important to the Republican revolution in the South:

> We have to force our leadership to deal more with social, cultural, and moral issues. They wanted them kept off the table, but they will be brought up. This week we passed a ban on partial birth abortions, repealed the assault weapons' ban, and began to deal with immigration. We are also going to get votes on school vouchers and prayer, so everything will come up. (Rae 1996a)

Congressman Funderburk partly got his wish in the summer of 1996 with the passage of legislation toughening up immigration procedures and the Defense of Marriage Act (DOMA) prohibiting homosexual marriages. These measures prevailed, however, only with the support of most Senate Democrats and the Clinton White House, which had succeeded masterfully in preempting the Republicans even on "family" and "values issues" in the 1996 election campaign. With the revolutionary energy of 1995 spent in the course of the budget battle, the new Republican congressional majority now faced the prospect of electoral disaster as their legislative program stalled in the Senate and public opinion turned hostile. In addition, the Republican freshmen had to face the prospect of an unprecedented advertising assault by the AFL-CIO intended to return a Democratic majority to the House (see Gruenwald and Wells 1996; Drew 1997, 69–78). While the southern GOP freshmen were somewhat less vulnerable—because of Clinton's continuing unpopularity and Labor's weak standing in most of their districts relative to the rest of the nation—they too were compelled to reassess their situation as the 1996 elections approached.

THE 1996 ELECTIONS

The Republican case for retaining control of the House in 1996 was based essentially on two premises: (1) "we did what we promised by 'cleaning up' Congress"; and (2) "you need a Republican Congress to keep a check on Bill Clinton." As the campaign progressed, the latter argument began to feature particularly prominently. The flurry of Senate-initiated legislative activity in the summer of 1996—including health insurance reform, a minimum wage hike, immigration reform, welfare reform, safe drinking water legislation, and DOMA—neutralized Democratic charges of a "do-nothing" Congress, but at the same time they damaged the presidential campaign of Robert Dole by boosting President Clinton's "moderate" or "centrist" credentials (Rae 1998, 182–90;

Drew 1997, 89–100; and Ceaser and Bush 1997, 97–100). Among the southern freshmen there was considerable discontent with the tenor of the Dole campaign, reflected in unease with a presidential candidate who did not share the experiences or outlook of the more conservative southern members of the freshman class. David Funderburk and Lindsay Graham were typical:

Dole was not my preferred candidate. He does not elicit enthusiasm from hardcore conservative supporters, but a majority of voters in my district would far prefer him to Bill Clinton. His wife is from North Carolina, and she is a very effective campaigner. Dole also has worked well with Senator Helms. He also is pro-tobacco and pro-farmer. He has been a longtime ally of those groups. Senator Dole came down to my district and got a tremendous reception. The enthusiasm is not there among true believers, but most people see him more aligned with their values than Bill Clinton. (Rae 1996a)

Bob Dole has failed to express how the U.S. would be different with him as President. I can answer but Bob Dole can't answer. It's got to be an agenda close to why we got elected in 1994. He needs to take stands on issues. Hell, I don't know where he stands now. Bill Clinton is beatable, but I couldn't have gotten elected in 1994 unless I stood for something. (Rae 1998, 188.)

On the reform front the Republicans could point to some record of achievement. In addition to significant modifications in the committee system, the 104th Congress passed the Congressional Accountability Act (making Congress subject to the same workplace regulations as other private and public institutions) and substantial reform in the area of gifts and lobbying of Congress (Salant 1995a, 3516–19; Salant 1995b, 3631–33). Congressional reform had also been a major theme of the 1994 GOP freshman class. One southern freshman who was particularly prominent in that movement was Tennessean Zach Wamp:

I am one of twenty-two members of the House who do not accept PAC [Political Action Committee] money, and one of four freshmen. I have a belief that the institution has grown corrupt over time. I support those people in the class who are really for change in this place. (Rae 1996i)

Congressman Wamp and other reform advocates would be disappointed, however, by the failure of the Republican Congress to enact significant campaign finance reform legislation, mainly due to the lack of consensus in Republican ranks on a reform proposal that would bring about significant change while not endangering Republican advantages in the areas of "soft money" and (post-1994) in PAC fundraising (Rae 1998, 170–76). Despite this, Congressman Wamp would continue to be one of the loudest voices of reform on the Republican side during the 105th Congress.

Campaign finance scandals in the Clinton reelection campaign, coupled with heavy Republican television advertising emphasizing the importance of "restraining" Clinton by reelecting a Republican House, succeeded in saving the day for the GOP (Drew 1997, 197–228; Ceaser and Bush 1997, 121–27). The

Republicans retained control of the House with a net loss of nine seats, 227–207 with one Independent. Of the 70 freshman Republicans running for reelection, 12 were defeated. Only three of the defeated freshmen were from the South—David Funderburk and Fred Heinemann of North Carolina and Steve Stockman of Texas. All three had been involved in some controversy. Heinemann was defeated by David Price, the longtime Democratic incumbent he had defeated in 1994, in a district carried by Clinton in the presidential race. Democrats had also pilloried him relentlessly for a remark he had made about his $133,600 congressional salary being a "lower middle-class" income (Barone and Ujifusa 1997, 1067). Funderburk had been involved in an auto accident where his claim that his wife, and not he, had been driving was denied by witnesses. Moreover, his Democratic opponent was a popular statewide elected official (Barone and Ujifusa 1997, 1062–63). Stockman had been one of the greatest surprises of the 1994 election when he defeated long-serving Democratic Judiciary Committee chair Jack Brooks. In Congress, Stockman attracted adverse publicity through his controversial ties to militia groups, particularly after his office received a fax from one of those groups on the day of the 1995 bombing of the federal office building in Oklahoma City. In a two-round election necessitated by court-ordered redistricting in Texas, Stockman won the first election 46–44 percent (while Clinton was carrying the blue-collar Beaumont-based district 48–45 percent), but lost the run-off two weeks later to Nick Lampson, a Democrat heavily backed by organized labor (Barone and Ujifusa 1997, 1360).

The other southern freshmen were reelected fairly easily, and in fact the Republicans still made a net pick-up of seats in the region. Thanks to continuing white Democratic retirements, the Republicans made a net gain of five seats in the South, winning the open seats vacated by Democrats Sonny Montgomery (MS), Bill Brewster (OK), Pete Geren and John Bryant (TX), Tom Bevill and Glenn Browder (AL), a new seat created by "re-redistricting" in Louisiana, and defeated Democratic freshman incumbent Mike Ward in Kentucky. Combined with gains from party switching, the Republicans now held an 82–55 edge in the region compared to 73–64 in 1994. Due to the relatively light freshman losses in the South and the continuing Republican advance, there was every indication that the southern conservative voice would predominate among the 58 survivors in the Republican sophomore class during the 105th Congress.

THE 105TH CONGRESS

The 105th Congress began with a furor over the future of Speaker Newt Gingrich, who had been censured and fined by the House for ethical violations committed while he was head of GOPAC, a political action committee that he had used to recruit Republican House candidates (see Carr 1997, 13–15; and Koszczuk and Carr 1997, 160–61). While a handful of Republicans (including three members of the class of 1994) refused to vote for Gingrich in protest, the southern sophomores stayed loyal to the Speaker, who was comfortably reelected to his post in January 1997. Gingrich's troubles did not end with his reelection to the Speakership, however. His continued unpopularity and several strategic mistakes engendered continued rumblings of discontent regarding his leadership during the spring and summer of 1997 (Barnes 1997, 10–12; Koszczuk 1997b, 1415–18). Moreover, as the Clinton White House had succeeded in dictating the issues of the 1996 election, with the Republican congressional campaign being based largely on "checking" a reelected Clinton, the GOP had no clear agenda or mandate for the 105th Congress as they had in the 104th. In frustration, a group of 11 Republicans (nine from the 1994 freshman class including the core southern conservative group: Tom Coburn (OK), Lindsay Graham, Steve Largent, Mark Sanford, and Joe Scarborough) defied the leadership in a March 22, 1997, House floor vote on the rule authorizing the budgets of the House's standing committees, which led to an extraordinary public dressing-down by the Speaker before the entire House Republican conference (Koszczuk 1997a, 679–81).

One major strategic error by the House Republican leadership that reawakened doubts about Gingrich was the "flood relief" fiasco in the early summer of 1997. This arose out of an attempt by the GOP leadership to hold passage of emergency relief for flood victims in the upper Midwest hostage to an agreement by the White House to abandon "sampling" as a method of determining the population in urban areas for the 2000 census. Republicans feared that sampling would produce an inaccurate count, inflating the urban population and costing them House districts in the post-2000 redistricting. The public perception, however, was that the congressional Republicans were delaying badly needed relief for essentially partisan ends, and after taking yet another public relations battering, the GOP was again forced to back down (Taylor 1997, 1362).

This re-echo of the 1995–96 budget debacle was too much for many conservative members of the Republican class of 1994, particularly Lindsay Graham, who with some other southern conservative stalwarts of that class including Steve Largent, began to think seriously about a challenge to the Republican leadership in the House. As Graham put it in an interview with Matthew Rees of the conservative magazine *The Weekly Standard*: "I'm basically tired of saying something on Monday and by Wednesday having to retract it" (Rees 1997b, 14–16). In the summer of 1997, these members actually mounted a coup attempt against Speaker Gingrich with the partial cooperation of some of the Speaker's closest lieutenants, including Republican Campaign Committee chair Bill Paxon of New York, majority whip Tom DeLay, and even majority leader Dick Armey, who eventually got cold feet and revealed the plot to Gingrich (Koszczuk 1997c, 1671–74; Rees 1997a, 20–22). Ironically, the Speaker's harshest critics inside his party were now to be found among the ranks of the conservative southern members of the 1994 freshman class, and his staunchest supporters were Republican moderates who felt that they had a better chance of a hearing from Gingrich than his more ideologically conservative deputies (Koszczuk 1997d, 1751–55).[3]

Gingrich's reputation among conservatives suffered further when he and Senate majority leader Trent Lott (MS) finally concluded a deal with Clinton in the summer of 1997 to balance the budget by 2002. The economic growth generated by the booming economy had reduced the level of "pain" needed to balance the budget and obviated the immediate need to deal with politically sensitive entitlement programs. Both parties were able to benefit from a deal that, at least temporarily, put the long-running budget issue to rest. Many conservatives, however, suspected that the deal had been conducted on terms largely favorable to the President rather than their own desire to reduce the size of government (Elving and Taylor 1997, 1831–36). The other major piece of legislation passed by the 105th Congress also seemed to violate the spirit of the Republican revolution of 1994. A massive highway bill reauthorizing federal surface transportation programs, written largely by House Transportation Committee chair Bud Shuster of Pennsylvania, provided billions of dollars in federal projects for individual House districts: just the kind of "pork barrel" legislation that Republicans had routinely criticized when they were in the House minority (Ota 1998, 1385–87).

Campaign finance legislation also continued to trouble Republicans during the 105th Congress. The Democrats had united behind the Shays-Meehan campaign finance reform bill (named for its cosponsors, Connecticut Republican Christopher Shays and Democrat Martin Meehan of Massachusetts), prohibiting the national political parties from collecting "soft money" or unrestricted donations from wealthy donors to finance national advertising campaigns. While some of the strongest campaign finance reform advocates in the House, such as Tennessean Zach Wamp, were members of the 1994 GOP freshman contingent, the GOP leadership perceived the Shays-Meehan measure as an assault on the Republican fundraising advantage in the area of "soft money" and strove mightily to keep the bill off the House floor. Facing the prospect of defecting Republicans producing a majority for a discharge petition to bring the bill to the floor without the leadership's consent, Speaker Gingrich changed tactics and allowed a floor vote on Shays-Meehan while also permitting a plethora of amendments that he hoped would either kill the bill or at least delay its passage so that the Senate would be unable to consider the measure prior to adjournment (Katz 1998a, 1379–81). While Shays-Meehan did eventually pass the House (with 51 Republicans, including a dozen sophomores, voting in favor) and the bill was reconsidered on the Senate floor in early September 1998, the delay did deny supporters of the bill sufficient time to get the necessary votes (60) to override a Senate filibuster, and the legislation died (Pope 1998, 2402).[4]

The second session of the 105th Congress was dominated by the Monica Lewinsky affair, Special Prosecutor Kenneth Starr's report, and the possible impeachment of President Clinton. The Lewinsky scandal certainly initially helped Republicans in that it derailed much of Clinton's ambitious 1998 agenda as set out in his state of the union address, and congressional Republicans saw no reason to help a president whom they believed had been fatally weakened.

Southern members of the class of 1994 were also among some of the earliest advocates of the president's impeachment, particularly Bob Barr of Georgia, who had been arguing for the impeachment of Clinton on other matters even before the Lewinsky scandal broke in January 1998. The Republicans also believed that Clinton's difficulties would lead them to an electoral triumph in the 1998 midterm elections as it was generally expected that the president's troubles would mobilize the Republicans' conservative base and demoralized Democrats would stay away from the polls. In accordance with this view, Republicans in the House largely reunited in condemnation of the president (Koszczuk 1998, 1127–31). The scandal also temporarily deflected attention from the stalled Republican policy agenda, to which the Senate and the Clinton White House still posed insuperable obstacles. After the submission of the Starr report, the House Judiciary Committee and the House floor, in largely partisan votes, voted to begin an impeachment inquiry into possible violations of the law by President Clinton (Katz 1998, 2712–15).

Despite their haste to end the second session of the 105th Congress and campaign, however, the Republicans still had to deal with the FY 1999 budget. Once again they had been unable to complete all the budget bills on schedule and thereby left themselves exposed to the threat of President Clinton's vetoes and another government shutdown. Fearful of a repeat of 1995–96 and the possible squandering of what appeared to be a golden electoral opportunity, the House Republicans, encouraged by Gingrich and Appropriations Committee chair Bob Livingston, decided to compromise with Clinton and agreed to many of his spending priorities (Taylor 1998, 2885–89). This left many conservative voices both inside and outside Congress distinctly unhappy, but again these became muted in anticipation of an electoral windfall at the polls and the larger Republican majority that might allow the House GOP to move once again on its policy objectives (Kristol 1998a, 10–11; Kristol 1998b, 9).

THE 1998 ELECTIONS AND THE DEMISE OF SPEAKER GINGRICH

The 1998 elections turned out to be something akin to a disaster for House Republicans—at least relative to the expectations they had held of substantial gains to consolidate their majority. For only the second time this century (the other occasion being 1934) the president's party gained seats in a midterm congressional election. The Democrats made a net gain of five House seats, further trimming the narrow Republican majority to 223–211 with one Independent.

While the GOP made no further advances in the South, they held their ground. All the southern Republican incumbents, including those from the class of 1994, were returned; the two parties each won an open seat from the other in Kentucky, and the Democrats won the open seat of retiring party switcher Mike Parker in Mississippi, while the Republicans picked up the seat of retiring Democratic veteran Bill Hefner in North Carolina. Two 1994 GOP House freshmen—Rick White (WA) and Jon Fox (PA)—were defeated in 1998, another three—John Ensign (NV), Mark Neumann (WI), and Linda Smith (WA)—resigned their House seats to make unsuccessful bids for the Senate, Sonny Bono of California died in a skiing accident, and another Californian, Frank Riggs, retired. Overall, 51 of the 73 members of the Republicans' 1994 freshman class remained in the House following the 1998 elections, still a very significant presence (23 percent) in the House Republican conference. Of the 51 survivors of the class of 1994, 21 (40 percent) were southerners, and members of the class made up over a quarter (26 percent) of the total number (82) of southern Republican House members. (For additional discussions of the 1998 elections, see chapters 2 and 5 in this volume.)

The major victim of the Republicans' 1998 House election debacle was Speaker Newt Gingrich. Gingrich had been responsible for the 1998 budget deal that had left many Republican conservatives dispirited and uncomfortable; he had also directed the strategy of the midterm election campaign that had relied on the Clinton scandals rather than a policy agenda to bring the Republicans electoral success. The perception that Gingrich—rather than Judiciary Committee chair Henry Hyde—was directing the Republican impeachment inquiry into President Clinton seemed to have both cost public support for impeachment and mobilized the Democratic base—minorities and Labor union members—to turn out in larger than expected numbers in November (Greenblatt 1998, 2983). As if to reinforce the point, Gingrich had directed that national television advertisements, specifically mentioning the Clinton scandals as a reason to vote Republican, be used in selected districts in the last week of the campaign. The national media attention given to the commercials only seemed to buttress Democratic arguments that the Republican agenda was about impeachment and nothing else, while the president and the congressional Democrats were really focusing on the issues that most concerned the country—education, health care, and social security (Berke 1998, A1).

The lingering discontent concerning Gingrich from the survivors of the 1994 Republican freshman class was manifested when Oklahoman Steve Largent, a long-standing critic, indicated that he would run against Gingrich as the Republican nominee for Speaker in the 106th Congress if no one else stepped up to the plate. Eventually Largent decided to run against majority leader Dick Armey, as a more seasoned Republican, Appropriations Committee chair Robert "Bob" Livingston of Louisiana, made it clear that he would challenge Gingrich. Although Livingston had a reputation for cultivating good relations with Democrats and had been instrumental in brokering the 1998 budget deal that had demoralized conservative Republicans in Washington and around the nation, conservatives were willing to accept him as Speaker to get rid of the unpopular Gingrich. Facing inevitable defeat, the Speaker and architect of the House Republican majority decided to step down (Katz 1998c, 2989–92).

In the House Republican leadership elections for the 106th Congress, majority leader Dick Armey held off strong challenges from Largent and Jennifer Dunn of Washington, defeating Largent narrowly (127–95) in the final balloting largely on the grounds that the Oklahoman was too radical and untested. While Republican whip Tom DeLay was returned unopposed, another Oklahoman member of the 1994 Republican freshman class, J.C. Watts, ousted incumbent John Boehner of Ohio for the position of House GOP conference chair. As the only black Republican Congressman, Watts's election helped give the congressional GOP a more diverse public profile. Finally, another southern member of the 1994 freshman class (albeit with a more moderate political profile reflecting his suburban Washington, D.C. district), Tom Davis of Virginia, was elected as chair of the House Republican Campaign Committee (Katz and Doherty 1998, 3161–66; the preceding chapter in this volume provides additional discussion of the leadership contests following the 1998 election).

Watts's and Davis's ascension to leadership positions and the near-election of Steve Largent showed that the House Republican class of 1994 continued to be a very powerful influence within the ranks of House Republicans. Whether the class as a whole would follow the path toward a more pragmatic approach on policy issues and greater accommodation to the values of Capitol Hill, indicated by the substitution of Bob Livingston, and ultimately Dennis Hastert in the wake of Livingston's scandal-related resignation,[5] for Gingrich as Speaker, however, remained to be seen.

CONCLUSION: A SOUTHERN CONGRESSIONAL PARTY?

In difficult times for the party during the 104th and 105th Congresses, Republican members from the Northeast and West often commented that the congressional Republicans party had become dominated by a southern conservative leadership that did not understand the different electoral context facing Republicans in other parts of the country (Rae 1998, 186–87). When it came time to replace the Georgia-based Newt Gingrich, however, the Republicans opted for another Deep South member, Bob Livingston of Louisiana. In fact the Republicans' leadership for the 106th Congress was more southern than ever with Texans Dick Armey and Tom DeLay continuing as majority leader and whip respectively, Oklahoman J.C. Watts as conference chair, and Florida's Tillie Fowler as conference vice chair. The only nonsoutherner in the leadership team was Chris Cox of California, the Policy Committee chair, although the suburban northern Virginia district of the new Campaign Committee chair, Tom Davis, bore more resemblance to those of northeastern suburban moderates than conservative Deep southerners.

Southern dominance of the major leadership positions, however, is an indication of the extent to which the Republican Party on Capitol Hill has become a white southern conservative party. In fact the culmination of the southern electoral realignment in House elections has left the South as the most Republican region in the country and the dominant element, regionally, ideologically, and culturally in the congressional GOP. This process was finally completed in the 1994 election cycle, when the Republican Party first won a majority of U.S. House seats in the South, thanks to the electoral successes of the members of the class of 1994. As mentioned in the previous section, of the 24 southern Republican freshmen elected in 1994, 21 (88 percent) were still in the House following the 1998 elections. In a freshman class conspicuous by its unprecedented degree of influence and public attention, southern conservatives such as Steve Largent, Lindsay Graham, Mark Sanford, and Joe Scarborough have been both the defining and dominant element. As the class began their third term in the House, despite several signs of pragmatic mellowing, the southern conservatives in the class still acted to a large extent as the "guardians of the flame" of the Republican "revolution" of 1994 and its ideals of a balanced budget, smaller government, and congressional reform.

On the first count, the Republicans could award themselves some degree of political success, and on the second, the Clinton administration's tilt away from "big government" liberalism—at least rhetorically—was some measure of the success of the 1994 Republican freshmen in altering the terms of public debate. As far as institutional reform is concerned, without the influence of the 1994 GOP freshmen, it is difficult to believe that far-reaching gift and lobby reform would have been enacted by Congress. Like their predecessors in the Democratic Watergate class of 1974, the Republican freshmen of 1994 may well have defined the rules and culture of Congress for a generation.

Such a redefinition would, of course, require that the Republicans consolidate their hold on the House, and after the results of the 1998 elections, with the Democrats requiring only a gain of six seats to regain control of Congress, prolonged Republican control appeared uncertain at best. Moreover, pledges made by many members of the Republican freshman class—such as Mark Sanford of South Carolina—to retire after a self-imposed term limit of three terms would, if fulfilled, reduce the class's numbers and dilute their influence.[6] The possibility of a large number of open seats in the South for the 2000 election in the wake of retirements by members of the Republican class of 1994 might also erode the overall Republican dominance in the region, particularly if a Democratic presidential candidate with regional appeal—such as Vice President Albert Gore of Tennessee—were to prevail in the 2000 presidential balloting.

Whatever the eventual outcome, there is no question that the Republican freshman class of 1994 has had a profound impact on American politics, and that the tone of the class was largely set by its large contingent of southern members, who consolidated the Republicans' status as the new majority party in the South in congressional elections and helped to redefine the national GOP in terms of white southern economic and cultural conservatism with a measure of populist reformism (also quintessentially southern, though not quintessentially Republican) thrown in. South Carolinian Mark Sanford, a typical southern member of the 1994 Republican freshman class, perhaps put it best while summarizing his motivations for being in politics: "I have always done what I believe to be a reflection of what the 'little guy' in the district wants: the guy without a voice who has a 14 foot boat and drives a pick-up truck" (Rae 1996f). In the

South, at least, the voters described by Sanford have stuck with the 1994 Republican freshmen, and that explains their continuing influence on Washington politics.

NOTES

1. Throughout this chapter the South is defined as the 11 former Confederate states plus Kentucky and Oklahoma.

2. *Congressional Quarterly Weekly Report*, January 13, 1996, 104–5.

3. According to Koszczuk, 15 Republican House members were at the seat of the conspiracy, 13 of whom were members of the 1994 freshman class, including southerners Tom Coburn (OK), Lindsay Graham (SC), Van Hilleary (TN), Steve Largent (OK), Sue Myrick (NC), Joe Scarborough (FL), and Mark Sanford (SC).

4. On final passage in the House, 61 Republicans including 16 members of the 1994 freshman class voted in support of the Shays-Meehan bill. Among this latter group were four southerners: Mark Foley (FL), Lindsay Graham (SC), Mark Sanford (SC), and Zach Wamp (TN). See *Congressional Quarterly Weekly Report*, August 8, 1998, 2206–7.

5. See Peters's discussion of this process through Livingston's resignation and the subsequent election of Hastert to the Speakership in the preceding chapter.

6. Thirty-five members of the Republican freshman class of 1994 voted for a congressional lifetime term limit of six years in 1997. Included in this group were 14 southerners: Ed Bryant (TN), Tom Coburn (OK), Tom Davis (VA), Lindsay Graham (SC), Van Hilleary (TN), Walter B. Jones (NC), Steve Largent (OK), Sue Myrick (NC), Mark Sanford (SC), "Mac" Thornbery (TX), Zach Wamp (TN), J.C. Watts (OK), Dave Weldon (FL), and Ed Whitfield (KY). See Rae 1998, 157.

8

It's the Variable, Dummy: The Evolution of Congressional Ideology, 1947–1996

FRANK B. FEIGERT AND MICHAEL AULT

Democratic theory rests, in part, on the assumption (if not the myth) that elected representatives will base their votes in Congress on constituent preferences, if not always accurately mirroring them—the so-called agent or delegate role (Wahlke et al., 1962, 276). These constituent preferences can either be expressed or perceived, however rightly or wrongly (Miller and Stokes 1963; Hedlund and Friesma 1972). Somehow, this behavior is supposed to accord with the notion that a legislator casts a roll-call vote in a fully informed manner, acting perhaps more rationally than those citizens who actually voted in the electoral process.

Yet, as we well know, a host of other factors may very well intervene (Clausen 1973; Van Doren 1990). Operating in an environment of uncertainty, legislators' search for constituent preferences is often limited by time and resources. Similarly, as agents of a diverse number of interests, the information received from several conflicting principals with policy preferences of their own may further confound the decision-making process. As a result, legislators must adjust to their complex and ever-changing environment, while maneuvering between the external pressures from local pressure groups and members of their own political party. While this adaptation is wrought with uncertainty, underlying ideological preferences may very well guide the casting of roll-call votes.

This chapter examines how congressional ideology has evolved in the post–World War II era. We explore the role of political parties, the trends in regional patterns, and the effects of institutional factors to assess the extent and type of change that has characterized the United States Congress in the past fifty years. Of particular interest in the context of this volume, we examine the interrelationship between ideological evolution and region within Congress. We begin with a brief outline of the most commonly used measures of congressional ideology and then discuss the relevant linkages between parties, regions, and congressional chambers. Using several descriptive and exploratory techniques on data from the U.S. House of Representatives and the U.S. Senate for the years 1947 to 1996, we then explore the linkages in greater and more rigorous detail. We find that despite the ebb and flow throughout the postwar period, party identification remains one of the most important indicators of congressional ideology in both the U.S. House of Representatives and U.S. Senate.

IDEOLOGY AND ITS THEORETICAL COMPONENTS

Ideology. Personal values—or what has come to be known as ideology—clearly have an influence on numerous types of political behavior. Whether one studies public opinion, voting behavior, judicial decision-making, or formal political theory, discussions of the role and consequences of political ideology are abundant. Until recently, however, it has been largely ignored as an empirical phenomenon in legislative research. Indeed, the well-regarded *Handbook of Legislative Research* (Loewenberg, Patterson, and Jewell 1985) does not index "ideology," per se, but only as a subcategory within the topics of coalition theory and committees.[1] The importance of ideology in comprehending congressional behavior, individual and collective, is recognized and stressed by a limited number of authors. Schneider (1979), for example, argues that during the 1970s, utilizing the role of ideology to understand congressional behavior was far more relevant than utilizing other policy content approaches. Such an understanding, he argues, "allows, in the aggregate, congressional and indeed governmental outcomes to be explained by reference to the ideological balance of forces in Congress" (1979, 147).

The oldest construct of congressional ideology is the Conservative Coalition (CC). The CC reflects the working alliance between Republicans and southern Democrats, and its scores have been reported by *Congressional Quarterly* since 1959. Initially, they were used to analyze the Senate (Manley 1973, 1977). Evidence in support of the coalition's presence and strength from 1925 to 1976 is developed by Brady and Bullock (1980, 1981). They refute the concept of a coalition in the formal sense but see its presence as a consequence of issue agreement. Hibbing (1982) finds evidence to suggest that legislators who hold more liberal or conservative positions are more likely to take early retirement than are moderates. More recently, using standardized CC scores from 1957 to 1982, he finds a general tendency toward increased conservatism with length of service, as "[e]ach term brings an average increase in support for the conservative coalition of about .02 standard deviations" (Hibbing 1991, 94). Fleisher, however, suggests that

> Conservative Coalition scores have become a less useful indicator of the level of ideological voting of southern Democrats than it was previously. By definition, the Conservative Coalition forms only when a majority of southern Democrats vote conservatively. Because of this definition, the Conservative Coalition support scores ignore the increasing number of votes on which southern Democrats vote for the liberal position. (1995, 331)

Hibbing also recognizes Fleisher's point in his earlier study but concedes that it is "practically definitional" (1991, 94). Another measure of ideology is the liberalism score compiled by the *New Republic* (Deckard and Stanley 1974).

More widely used as a measure of congressional ideology is the annual score reported for each member by Americans for Democratic Action (ADA). This score, reported since 1947, is based on the number of times a legislator voted "correctly" on a selected number of roll calls on "a broad range of issues" (Poole and Daniels 1985, 374). These include "foreign policy, civil liberties and democracy, race, and economic issues" (Schneider 1979, 56). Coleman (1996) uses both ADA (1960–84) and CC (1959–88) scores for the House and concludes that they tell the same story of increasing northern Democratic conservatism. Due to either necessity or choice, a common problem with studies based on ADA scores is that they are often limited to a relatively short timespan. As we discuss below, short-term analyses risk overstating trends in congressional ideology that might only occur during limited periods. Extending the analysis to include all available years, we argue, will foster an understanding of the short- and long-term dynamics that have occurred in both chambers of Congress.

Examples of using ADA scores as independent variables include those of Campbell (1982), Krehbiel (1995), and Schneider (1979).[2] Schneider uses ADA scores to develop broad classifications of liberal, moderate, and conservative categories of congressional ideologies and then examines the behavior of a subset of House members.

By contrast, a number of studies use ADA scores as a dependent variable. Fleisher examines such scores for odd-numbered years (1981–87) for the House, focusing on various aspects of constituency (Proportion Black, White Mondale Vote, Urbanization, and GOP Congressional Vote) as explanatory variables. For southern Democrats, these variables account for 40 to 48 percent of the variance, while for northern Democrats the fit of 22 to 38 percent is less robust (1995, 337–38). More extended in terms of time is Hood, Kidd, and Morriss (1996), who focus on southern Democratic senators between 1955 and 1995, in the context of changes brought about by the Voting Rights Act of 1965. Shaffer (1980) also examines ADA scores as the dependent variable, relating them to party, region, and chamber, 1965 to 1976.

Yet, in spite of these previous discussions, ADA scores are something of an idiosyncratic phenomenon in congressional research. Analysts may cite the annual scores for an individual (for example, Shaffer 1980), or perhaps for groups such as southern Democrats or all House Republicans, but most studies have been limited to either a single chamber or a limited time period. In fact, lacking in the literature is a discussion of how congressional ideology has evolved (in both chambers) throughout the postwar period. Such a discussion, we believe, is a necessary step toward understanding the extent and type of change that has characterized the United States Congress and should go a long way toward cumulative development in the burgeoning area of legislative research.

Party Influence. Fairly early in the empirical study of legislative behavior, the responsible party model debate provoked a host of studies refuting the claim of APSA's Committee on Political Parties (1950) that congressional parties were irresponsible, if not indistinguishable (Stedman and Sonthoff 1951; Turner 1950, 1951). A later school of inquiry concludes that party is not an important variable in understanding congressional voting behavior, and its importance is, indeed, declining (Clubb and Traugott 1977; Clubb, Flanigan, and Zingale 1980; Brady, Cooper, and Hurley 1979; Sinclair 1977, 1978). In this vein, Brady and Althoff suggest that, during the period from 1890 to 1910, "American congressional parties, unlike those in the contemporary House, exhibited certain important characteristics of a responsible party system" (1974, 754). Interestingly, this school of thought, part of the party decline school, is at odds with Broder's conclusion that the roughly 40 percent of roll calls in the 1960s meeting the majority versus majority criterion is evidence that "[p]arty lines and party loyalties play more of a role in the decision making of Congress than we sometimes imagine" (1971, 217). A recent study comparing party voting between the House and Senate over three congresses between 1969 and 1988 concludes that, in terms of domestic, foreign policy, and defense-related votes, "party voting was stronger in the House in all of the three Congresses," although lower partisanship was displayed in each chamber on foreign policy votes (Rohde 1992, 43).[3] Moreover, Hurley and Wilson conclude that for more than a century, party voting in both chambers generally declined (1989, 246). Democratic unity in the Senate is seen as having a regional basis, dependent on the "size of the Democratic contingent," while Republican unity derives from "membership turnover and presidential partisanship" (1989, 225).

Regional Influence. A considerable body of congressional voting research investigates the relative influence of state House delegations (Born 1976; Vessel 1964; Snows 1966). As Ripley (1988, 229, note 2) points out,

> The concept of "state delegation" in the Senate is meaningless since there are only two senators per state. Senators from a state cooperate explicitly with House members from the same state only sporadically. Various interest-based caucuses, both within the House and occasionally including senators, absorb what might be thought of, in principal, as regional interests. Political scientists, reasonably so, use region as an analytical category for understanding congressional behavior, especially on roll calls, but regional considerations only rarely serve to motivate concrete individual behavior in Congress in the late Twentieth Century.

Conventionally, such analyses focus on distinctions between the South and the rest of the nation.

Deckard and Stanley (1974) provide a unique analysis in this regard. Starting with four regional groupings (for example, South, East, Midwest, West) for the House, they collapse the latter three into a single non-South category for Democrats. A dummy variable of "South" explains 12.5 to 48.5 percent of the variance in Democratic party unity scores, with greater explanation coming since 1961. Correlations between party unity and the *New Republic* scores used as a measure of liberalism are quite strong, ranging during the period from 1945 through 1970 from .57 to .87. Using a dummy variable of "East" for the GOP, 6.7 to 30 percent of party unity since 1961 can be explained by the regional variable. Correlations between party unity and the *New Republic* scores are also strong, ranging from -.25 to -.77 (1994, 253–59). They suggest "that at certain periods, region and ideology merge as explanatory devices in American politics whose importance should not be overlooked. The period since the Eighty-sixth Congress appears to be one of increased ideological hostility between sections of the two parties and these sections are primarily regional" (1994, 264). Shaffer (1980) provides a more exhaustive analysis in terms of region, employing a six-fold regional breakdown for the years 1965–76.

Suffice it to say that the overwhelming bulk of the literature examining regional influences concludes that southern legislators are uniquely conservative in their voting patterns, forming the bulwark of the Conservative Coalition discussed above. We address this issue, as an empirical question, in the analyses that follow.

Chamber Influence. Although "Congress is the most widely studied legislative institution in the world" (Poole and Daniels 1985, 373), and a staple of courses on Congress is the set of institutional differences between its two chambers, scholars have all but avoided discussion of the differences in roll-call patterns that emerge between the two chambers. One possible exception is Poole and Daniels (1985), who employ spatial modeling for the 1959–80 period. Yet, they place House and Senate members in

> a common configuration. . . . In only two instances were the configurations different enough to cast doubt on the assumption of comparability. Although we have not exploited it here, having the House and Senate members in the same spatial configuration makes cross-chamber comparisons of roll-call voting within and between issue domains possible. (Poole and Daniels 1985, 397)

Examining House party unity scores from 1965 to 1978, Abramowitz finds that "reports of the demise of the southern Democratic revolt in Congress have been greatly exaggerated" (1980a, 752). Patterson and Caldeira (1988) find substantial differences in party voting between the House, where there is no clear trend, and the Senate, where there is significant decline from 1949 to 1984. But, they also note, the two chambers had virtually the same means, standard deviations, and standard errors. As they point out, however, differential norms, rules, and electoral context may account for some of these differences. In short, they do not provide a direct test of the impact that the chambers may have on member's party voting patterns, much less the ideological dimensions reflected by roll-call votes.

Given these influences—party, region, and chamber—we now examine the evolution of congressional ideology. Using the period of 1947 to 1996 for both houses of Congress, we investigate the relationship between party, region, and chamber and the changes that occurred in the structure of congressional ideology. The size and inclusiveness of our database allow us to assess trends and changes in the relative weight of each of the variables over the entire fifty-year period. While, ideally, we would like to specify a complete model of the factors influencing congressional ideology, we choose to limit this study to a descriptive and exploratory analysis, leaving a multivariate test of each influence for another study.

DATA AND FINDINGS

Our measure of congressional ideology is the annual ideological score compiled by the Americans for Democratic Action (ADA). Under this scheme, a score of 0 counts as most conservative and a score of 100 as most liberal (the latter merits, in the ADA's analysis, a description as a "hero" or "heroine"). These data cover all members of Congress from 1947 to 1996. During this period, 2,196 individuals served in the House, and 442 served in the Senate.[4] Our initial task is to determine the extent to which the South/non-South distinction can be usefully employed to specify ideological differences in Congress. Figures 8.1 (House) and 8.2 (Senate) provide a basis for comprehending short- and long-term trends in the South and non-South. Taken as a whole, the mean ideological scores for the South and non-South in each chamber indicate a broad range of ideology over time. Focusing on the House (Figure 8.1), we see that in

Figure 8.1
House ADA Scores by Party and Region

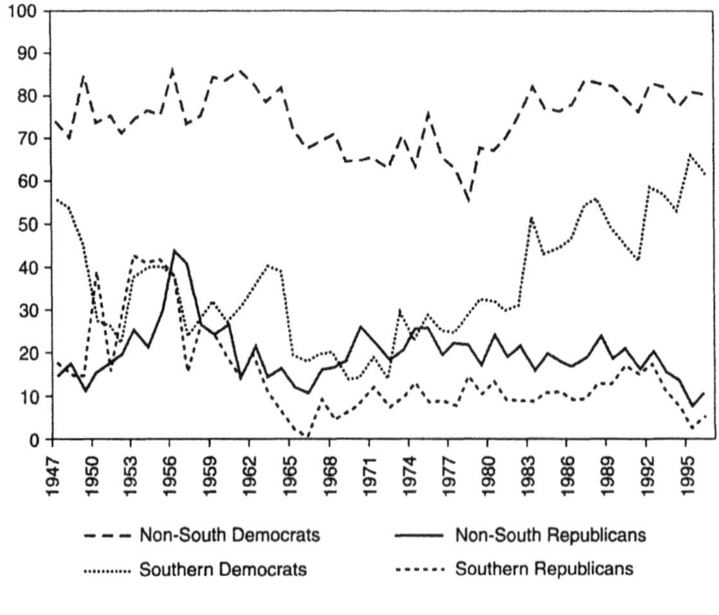

the late 1940s, the South tends to be more liberal than the non-South. But beginning in the 1950s, and continuing throughout the rest of the period, the South is consistently more conservative than the non-South. Interestingly, beginning in 1965 and ending in 1972, the mean ideological scores dropped to record lows (averaging around 15 for the eight-year period), indicating a strong conservative shift by southern House members. After 1972, however, we see a convergence between scores in the South and the non-South, with southern members becoming less conservative. Average scores for southern members during 1973–96 hovers around 30, while the average for nonsouthern members is approximately 50.

A similar pattern exists in the Senate (Figure 8.2). Throughout the early period, mean ideological scores for southern and nonsouthern Senators are virtually interchangeable. But, beginning in 1958 and continuing through the rest of the period, the South again is consistently more conservative than its nonsouthern counterparts—the greatest disparity occurring during the late 1960s and early 1970s. During the period 1964–76, the average is around 16. After 1976, however, southern scores converge with those from the non-South. The average of the mean ideological scores for the South is almost 33, while the average of the mean ideological score for the non-South is around 51.

To investigate the relationship a bit more closely, Figures 8.3 and 8.4 illustrate the evolution of ideology in the South and non-South according to party identification across each chamber. Focusing first on House Democrats (Figure

Figure 8.2
Senate ADA Scores by Party and Region

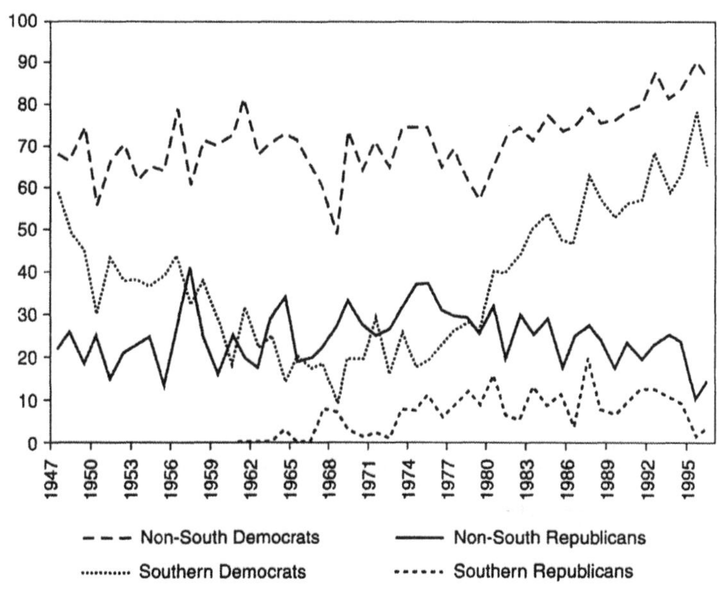

8.3), we see that during the early period from 1947 to 1950, southern Democrats tended to be fairly liberal in their congressional ideology. Beginning in 1950, however, they became more conservative, moreso than their southern Republican counterparts for the years 1952 to 1955. Moreover, comparing Figures 8.3 and 8.4, from around 1965 to 1978, there appears to be some homogeneity of ideology between southern Republicans and southern Democrats, with both groups exhibiting very conservative ideologies. The average of the mean ideological scores for this fourteen-year period for the southern Republicans is 8, and for southern Democrats it is 21. Yet, after a brief period in 1979, during which southern Republicans were actually more liberal than their southern Democratic counterparts, a widening of the gap between the two parties occurred. The average of the mean ideological scores for the years 1979 to 1996 is nine for southern Republicans and 48 for the southern Democrats. This seventeen-year trend reflects the distinctions between the two parties that one would typically expect to observe in other regions.

Turning to the non-South, we see that there has always been a clear demarcation between the two political parties in the House. Although there have been times when nonsouthern Republicans have exhibited fairly middle of the road ideological postures (for example, 1956–58), for the most part, nonsouthern Republicans have tended to be fairly conservative. The average of the mean

Figure 8.3
Democratic ADA Scores by Chamber and Region

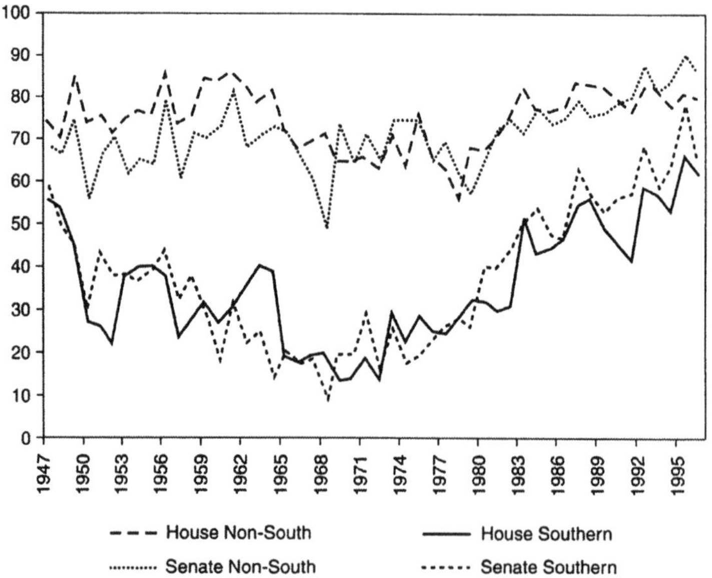

ideological scores for nonsouthern Republicans for the entire period is 20, while for the southern Democrats it is 75. Clearly, in nonsouthern regions for the Senate, congressional ideology has also closely mirrored party identification.

An examination of the Senate reveals a similar pattern. Aside from the fact that no Republican was elected to the Senate in the South prior to 1961, the fluctuations in ideology after 1961 closely resemble the scores for the House. The average of the mean ideological scores for southern Republican senators is a staunchly conservative six, while for southern Democratic senators it is 38. Similarly, as we observed in the House, ideological scores for nonsouthern senators (both Republican and Democratic) reflect clear differences based on party identification.

Taken as a whole, it is apparent that, regardless of chamber or region, GOP members are overwhelmingly more conservative than are Democrats. Despite some years in which there are major differences within each party, there are certain ideological threads that bind. On the other hand, images of the GOP as having become an ideologically unified party only in the "Era of Newt" simply do not square with the long-term analyses presented here. And, it is also apparent that, given the convergence taking place within each party, whether in the House or Senate, the Congress is becoming an institution increasingly driven by ideology.

Figure 8.4
Republican ADA Scores by Chamber and Region

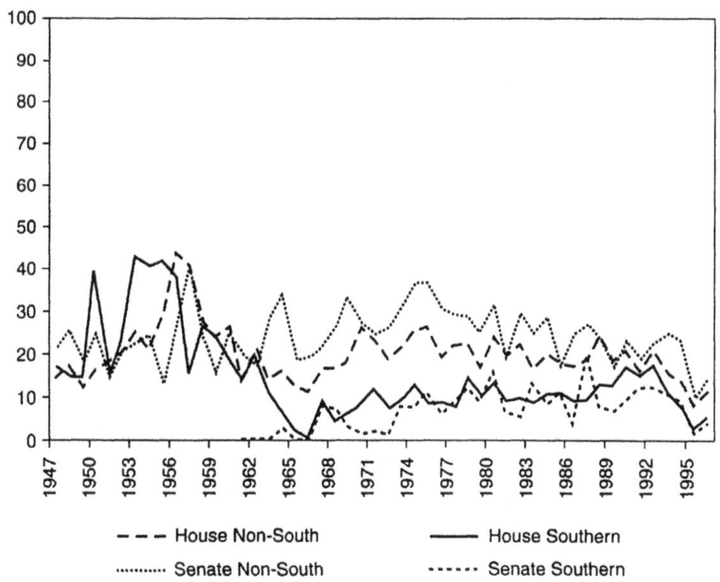

DISCUSSION AND ANALYSIS

There are some important generalizations to be derived from the data. For one, there are broadly similar patterns between the House and the Senate. Included is the fact that southern Democrats, long considered the absolute bastion of conservatism, are at various times among the more liberal groups in Congress. This was true from 1947 to 1949 in both chambers, perhaps because matters other than civil rights dominated the legislative agenda. And, for the last 25 years, it has become increasingly true again. As southern Democrats have been increasingly and successfully challenged by Republicans, a rough parity in numbers has been achieved, with the GOP holding a slight edge in each chamber since 1995. The increase of mean liberalism among southern Democrats in both houses is obviously attributable, at least in part, to the fact that African Americans and Hispanics have come to supplant many of the old-line conservative Democrats (see Bullock 1995). And it is necessary to recall that the South has a distinctly populist tradition on some matters, if not on race, as the scores for the immediate postwar period suggest. Ranking ADA scores in diminishing order for the entire time period reveals the following:

Non-South Democrats (House)	74.6	Non-South Republicans (Senate)	22.5
Non-South Democrats (Senate)	71.3	Non-South Republicans (House)	20.3
Southern Democrats (Senate)	37.7	Southern Republicans (House)	14.6
Southern Democrats (House)	35.4	Southern Republicans (Senate)	6.7

We observe that, on average, Democrats from the South and the non-South are consistently more liberal than Republicans. In other words, regardless of chamber or region, it appears that party is clearly an important and relevant indicator of congressional ideology. The role of region, however, appears to help differentiate within each party. That is, on the one hand, nonsouthern Democrats in the House and Senate share a mostly liberal ideology, while Southern Republicans in the House and Senate share a mostly conservative ideology. On the other hand, Southern Democrats share moderate ideologies, making them less liberal than their nonsouthern counterparts, but importantly, they also are less conservative than all the Republicans.

Regardless, it is quite clear that *inter*-party distinctions exist and may be increasing, while *intra*-party distinctions have been decreasing. Regional differences have come to be more muted within each party, and since 1977 in the House, there are only two instances (1982 and 1983) in which regional differences between Democrats exceed the fifty-year average of 39. Since 1977, in the Senate, there are no such regional differences that exceed the fifty year average of 34. Republicans have considerably less regional difference in ideology (5.7 in the House, 19.5 in the Senate), with a general tendency in the last dozen years toward smaller distinctions. In short, the parties are becoming more ideologically unified within each chamber, thus lending the potential for even more fractious debate. Over the fifty-year period, there is a much greater distinction among Democrats in both houses of Congress based on South versus non-South. This difference is narrowing, but not as quickly as it has been among Republicans.

Given that nonsouthern Democrats are the most liberal over time, and that Republicans in both chambers are most conservative, it is the changing nature of southern Democrats that is most distinctive. Specifically, starting with the end of the 1970s, and continuing for almost two decades, there is a convergence of mean ADA scores for both southern and nonsouthern Democratic legislators in terms of their liberalism. This has not happened because nonsouthern members have become more conservative or centrist. Rather, southern Democrats are becoming increasingly liberal over time.

How can this be explained? The number of southern Democrats has been sinking. Following the 1994 elections, for example, southern Democrats comprised less than a majority of their region in both chambers. While not marginalized in any real sense, it is obvious that the trend is such that remaining Democrats from the South are more liberal in their voting behavior than were those who preceded them. Conservative southern Democrats have either retired, lost at the polls or, in a few cases, converted to the GOP. Additionally, as Fleisher notes,

> As Republican strength in southern districts increases over time, it may force more southern Democrats to respond by voting more often for policies that satisfy blacks and progressive whites. . . . [They] must be more aware of the electoral role played by blacks than was the case 25 years ago. . . . [Further] conditions in the late 1970s and 1980s presented the Congress with a different legislative agenda than was previously the case. (1995, 339)

We must point out, however, that similar changes confront the newly emergent southern GOP, members of which have responded by voting in an even more conservative and constrained manner than either their Democratic predecessors or their nonsouthern fellow partisans.

What can be made of these changes in terms of a liberalism/conservatism distinction? In both chambers, Republican ADA scores are more tightly constrained than are those for the Democrats. Issue agreement may very well be the basis for this apparent cohesion and agreement among Republicans. Examining the rank-order of standard deviations of the ideological scores we observe the following pattern:

Southern Democrats (Senate)	37.7	Non-South Democrats (House)	20.6
Southern Democrats (House)	22.8	Non-South Republicans (House)	19.6
Non-South Republicans (Senate)	22.5	Southern Republicans (House)	16.8
Non-South Democrats (Senate)	20.7	Southern Republicans (Senate)	6.1

Clearly, southern Republicans in the Senate are the most tightly constrained, with an average standard deviation of 6.1. Even southern Democrats in the

Senate, whose average standard deviation is 37.7, demonstrate loosely cohesive ideological patterns.

Continuing, Tables 8.1 (House) and 8.2 (Senate) show grouped ADA scores and standard deviations organized by region and party. What is immediately apparent is that a majority (53.2 percent) of the representatives have narrowly constrained (std. dev. > 10) ADA scores. A nearly alike proportion of senators (49.3 percent) have low standard deviations. In the aggregate, no matter whether liberal or conservative, our elected representatives tend to vote within a relatively low dispersion of ADA scores.

Table 8.1
Distribution of House ADA Scores and Standard Deviations by Party and Region

Party and Region with	*Standard Deviations*			
grouped ADA scores	*0–9.9*	*10.0–19.9*	*> 20*	*N*
Nonsouthern Democrats				
0.0–19.9	2.3%	0.9%	1.0%	13
20–39.9	2.9	4.1	7.1	31
40–59.9	6.8	14.4	28.3	100
60–79.9	21.5	47.2	57.6	290
80–100	66.5	33.4	6.1	367
N	382	320	99	801
Southern Democrats				
0.0–19.9	38.6	22.3	7.4	103
20–39.9	14.2	29.1	39.7	109
40–59.9	16.5	19.1	36.8	88
60–79.9	7.1	13.2	7.4	43
80–100	23.6	16.4	8.8	72
N	127	220	68	415
Nonsouthern Republicans				
0.0–19.9	83.0	39.2	1.6	565
20–39.9	13.9	39.6	40.3	208
40–59.9	1.8	13.4	41.9	72
60–79.9	0.9	6.7	16.1	33
80–100	0.3	1.1	—	5
N	553	268	62	883
Southern Republicans				
0.0–19.9	96.9	54.5	50.0	133
20–39.9	2.3	27.3	50.0	7
40–59.9				0
60–79.9				0
80–100	0.8	18.2	—	3
N	130	11	2	143

Source: Compiled by authors.

Examining this phenomenon by party and region, we see the expected differences across region, at least for Democrats. Nonsouthern Democrats are considerably more liberal than their southern brethren, a not unexpected finding. What dispersion there is, as measured by standard deviations, is greatest for Democrats in general, regardless of chamber and regardless of region. A majority of Democrats, southern or nonsouthern, House (57.3 percent) or Senate (65.4 percent), have standard deviations greater than 10.0. On the other hand, 66.5 percent of all House Republicans and 64.3 percent of their Senate colleagues have standard deviations less than 10.0. Region, however, fails to differentiate

Table 8.2
Distribution of Senate ADA Scores and Standard Deviations by Party and Region

Party and Region with grouped ADA scores	*Standard Deviations* 0–9.9	10.0–19.9	> 20	*N*
Nonsouthern Democrats				
0.0–19.9	1.9%	1.1%	0.0%	2
20–39.9	0.0	7.4	0.0	7
40–59.9	1.9	27.4	36.8	34
60–79.9	13.5	41.1	52.6	56
80–100	82.7	23.2	10.5	67
N	52	95	19	166
Southern Democrats				
0.0–19.9	34.5	25.0	14.3	19
20–39.9	48.3	9.4	0.0	17
40–59.9	10.3	37.5	42.9	18
60–79.9	6.9	28.1	28.6	13
80–100	0.0	0.0	14.3	1
N	29	32	7	68
Nonsouthern Republicans				
0.0–19.9	82.1	29.2	33.3	114
20–39.9	15.2	37.5	33.3	45
40–59.9	0.9	20.8	33.3	17
60–79.9	1.8	11.1	0.0	10
80–100	0.0	1.4	0.0	1
N	112	72	3	187
Southern Republicans				
0.0–19.9	100.0			23
20–39.9				0
40–59.9				0
60–79.9				0
80–100				0
N	23			23

Source: Compiled by authors.

significantly among Republicans as the overwhelming majority of them, regardless of chamber, vote in the most conservative and constrained manner.

We extend this sorting of the various influences by examining, in Table 8.3, the extent to which annual ADA averages are intercorrelated. As expected, interparty correlations are essentially nil, regardless of region or chamber. On the other hand, one might expect that the normally fractious Democrats would display, particularly in the South/non-South distinction, substantially less cohesion than the Republicans, in either chamber. Such is not the case, by any means. The only correlations that are similar are those between Senate southern Democrats and House nonsouthern Democrats, on the one hand, and those for House Republicans, southern or nonsouthern, on the other. For the Democrats, these are the *lowest* intraparty correlations, and for the Republicans these are the *highest.* Indeed, for the GOP, correlations are nominal at best, while for the Democrats region appears to have a truly important effect. The R-squared for Senate and House southern Democrats is an astonishingly high .749. And yet, the correlation between House members, regardless of region, is a robust .415. This is matched by a .428 for the Senate, between southern and nonsouthern regions.

Next, we examine the correlations between members' ADA scores, their party affiliation and members' chamber, by region. Table 8.4 indicates strikingly strong and significant correlations between members' ADA score and their party affiliations. This remains true even when we statistically control for members' regional categories as measured by a five-category variable (for example, South, Border, West, Midwest, and Northeast). The probability that these results are

Table 8.3
Correlations (R^2) of Yearly ADA Scores by Party, Chamber, and Region

Chamber and Party	*H N-S*	*H S*	*S N-S*	*S S*	*H N-S*	*H S*	*S N-S*	*S S*
H N-S D								
H S D	**.415**							
S N-S D	**.287**	**.359**						
S S D	**.246**	**.749**	**.428**					
H N-S R	.001	.071	.031	.035				
H S R	.045	.002	.047	.003	**.241**			
S N-S R	.145	.130	.055	.187	**.161**	**.025**		
S S R	.006	.127	.004	.161	**.105**	**.111**	**.005**	

*Chamber is indicated by H for House, S for Senate; retion is N-S for nonsouthern, S for southern; party is D for Democrats, R for Republicans. Hence, for the first entry, H N-S D is House, nonsouthern Democrats. Same-party correlations are in boldface.
Source: Compiled by authors.

Table 8.4
Correlations Between Ideology, Party, and Chamber by Region, 1947–1996

	House	*Senate*	*Both*	
	ADA/Party	ADA/Party	ADA/Party	ADA/Chamber
All Regions	.61*	.59*	.61*	-0.0015
South	.39*	.45*	.40*	-0.0009
Non-South	.78*	.73*	.77*	-0.0107
Border	.60*	.61*	.60*	0.0164
West	.83*	.76*	.81*	-0.0697*
Midwest	.83*	.85*	.84*	0.0363*
Northeast	.73*	.66*	.72*	-0.0056

*p < .01
Source: Compiled by authors.

obtained simply by chance is less than one percent for all regions in the House and Senate. Surprisingly, however, the correlations between members' ADA scores and their chamber (column 4) yield quite weak relationships. Even in the case of the West and Midwest, where we observe statistically significant relationships, the correlations are extremely weak (-0.07 and 0.04, respectively).

CONCLUSIONS

Our analysis of postwar trends in congressional ideology leads us to several conclusions. First, in terms of the literature on the role of parties in Congress, it is clear that ideological distinctions between the two parties are both profound and have been increasing since the 1980s. While nonsouthern Democrats are historically the most liberal group in either chamber, southern Democrats are showing a convergence with their fellow partisans in the last twenty or so years. Regardless of chamber or region, Republicans in the House and Senate are considerably more conservative than southern Democrats once were. Hence, we are presently witnessing an increasing ideological polarization of the parties. Examining the data on an annual basis, party is clearly the most significant determinant of ideology. And, for those of the party decline school, it is well to remind ourselves that an extension of the scope of previous analyses suggests that party cohesiveness characterizes the ideological makeup of Republicans and Democrats in both the House and the Senate.

Not at all surprisingly, we find an historic basis for concluding that southern senators and representatives can be uniquely differentiated from their brethren in Congress. However, when we examine regional differences, whether dichotomized (South vs. non-South) or on the more conventional basis of five regions, we find that these have become more muted in both parties, in either chamber, than once they were. This, it seems, helps to illuminate Peters's discussion in this volume (chapter 6) of the role of region the contemporary House of Representatives. Region does, indeed, contribute to aggregated ideological scores, but considerably less than does party, whether we examine this on an annual or long-term trend basis.

Of interest is the relatively small, if not indistinct, contribution to ideological variance found when we consider chamber. Given the different institutional rules, norms, and larger contexts, one might have expected that chamber effects would have been more evident, as suggested by Poole and Daniels (1985, 397). These are clearly diminished for southern Democrats, as demonstrated by the high correlation seen in Table 8.3 and the insignificance of chamber when, in Table 8.4, we use South/non-South as a dummy variable. And, the simple correlation of .61 for party across all regions contrasts sharply with the low and insignificant correlation for chamber. Building on Fleisher's work using district-level data, we have attempted to explain congressional ideology with the use of just three variables. We believe the next step toward building cumulative knowledge in the field of legislative research is to specify a complete multivariate model of congressional ideology.

NOTES

1. Part of the problem may derive from the relative paucity of studies to that date employing ideology as an explanatory variable. Collie (1985, 483–84) provides a useful review of these.

2. Van Doren (1990) also utilizes ADA scores as independent variables, 1947–76, while critiquing their usage, or any individual-level data to explain aggregate congressional decisions.

3. For a useful review of the party-in-decline literature, see Rohde (1991a, 8–11). He also points out a "remarkable resurgence of partisanship in the House," peaking in 1987 (1991, 14).

4. The principal data source is Sharp (1997). This was augmented for 1995 and 1996 by Duncan and Lawrence (1997). Scores for those who left Congress were supplemented from *ADA Today* 51 (March 1996) and 51 (November 1996). Fourteen representatives converted and are counted twice; 12 of these are former Democrats, of whom 10 came from southern states, mainly in the last 20 years. Four senators (Morse, OR; Thurmond, SC; Shelby, AL; Campbell, CO) converted and are doubly counted, dating from their party conversion. While potentially important in terms of partisan control, the phenomenon of congressional conversion is much less prevalent than one might conclude, given the journalistic attention it generates. Excluded are Senator Harry F. Byrd, Jr. (VA), who became an Independent in 1970 and three House Independents as well (Marcantonio, NY; Isacson, NY; Sanders, VT).

9

Testing Hypotheses on Increased Ideological Polarization in U.S. House Delegations from the South after Redistricting

ALLISON L. HAYES AND KENNETH A. WINK

The research proposition is straightforward: ideological polarization should have increased after the creation of majority-minority districts. As district lines are drawn to increase the chances that minority candidates are elected, the districts surrounding the majority-minority districts should favor Republicans. If Republicans and African-American Democrats are elected in larger numbers after racial redistricting, the cohort elected after the redistricting should be polarized into more liberal and conservative wings.

A number of hypotheses can be tested in support of the major proposition. In order to accept the scenario stated previously, one must first determine that more African Americans and more Republicans were elected after racial redistricting. Thus, the first hypothesis is that there were more African Americans and Republicans elected in 1992 than in 1990.

Two other hypotheses relate to the pattern of roll-call voting before and after racial redistricting. The second hypothesis for which there should be some evidence is that the standard deviation of some measure of ideological roll-call voting for states affected by race-based redistricting should have increased after redistricting. Regardless of whether the mean score of the measure of ideology increases or decreases, the scores should be more dispersed around the mean if voting patterns are becoming more polarized. Third, after controlling for party, the major shift in the standard deviation of the ideology measure should primarily reflect more polarized voting in the Democratic cohort, particularly in states affected by racial redistricting. Assuming that African-American Democrats will exhibit a more liberal voting pattern than will white Democrats, as African Americans become a numerically larger part of the Democratic cohort, the standard deviation of the ideological voting measure should increase for Democrats. Note that polarization in the southern delegation should be increased independent of changes in Republican voting patterns. With regard to the theory of increased polarization, evidence can be supportive simply if more Republicans are elected to office.

As the discussion implies, the methods employed to test the hypotheses involve examination of descriptive statistics related to roll-call voting in the U.S. House before and after racial redistricting. In this quasi-experiment, we compare descriptive statistics for southern states that were involved in creating majority-minority districts with those that were not. These fourteen states all contain relatively substantial minority populations, have tended historically to support the Democratic party, and share other similar socioeconomic, cultural, and historical patterns that make them distinct from the rest of the nation. Thus, we hope to isolate different patterns of polarized voting based as nearly as possible on only whether or not the state experienced the creation of new majority-minority districts before the 1992 election.[1]

The measure of ideology chosen for this study is the annual Americans for Democratic Action (ADA) score for each representative. To attempt to minimize measurement error that might result from an unusual voting pattern for a particular representative in a given year, mean scores are calculated for each representative. The measure of ideology before racial redistricting is calculated by averaging the 1991 and 1992 mean scores of each member. The measure of ideology after racial redistricting is the mean of each representative's 1993 and 1994 ADA score. Since the ADA is a liberal group that rewards with high scores those who vote the liberal position on key pieces of legislation in a given year, representative mean ADA scores that are high represent liberal roll-call voting and low mean scores represent conservative voting.

The use of ADA scores is common in studies of congressional roll-call voting in general and in studies that are specifically concerned with the representation of African Americans in Congress (for example, Fleisher 1993; Sharpe and Garand 1995; Whitby 1987). Lublin (1997) contended that a more complex measure of ideology, such as the Poole-Rosenthal score, which standardizes individual ideological positions on all votes taken over several years, is a more appropriate measure of a representative's ideological position. However, Lublin noted that interest-group ratings such as ADA scores correlated quite highly with the Poole-Rosenthal scores. Furthermore, the results of Lublin's research were "virtually identical" when he substituted interest group ratings for the Poole-Rosenthal scores as the dependent variable in his models (Lublin 1997, 79). Because of the relatively straightforward interpretation of ADA scores and the ease with which they can be obtained, we employ ADA scores in our analysis.

The data on roll-call behavior and on the makeup of the southern U.S. House delegation were taken from the 1994 and 1992 editions of the *Almanac of American Politics* (Barone and Ujifusa 1993, 1995).[2] The *Almanac* contains demographic data, election data, and descriptive information about the states and the congressional districts. In addition, the *Almanac* is a good source of information concerning redistricting since it includes maps illustrating the latest district lines and narrative accounts of the creation of the new lines.

RESULTS

The results are as expected, and they provide strong support for the theory that racial redistricting results in polarized roll-call voting in the U.S. House of Representatives. The results for representatives from all states are reported in Table 9.1. First, as noted by many other observers, there were more African Americans and more Republicans elected in the southern U.S. House races in 1992 than in previous years. The number of African-American Democrats increased from seven in 1990 to nineteen in 1992. Likewise, the number of Republicans rose from forty-seven in 1990 to fifty-four in 1992. Thus, there is tentative empirical support for the first hypothesis.[3]

Second, the evidence does suggest that voting became more ideologically polarized in the cohort as a whole after redistricting. The standard deviation of the ADA scores was 27.5 in 1991 and 1992; in 1993 and 1994, the standard deviation increased to 31.5. As Table 9.1 illustrates, the mean ADA score before redistricting was 39.6, and the mean after redistricting was 38.6. Applying the

Table 9.1
Mean ADA Scores for Southern U.S. House Members, by Race and Party, 1991–92 and 1993–94

Group	*Frequency*	*Mean*	*Standard Deviation*
1991–92			
White Democrats	80	51.2	9.7
Black Democrats	7	87.9	7.6
Latino Democrats	4	63.8	15.3
All Democrats	91	54.6	21.3
Republicans	47	10.6	8.3
Total	138	39.6	27.5
1993–94			
White Democrats	68	48.9	21.1
Black Democrats	19	88.1	8.6
Latino Democrats	4	52.5	16.8
All Democrats	91	57.2	24.7
Republicans	54	7.1	6.8
Total	145	38.6	31.5

Source: Compiled by authors.

respective standard deviations to the means, one discovers that the range from one standard deviation above the mean to one standard deviation below the mean produced a range of from 12.1 to 67.1 in 1991 and 1992 and 7.1 to 70.1 in 1993 and 1994. Thus, roll-call voting in the cohort as a whole was more polarized into liberal and conservative wings after racial redistricting.

Third, the evidence also supports the assumption that the ADA scores of Democrats will become more polarized as African-American Democrats increase in numbers. The ADA scores for all Democrats exhibited a standard deviation of 21.3 in 1991 and 1992 and 24.7 in 1993 and 1994. Furthermore, the standard deviation of Republican ADA scores actually declined from 8.3 in the first period to 6.8 in the latter years.

The third hypothesis is also confirmed by examining the mean ADA scores of African-American Democrats, white Democrats, and all Democrats in both periods. As noted in Table 9.1, there are large differences in the voting patterns of African-American Democrats and white Democrats in both periods. White Democrats have ADA scores of 51.2 and 48.9 in the respective time periods. During these same years, African-American ADA scores are 87.9 and 88.1, respectively. The mean ADA scores for all Democrats increased from 54.6 to 57.2 despite the slightly more conservative voting patterns of the two cohorts of Democrats. The more liberal and more ideologically polarized voting pattern of Democrats as a whole after racial redistricting can only be attributed to the influx of African-American Democrats elected in 1992.

In addition to the fact that all three hypotheses concerning the effects of racial redistricting appear to be supported in the aggregate, another interesting point should be noted from Table 9.1. The mean ADA scores of Republicans declined from 10.6 in 1991 and 1992 to 7.1 in 1993 and 1994. One explanation for this 33 percent decline in mean ADA scores for Republicans is grounded in the possible consequences of the use of majority-minority districts. As African-Americans are packed into majority-minority districts, the surrounding House districts become more white. Republicans elected in these districts have less incentive to pay attention to the concerns of African Americans or to the underprivileged because there are fewer such constituents to whom they must be responsible. Regardless of whether the new, overwhelmingly white districts produced new Republican House members or made already Republican-leaning districts safer for Republican incumbents, Republican representatives were voting more conservatively as the more liberal constituents in their districts were ushered into majority-minority districts.

The descriptive statistics associated with ADA scores are reported by state in Table 9.2. In this manner, one can identify the differences in ADA scores between those states in which racial redistricting occurred and those without racial redistricting after the 1990 census. Note that mean ADA scores declined in five of the six states that did not engage in racial redistricting and in five of the eight states that were involved. While the direction of change in mean scores between racially redistricted states and states that were not so redistricted does not appear

Table 9.2
Mean ADA Scores for Southern U.S. House Members, by State, 1991–92 and 1993–94

State		*Frequency*	*Mean*	*Standard Deviation*
Alabama*	1991–92	7	31.4	18.5
	1993–94	7	29.3	29.5
Arkansas	1991–92	4	45.0	28.5
	1993–94	4	33.8	33.2
Florida*	1991–92	19	38.6	30.5
	1993–94	23	37.5	31.8
Georgia*	1991–92	10	43.5	25.3
	1993–94	11	38.0	37.8
Kentucky	1991–92	7	40.7	29.0
	1993–94	6	40.4	23.2
Louisiana*	1991–92	8	21.3	27.5
	1993–94	7	33.2	41.7
Mississippi	1991–92	5	35.5	23.3
	1993–94	5	40.4	27.7
Missouri	1991–92	9	56.1	35.3
	1993–94	9	49.2	38.1
North Carolina*	1991–92	11	40.4	25.7
	1993–94	12	47.3	35.2
Oklahoma	1991–92	6	40.8	31.1
	1993–94	5	33.5	33.5
South Carolina*	1991–92	6	47.5	22.3
	1993–94	6	40.0	35.5
Tennessee	1991–92	9	41.4	27.1
	1993–94	9	38.6	24.9
Texas*	1991–92	27	39.0	28.9
	1993–94	30	37.3	30.7
Virginia*	1991–92	9	39.4	25.8
	1993–94	11	37.5	31.4

Note: An asterisk denotes states that were affected by racial redistricting after the 1990 decennial census.
Source: Compiled by authors.

to be substantial, there does appear to be a difference in the standard deviations of the means. All eight of the states that experienced racial redistricting illustrated an increase in the standard deviation of ADA scores. Only four of the six states that were not involved in race-based redistricting saw a similar increase.

In Tables 9.3 and 9.4 the findings reported in Table 9.2 are aggregated; the results are similar. In Table 9.3, the mean ADA scores of representatives are aggregated by state, and the state medians are reported. State median ADA scores and their change from 1991–92 to 1993–94 are similar for states that experienced racial redistricting and for those that did not. For the affected states, the median state ADA score of 39.2 in the first period declined by 1.7 points to 37.5 in the latter period. Similarly, unaffected states exhibited a 41.1 median ADA score that declined 1.6 points to 39.5 in the later years. However, there is quite a difference in the changes in the median state standard deviations between effected and unaffected states. States that did not experience racial redistricting actually exhibited a larger median standard deviation in the earlier period—28.8—than the 25.8 obtained by affected states. However, in the latter period,

Table 9.3
Median State Delegation Mean ADA Scores for Southern U.S. House Members, by Whether State Was Affected by Racial Redistricting, 1991–92 and 1993–94

	Affected by Racial Redistricting		*Not Affected by Racial Redistricting*	
	1991–92	*1993–94*	*1991–92*	*1993–94*
Frequency of states	8	8	6	6
Median of state means	39.2	37.5	41.1	39.5
Median of state standard deviations	25.8	33.5	28.8	30.5

Source: Compiled by authors.

Table 9.4
Mean ADA Scores for Southern U.S. House Members, by Whether State Was Affected by Racial Redistricting, 1991–92 and 1993–94

	Affected by Racial Redistricting		*Not Affected by Racial Redistricting*	
	1991–92	*1993–94*	*1991–92*	*1993–94*
Frequency	97	107	40	38
Mean	37.8	37.9	44.1	40.4
Standard deviation	26.9	32.4	28.7	29.1

Source: Compiled by authors.

states that were affected by race-based redistricting witnessed a 7.7-point increase in their median standard deviation (to 33.5) while unaffected states saw only a 1.7-point increase in their median standard deviation (to 30.5).

The results of Table 9.4 are similar to those noted above. Table 9.4 reports results by aggregating representatives into two groups—those who represented states affected by redistricting and those who represented unaffected states. The means and standard deviations in this table weigh trends in large states more heavily since they are based on the voting behavior of individuals rather than state delegations, and thus there is some deviation from the findings in Table 9.3. However, particularly with regard to the standard deviations of ADA scores, the findings are substantially alike. States that were affected by race-based redistricting witnessed a 5.5-point increase in their standard deviations (from 26.9 to 32.4) while states that were not affected by racial redistricting witnessed only a 0.4-point increase in their standard deviations (from 28.7 to 29.1). Table 9.4 does report more dramatic changes in means than does Table 9.3. Whereas unaffected states witnessed a 3.7-point decline in mean ADA scores (from 44.1 to 40.4), states that engaged in racial redistricting experienced only a 0.1-point increase in mean scores (from 37.8 to 37.9).

What these findings suggest is that racially redistricted states in the South, compared with other southern states, witnessed virtually no change in ADA scores in the aggregate but did witness a relatively sharp increase in the standard deviation of the mean scores. Although not reported in the tables, it should also be pointed out that Republicans picked up no additional seats after the 1992 election in states that did not create minority districts, but they gained an additional seven seats in those that did. Likewise, African-American representatives gained no seats in states that did not engage in race-based redistricting but were the victors in twelve additional races in states that created majority-minority seats for the 1992 election. Finally, it should also be noted (again, not reported in tables) that the standard deviation for Democratic representatives' ADA scores decreased by 2.3 points in states that did not create majority-minority districts but increased by 4.8 points in states experiencing race-based redistricting. Thus, after controlling for whether southern states did or did not engage in race-based redistricting, all the hypotheses appear to be confirmed. Race-based redistricting seems to benefit Republican and African-American candidates and appears to produce a more ideologically polarized body of representatives.

IMPLICATIONS OF RACIAL REDISTRICTING

Racial redistricting has implications for minority representation and for the process of governing. Unquestionably, the efforts by the federal courts and the Justice Department to ensure that minority voting power is not diluted has resulted in the election of more African-American representatives to the U.S. House of Representatives. Certainly, symbolic representation of African Americans has been increased as the number of African-American representatives has increased. However, has policy representation increased for African Americans as a result of race-based redistricting? Our evidence, which is consistent with the findings of Sharpe and Garand (1995) and Lublin (1997) suggests that in the short run more liberal voting patterns do not occur, at least in the South. However, advocates of race-based redistricting could point out the fact that the trend toward more conservative voting patterns among southern members of Congress was slightly more muted in states that did engage in racial redistricting.

Furthermore, how will racial redistricting affect the ability of House members to form winning coalitions in support of important pieces of legislation? Within the House, race-based redistricting should promote more cohesive voting among members of the respective parties and more party-line votes on individual pieces of legislation. Some observers would note that this is merely normal behavior in a democracy and that ideologically distinct parties offer a responsible party model in which parties offer choices to voters and then implement highly defined policies after winning an election. For example, Poole and Rosenthal (1984) have provided empirical support for the proposition that Democratic and Republican senators took ideologically distinct positions and supported different coalitions of voters from 1959 to 1980. Petrocik (1981) has also documented the fact that the respective parties have represented distinct blocs of voters since the New Deal realignment, even though the New Deal coalition has become weaker over time.

Others, however, note that American congressional parties have been far from cohesive and that flexibility and pragmatism are important. As an example, Melissa Collie (1989) has noted that increases in party voting in the U.S. House in the 1980s actually consisted of a break in an unsteady trend toward a more "individualistic" brand of roll-call voting that had slowly developed after the 1930s. Furthermore, Collie (1988) suggests that bipartisan coalitions forming around ad hoc issues became more common as the strength of partisanship in the electorate and in congressional roll-call behavior slowly declined from the post–World War II period through 1980. If one takes the position that bipartisan coalition building is important in Congress, then our results suggest that race-based redistricting may make it more difficult to fashion pragmatic, centrist solutions to problems.

Placing legislative politics in a larger perspective, there is strong evidence that the increasingly common defeats and retirements of white southern Democrats on the heels of race-based redistricting will make it more difficult for Democratic and Republican presidents to fashion ideologically moderate winning coalitions in Congress. Every president from 1953 to 1986 (with the exception of Eisenhower and Johnson) could count on white southern Democratic congressional support roughly half the time. Coalition building involved framing legislation that could be supported by northern Democrats and enough southern Democrats to win a majority or to build a more conservative coalition of Republicans and a large majority of southern Democrats (Edwards 1989).

In addition, while some would note that southern Democrats have at times obstructed important initiatives such as civil rights legislation in the 1960s, more recent survey evidence from the 1970s and 1980s indicates that southern Democrats are actually ideologically moderate (Erikson, Wright, and McIver 1993). Ironically, moderate coalition building in the contemporary period would seem to depend on the existence of two groups—southern Democrats and Republicans from the northeast—who historically have had very little in common. Moderate, bipartisan attempts to balance the budget have already seemed to center around southern Democrats and northeastern Republicans such as in the Gramm-Rudman-Hollings legislation of 1985. Though the impact of the 1985 act was somewhat awkward, bipartisan efforts to solve budgetary and other important political problems are going to continue to be necessary in the future.

Furthermore, while some might favor the formation of responsible parties that are ideologically distinct, such a formula is no guarantee that a clear winner will emerge from each election and pass desired legislation in a fashion that is consistent with a majoritarian democratic model. In fact, one reason coalition building by the president is so important today is because of the tendency of voters to opt for divided government. Leaving aside the question of whether voters actually desire divided government, the fact remains that divided government has been a common feature of American democracy over the last few decades (Fiorina 1996). It would seem that the demise of the white southern Democrat might make moderate, bipartisan coalition building more difficult in the future.

Finally, with regard to southern politics, race-based redistricting would seem to be the perfect formula to increase Republican Party identification as well as to increase Republican electoral strength throughout the South. As white southern Democratic members of Congress become increasingly rare, some white southern Democrats may opt to support the Republican Party. Such defection of southern Democrats becomes likely, as has been seen in states like South Carolina, as more conservative Democrats become convinced that the national Democratic Party has moved "too far to the left." Furthermore, the increasing tendency of southerners to vote along class lines (which, according to Nadeau and Stanley [1993] began in the mid-1970s) combined with the decreasing numbers of moderate southern Democrats in Congress virtually assure that Republicans will continue to prosper electorally and with regard to voter registration in suburban districts throughout the South.

In conclusion, though the creation of majority-minority districts may increase the numbers of African Americans in Congress, there is certainly no guarantee that African-American policy prescriptions will be implemented more frequently because of the existence of these districts. To the extent that they increase the likelihood that Republicans will be elected from surrounding districts, race-base redistricting may in fact simply produce a more bipolar congressional delegation. Indeed race-based redistricting seems to have a polarizing influence on voting patterns in southern House delegations. Finally, race-based redistricting may not only serve to increase the numbers of Republican House members, but they may exacerbate the tendency of white southerners to defect to the Republican Party.

NOTES

1. In fact, both Deep South states and other southern states can be found in each respective category of redistricted states. States that were affected by racial redistricting in 1992 were Alabama, Florida, Georgia, Louisiana, North Carolina, South Carolina, Texas, and Virginia. States in which no new majority-minority districts were created for the 1992 election were Arkansas, Kentucky, Mississippi, Missouri, Oklahoma, and Tennessee.

2. For purposes of this study, we included as southern states the eleven former Confederate states and Oklahoma, Kentucky, and Missouri. The survey research pooled by Erikson, Wright, and McIver (1993) served as a guide for determining which states to include. We included Oklahoma because it has many ideological and partisan characteristics that are similar to states of the former Confederacy. Kentucky was included because it is a border state with a sizeable African-American population and a strong tradition of Democratic party dominance similar to other southern states. We included Missouri because it is a border state with a sizeable African-American population. We excluded Maryland and West Virginia from the analysis because citizens in these states have more liberal ideological leanings than do citizens in southern states.

3. For purposes of this analysis, the Sixth District of Oklahoma is excluded from the 1993–94 data. In this district, conservative Democrat Glenn English served in 1993 and Republican Frank Lucas served in 1994. Rather than attempt to provide an average score for the district, or include the district twice in the 1993–94 period, we decided to exclude the district from the analysis altogether. For purposes of the discussion of the numbers of Democratic and Republican representatives, we also exclude this district since it is cannot be clearly labeled as a Democratic or Republican district.

10

Payback or Continuity? GOP Support of the Religious Right in the House of Representatives

MARK CALEB SMITH

Few scholars would dispute, it seems, the revolutionary nature of the congressional elections of 1994. These contests allowed the Republican Party to seize control of both houses of Congress for the first time in four decades and seem destined to provide legislative scholars with a lynchpin electoral event which will be studied for many years to come—along with the similarly earth-shaking Democratic "Clinton coattail" gains of 1998. For as much of a puzzle as 1994 might have posed to scholars, however, the popular press had no such difficulty in quickly identifying the factors behind the Republican landslide. *Time*, *Newsweek*, and *U.S. News and World Report* all quickly jointly credited the win to both Newt Gingrich's Contract with America strategy and the GOP's foot soldiers, who garnered significant grassroots support from important groups within the party's conservative coalition (Stacks 1994; Lacayo 1994). The party faction most often cited for supplying such political muscle was the Religious Right.

"Replacing the Democratic liberals was a herd of Republicans ranging from the born-again to the libertarian," one publication quipped (Stacks 1994, 48). Another proffered that "[t]he Democrat's special interests are soon to be replaced by an equally long list of Republican ones; agriculture, the oil industry, the gun lobby, the Christian Right" (Fineman 1994, 37). A *Time* writer, in turn, said that the 1994 elections "marked the biggest year ever for the Christian Coalition" (Farley 1994, 62). Muscle, however, does not come cheaply to those who benefit from it. The central principle seized upon by many media pundits was that from the flexing arm eventually comes an extended hand. As a loyal segment of the controlling party, this line of reasoning suggested, the Religious Right could expect a certain amount of legislative "payback" for its hard work.

Did the Religious Right get a boost of support due to the 1994 elections? If so, from where did the payback come? An attempt to answer these questions through the analysis of available contribution and voting data is the purpose of this essay. The concept of political payback, however, must first be defined, and the post-1994 success of the Religious Right's legislative agenda seems the most reasonable place to begin the search for such a definition. Legislative success of this agenda, however, may not be a function of payback. Instead, it may simply mark a degree of continuity in the Republican-Christian Coalition relationship, and therefore be nothing more than a sign of the change in the partisan control of Congress. The legislative preferences of the Religious Right may therefore so closely mirror those of the Republican Party in general that payback may be the same thing as governance; GOP support for the Religious Right could be merely an expression of its inherent conservatism, and not a gesture of thanks for support in a specific electoral contest.

One possible approach to evaluating whether the Christian Coalition experienced a payback effect from GOP congressional leadership is to compare the Republican Party's support for the Religious Right with that of another conservative organization of a more secular design. Controlling for issues on which these secular and religious interests have the same perspective, if differences in the treatment of these two groups emerge—specifically, if the Religious Right gets more than just conservative GOP support while the secular group does not—a case for payback may be made. Not only must this comparison be made in the 104th Congress, when the Republicans took control, but it must also extend back to the 103rd; as such, individual Republican support for the agendas of these groups may be evaluated both pre- and post-1994, as members of the minority and majority party in Congress. If a pattern of electoral payback may be found with Republican ranks, support for the Religious Right would theoretically increase after the election, while support for the other organization or group would remain essentially the same.

The U.S. House of Representatives seems to be the logical choice of a location in which to search for this pattern, given its hierarchical structure and the degree of leadership control which marks partisan battles within the chamber. It provides the benefit of more cases for analysis than does the Senate, and has been exclusively used in a long history of critical legislative studies because it is larger and more rapidly responsive to constituency pressure than the upper chamber (Kingdon 1989; Loomis 1998). Republican House members alone will be included in this analysis because they are presumably the members of whom payback to the Religious Right would be expected from party leadership.

VOTING DECISIONS AND LEADERSHIP POWER

The term "support," in the way it is used in this essay, is nothing more than a string of congressional voting decisions. There are mountains of literature on how legislators make such determinations. This review does not pretend to be exhaustive, but it instead focuses on the factors relevant to this situation. *Constituency* regularly emerges as one of the primary influences on legislative behavior. Mayhew (1974a) and Fiorina (1974) argue that legislators have several goals, some of which, like good public policy and influence within the chamber, are dependent upon reelection. Getting reelected depends, of course, on pleasing the constituency. Fenno (1978) goes a bit farther when he argues that it is impossible to understand a legislator's actions outside of her perception of her constituency. The legislator generally goes to great lengths to please his most loyal supporters, for their backing is required for reelection.

Naturally, congressmen from competitive districts may feel more constrained by their constituency than those who easily win their bids to stay in office. After all, competitive districts tend to reflect heterogeneous concerns that must be balanced by the member. Members from competitive districts, the argument goes, are more likely to defect from the party line, which in this instance would be support for the religious right, in order to please enough of their constituency to get reelected. Kingdon (1989) and Fiorina (1973) find that when control variables like party and seniority are introduced, the relationship between competitive districts and voting behavior disappears.

Much has been made in this light about the abundance and causes of safe seats in Congress (Mayhew 1974b; Bullock 1975; Ferejohn 1977; Fiorina 1977), but it is difficult to say how these findings will translate to the new Republican majority. The Republican Party, especially in the 1996 elections, was under a great deal of pressure to maintain its majority status in the face of Bill Clinton's reelection bid, and 1996 was the first year Republican candidates were forced to return to their districts and run on their record, as opposed to campaigning against the Democratic majority. These factors may have constrained representatives from competitive districts, pulling them away from doggish loyalty to the goals of party leadership and pushing them instead toward a more individually crafted response to constituent concerns.

This perception must be balanced, however, against the possibility that 1994 was a critical election. Brady (1978) has explored these types of elections, arguing that in the face of revolutionary policy shifts as effected by a new regime, constituency pressures on individual members of Congress are diminished. It is therefore possible that what has previously been established about the importance of short-term constituency demands may not have been of paramount concern among Republican House freshmen immediately after the 1994 elections; the Contract with America, so to speak, still had enough steam to propel the Republican locomotive forward into 1996.

Another potentially important factor in the decisional process employed by congressmen centers around interest group involvement. Kingdon (1989) argues that interest groups are not very important when party and constituency effects are controlled. Also, potential group influences are essentially zero if there is no connection between the representative's district and the group. Several problems arise when these results are applied to the study of the Religious Right and its impact on members of the 104th Congress. The first hurdle is the diversity of the movement itself; scholars have not yet defined the Religious Right with a common voice, and early evidence suggests that "the movement" may actually be a confederation, of sorts, of smaller movements (Guth and Green 1991; Kuzenski 1998; Layman 1999). The groups that may comprise the faction—fundamentalists, evangelicals, charismatics, and others by a host of other names—have not been adequately measured at the congressional district level. As a result, it is impossible to estimate the number of the potential members in the Religious Right within a district. As a political movement, the Religious Right may be categorized as a "potential group," as defined by David Truman (1951). These groups manage to influence the legislative process even though they are not explicitly organized. While this categorization may be proper, it begs the problem of measuring such indirect influence on congressmen.

Even if the Religious Right is a potential group, as Truman has suggested, there are some organized lobbies that represent at least *segments* of the movement. Moen (1989) looked at the influence of the lobbying arm of the Moral Majority and other groups during the 97th and 98th Congresses. He argues that the Religious Right was successful, in conjunction with the Reagan White House, in shaping Congress's social agenda. Even though none of the movement's favored legislation passed, it managed to make its presence and positions known to congressmen. Cohodas (1984, 538), writing in *Congressional Quarterly Weekly Report*, noted this presence when she chronicled the ambience surrounding the Senate's debate on school prayer; the Religious Right's vigils and rallies created "the atmosphere of a revival meeting around much of the capitol."

The most influential contemporary group that might be viewed as representative of the Religious Right is the Christian Coalition. Defining the coalition's activity, however, is problematic because of the decentralized nature of the organization. This grassroots philosophy is seen in the coalition's sheer number of 1,617 chapters, with at least one in every state. Even if the Christian Coalition is pulling all those strings from Washington, it seems unlikely that it can effectively monitor or control the actions being carried out at the chapter level. In spite of this reservation, there is some evidence that there was a concerted effort by the coalition to effect a general legislative agenda. The rival group, People for the American Way,[1] claims the Christian Coalition focused its attention, through voter guides and other means, on 84 congressional districts during the 1996 election. By tackling at least 20 percent of all House districts, the coalition has established a beachhead from which to sway the governmental process. As a result, it seems that any study that claims to measure Congress's support of the Religious Right must incorporate some assessment of how strong the Religious Right is within that district.

Several scholars have noted the regional differences in congressional voting behavior. Sinclair (1985) and Asher and Weisberg (1978) have each revealed the disparities between southern and nonsouthern Democrats, the former exhibiting more conservative and moralistic-religious issue positions than the latter. It is logical to assume that the same general pattern holds true in the party opposite, and that southern members are also the most conservative faction in the now majority *Republican* Party. There were 48 southern Republicans in the U.S. House in the 103rd Congress, and 69 in the 104th. In order to test for this assumed greater degree of conservatism, a distinction should be made between southern and nonsouthern congressmen in subsequent analyses. This suggestion is augmented by the fact that the groups most associated with the Religious Right are concentrated in the South. In one recent large national survey (Pew Foundation 1996), 49 percent of all white evangelical Protestants were located in the South, and southern respondents were consistently more conservative than any other region in terms of religious beliefs and activities. The potential for constituent effects on congressional support for the Religious Right is obvious, and it merely lends credence to the idea that a regional variable should be included in this analysis.

There is one other variable that could be important in the effort to identify the existence of payback behavior, and it should therefore be included in a model designed to test for such a phenomenon's presence in the Republican House. If payback is due to electoral help, it seems that the pressure to follow through would be greatest on freshmen legislators for two reasons. First, freshmen may feel they owe their very presence in Washington to prominent factions within the party (Kingdon 1989). This gratitude might translate into legislative loyalty. Second, the 1994 election carried 73 GOP freshmen into the House of Representatives. Theoretically, freshmen legislators are more closely tied to their districts and supporters. This tendency might force the newcomers to pay close attention to the Religious Right's muscle manifested in 1994. As a result, this "freshman effect" may be strongest during the 104th Congress.

This reasoning may or may not bear fruit. Fenno (1978) argues that legislators use their first several terms to build trust with their constituents and their supporters, which would make them especially difficult to target for payback if they descend from contentious districts. However, it is widely assumed that the 1994 Republican freshmen were staunchly conservative, with Reagan as their role model and Gingrich as their leader. This loyalty might predispose this particular class of new legislators to follow along with party initiatives that seek to offer reparations to the mighty Religious Right. Regardless of which of these perceptions is more accurate, there appears to be a need for a seniority-based variable in the research design.

RELIGION AND CONGRESSIONAL VOTING BEHAVIOR

While there are other traditional variables that are occasionally used in the study of congressional voting,[2] they will not be considered in this analysis. Other variables, however, that are generally ignored when legislative behavior is explained, are at the center of this research question. If support for the Religious Right is under scrutiny, there is a possibility that the legislator's religious sympathies may come into play. Benson and Williams (1982) consider the place of religion on Capitol Hill, and they find that religion does matter in legislative policy decisions. While their findings are intriguing, Benson and Williams test only for a correlation between religious orientation and political behavior, and they do so without the aid of control variables. It is of little wonder, then, that the pair found a consistent relationship between orientation and voting behavior. How persistent these associations would be in more stringent circumstances is unknown because the study has not been repeated or clarified. Since their results are based on extensive interview data, the specificity of their religious items are not available here. That does not spell the end of a consideration of a measurement of religious affiliation, however; various publications contain biographical information relating to members of the U.S. Congress, which allows for the inclusion of a personal religion variable for these members. While not perhaps an ideal measurement of the *degree* of religiosity expressed by any given member of Congress, it at least insures that religion will not be cast aside when support for the Religious Right is considered.

MODELING PAYBACK BEHAVIOR

Based on the findings of previous studies noted above, what might one expect in an analysis of Republican support for the Religious Right? If payback is occurring, the following hypotheses seem reasonable and will be tested in this analysis:

H_1: The Religious Right received an increase in support after the Republicans gained control of Congress.
H_2: Republican support for the Religious Right is greater than support of secular conservatism due to the degree of payback exacted.

If supported, these hypotheses would show that support for the Religious Right is not merely a function of the general conservatism of GOP legislators, but that other forces are at work that favor religious over secular conservativism in the post-1994 Congress.

These first two hypotheses deal with whether or not payback is taking place in the House of Representatives. The remainder of the hypotheses I suggest attempt to predict the type of support the Religious Right and conservatives in general receive from particular Republican groups. Based upon what is known of legislative voting behavior, what groups might be expected to support the Religious Right and how might they differ from those supporting a generally conservative agenda? The literature suggests that safe districts should not matter if party and seniority are controlled (Fiorina 1973; Kingdon 1989), which they will be in this analysis. Based on this premise, it is possible to test several additional hypotheses:

H_3: The safety of a legislator's seat is not related to support for either the Religious Right or for conservatism in general.
H_4: Status as a freshman will be positively correlated to support for the Religious Right, particularly during the 104th Congress.

Freshmen will feel the most loyalty to the Religious Right because of their conception that they may not only owe their seats to the movement, but also their majority status. Freshmen are also more reliant on the party leadership than more senior members, for freshmen must win coveted committee assignments. Given this reliance on their leaders, the freshmen will likely reflect the conservative nature of the House leadership.

H_5: Status as a freshman will be positively related to support for a conservative agenda, particularly during the 104th Congress.

H_6: Religion will play a larger role in member's support for the Religious Right than it will in their support of a general conservative agenda.

Given the religious nature of some of the Religious Right's positions, such as on abortion and prayer in school, it seems reasonable to argue that members will rely more on their religious affiliation for these types of decisions than they will in their evaluation of a conservative agenda. Regional differences may also play a part. Due to the fact that the South is conservative and home to much of the Religious Right, regional factors are theoretically likely be important. As such:

H_7: Southern legislators will strongly support both the Religious Right and a conservative agenda.

H_8: Members from districts in which the Religious Right is active will strongly support the Religious Right.

As was previously noted, the House of Representatives is the backdrop for this study, while individual congressmen are the units of analysis. The 103rd Congress is compared to the 104th Congress so that changes over time may be analyzed. The number of Republicans is computed according to the Christian Coalition's list; this method of calculation was chosen because of the numerous Democratic defections after the House changed hands. In the 103rd Congress there were 176 Republicans, according to Christian Coalition statistics, while in the 104th there were 234. Support for the Religious Right is most accurately represented by support for the Christian Coalition (CC), while support for the American Conservative Union (ACU) will serve as a proxy for support of conservatism in general.[3]

Legislator support scores for the CC and the ACU will serve as dependent variables throughout the analysis. The scores were furnished by each organization, and they range from 0, which shows no support for the organization, to 100, indicating total support. Scores were provided for the 1994 and 1996 elections. The 1994 scores reflect the activity during the 103rd Congress, while the 1996 scores do the same for the 104th. The ACU furnishes scores for each year of a term, so individual legislators' scores were added and divided by two to represent the score for the entire term.[4]

Data for the independent variables came from *Congressional Quarterly*'s *Politics in America* (1994 and 1996), and the coding was relatively straightforward. Constituency concerns were captured in at least two ways. Safe districts were defined as those in which the legislator received at least 55 percent of the vote. Safe districts are scored as "1" for safe and "0" if it is not. In the 103rd Congress, 132 of the GOP's 176 seats were safe, while in the 104th, 187 of the 234 seats were. Even though safe districts should free incumbents to support the Christian Coalition, the lack of a safe seat should not constrain a member if legislative payback is taking place. As such, this variable should not be related to support for the Christian Coalition, nor will it be related to support for the ACU.

Constituency effects, as defined by the People for the American Way, were measured by the presence of the Christian Coalition in the district. Of the 84 districts in which the group was active in 1996, 48 were Republican. Since data exist only for the 1996 election, it was assumed that the activity was generally the same for the 1994 election. Therefore, any district that showed activity in 1996 will show the same level for 1994. A district that has a Christian Coalition presence is coded as "1," while those without it register as "0." This crude variable will at least allow some semblance of group pressure to be included in the analysis, and it should be positively related to support for the Christian Coalition.

Region is also simply coded as "1" for legislators from the South and "0" for those in other regions. The region was defined in the traditional sense, with Alabama, Arkansas, Florida, Georgia, Louisiana, Mississippi, North Carolina, South Carolina, Tennessee, Texas, and Virginia all counting as part of the region. In the 103rd Congress, 48 (27.3 percent) Republican legislators were southern, while in the 104th 29.4 percent, as well as key elements of the leadership—Speaker Gingrich and Majority Leader Armey especially—were from the South. This variable, because of the conservative nature of the region and the preponderance of groups sympathetic to the Religious Right, will likely remain strong in each facet of the upcoming analysis.

Freshmen are coded as "1" and nonfreshmen are "0." In the 103rd Congress there were 51 freshmen, and in the 104th 73 newcomers entered the House. Because of the group's loyalty to a major party faction and to the conservative House leadership, it was expected that this group's policy leanings would be positively related to support for the Christian Coalition and the ACU. Support should increase after the 1994 election; as such, the variable should have larger coefficients in the 104th Congress than for the 103rd. This is due to the general conservatism of the freshmen and their loyalty to the newly elected House leadership.

Religion presents more of a challenge. The information in *Politics in America* is basic, but it must be used. The biographical sketches supplied include an item concerning the member's religion. Most answers provided are very general, like "Baptist," "Methodist," or "Protestant." Others are more specific, like "Southern Baptist," "United Methodist," and "Christian Reformed." Given the varying levels of specificity, the only option is to use the most general categories offered. In the end, four categories emerge—Protestant, Catholic, Jewish, and Nontraditional. While the first three are self-explanatory, the fourth includes Mormons, Christian Scientists, Unitarians, and Seventh Day Adventists. A series of dummy variables was constructed so that a Baptist member, for example, would be coded as "1" for Protestant and "0" for all other categories. In the 103rd Congress, 67 percent of the congressmen (118) were Protestant, 23 percent (40) were Catholic, 8 percent (14) were Nontraditional, and 2 percent (4) were Jewish. In the 104th, the numbers increased but the percentages stayed nearly the same; 67 percent (157) were Protestant, 24 percent (56) were Catholic, 7 percent (17) were Nontraditional, and 2 percent (4) were Jewish.

Religion should play a significant role in support for the Christian Coalition. Catholic and Jewish affiliation should be negatively related to support for the heavily Protestant Christian Coalition. This constraint on legislative behavior should not be as important when support for the ACU is analyzed, given the generally conservative nature of Republicans in general.

ANALYSIS

By looking at descriptive statistics, several differences in support for the ACU and the Christian Coalition emerge. During the 103rd Congress, the two entities received strikingly similar types of treatment from House Republicans. Of the three measures of central tendency, there is virtually no difference in the way the Christian Coalition and the American Conservative Union were handled. Support for the Coalition was more variable, however, as seen by the larger standard deviation and the lower minimum value. However, both organizations received high amounts of support. The variability in that support, as represented by the standard deviation, is somewhat large for each organization, but not exceedingly so. The use of the standard deviation is particularly sensitive to outliers, of which there are several in each group, so the size of the deviation is not surprising.

According to the data, changes took place during the 104th Congress. The American Conservative Union showed virtually no shift in its support. The variability of its support changed, but not by much—it went down 6.63 percent. The mean did not appreciably change from the 103rd to the 104th Congress. Neither change, in the mean or in the variance, is statistically significant.

The Christian Coalition, on the other hand, was the beneficiary of a sizable increase in backing. The average Republican increased support of the coalition by 8.2 percent, while the variability in CC support went down 37 percent. Each change was statistically significant. In the most basic terms, payback, or something akin to it, is taking place. A general secular conservativism does not appear to be driving this phenomenon; ACU support does not reflect the sort of increase that would be expected if this alone was the source of the observed

Table 10.1
Support for the Christian Coalition and the American Conservative Union during the 103rd and 104th Congresses

	103rd	*104th*	*% Change*	*p-value*
Christian Coalition				
mean	86.483	93.570	+8.2	.0000[a]
median	91.000	100.00	+10.1	
mode	100.00	100.00	0	
min.	21.00	36.00	+71.4	
max.	100.00	100.00	0	
std. dev.	17.735	11.173	-37.0	.0000[b]
American Conservative Union				
mean	86.668	86.443	-0.2	.8696
median	91.000	90.000	-1.1	
mode	100.00	96.000	-4.0	
min.	34.000	27.500	-19.1	
max.	100.00	100.00	0	
std. dev.	14.138	13.201	-6.63	.326

[a]To determine whether these means were different, a difference in means test was run. The tests were two-tailed, alpha=.05. Also, a proportional test for the difference in means was used to see if there would be any change in the results. The p-value for this test was .0153 for the coalition and .9473 for the ACU.

[b]A test for the equality of variances was used to see if the squared standard deviations were significantly different from one another. The tests were two-tailed, alpha=.05.

Source: Compiled by the author.

changes in behavior. Therefore, hypotheses 1 and 2 appear to be confirmed by the above data.

A subsequent regression analysis displays some interesting findings in pursuit of the validity of other hypotheses I have suggested. The South/non-South distinction is the most important variable for the Christian Coalition in the 103rd Congress. Being a legislator from the South means nearly an 11-point jump in support of the coalition, even after the effects of freshman status, safe districts, the presence of the Christian Coalition in the district, and religious affiliation are controlled. In terms of predictive power, however, the southern distinction is the most important variable in the equation as evidenced by its large beta value.

The 104th Congress brought about one major change in the coalition's support. The value of freshmen grew in importance, seemingly at the expense of the South and Jewish variables. While both of the latter remained strong and consistent, they were nevertheless diminished when compared to the 103rd Congress. In terms of predictive power, the freshmen variable eclipsed all other variables in the model. This surge lends a good deal of credence to the idea that payback was "in the air," so to speak. The newcomers supported the Christian Coalition

Table 10.2
Support for the Christian Coalition and the American Conservative Union during the 103rd and 104th Congresses

	Variable	*b*	*beta*	*sig. level*[a]
Christian Coalition				
103rd Congress	South	10.77	.2712	.0004
	Fresh	2.43	.0622	.4262
	Safed	-3.11	-.0761	.3375
	Coalpres	-1.30	-.0277	.7099
	Prot	-2.15	-.0572	.6564
	Jewish	-19.98	-.1684	.0409
	Catholic	-4.69	-.1110	.3753
N = 176, Adj.R^2 = .12				
104th Congress	South	3.44	.1401	.033
	Fresh	3.69	.1539	.048
	Safed	1.25	.0445	.565
	Coalpres	2.65	.0960	.135
	Prot	1.87	.0788	.503
	Jewish	-12.69	-.1473	.036
	Catholic	-.2801	-.0107	.926
N = 234, Adj.R^2 = .09				
American Conservative Union				
103rd Congress	South	8.63	.2726	.000
	Fresh	1.91	.0614	.428
	Safed	-2.20	-.0675	.391
	Coalpres	1.08	.0289	.695
	Prot	-4.35	-.1452	.256
	Jewish	-18.85	-.1993	.015
	Catholic	-7.85	-.2334	.061
N = 176, Adj.R^2 = .14				
104th Congress	South	5.12	.1763	.005
	Fresh	7.24	.2551	.001
	Safed	3.01	.0906	.219
	Coalpres	2.43	.0745	.223
	Prot	-2.73	-.0971	.386
	Jewish	-25.05	-.2460	.000
	Catholic	-7.79	-.2518	.022
N = 234, Adj.R^2 = .18				

[a]All tests were two-tailed, alpha = .05.
Source: Compiled by the author.

agenda more than southerners, Protestants, those with safe districts, and even those members with a heavy CC presence in their own district. Hypothesis 4, which predicts the positive relationship between status as a freshman and support for the coalition, is thus supported by an analysis of the data. Religion, on the other hand, is relatively unimportant except among Jewish Republicans; Protestant and Catholic designations were not helpful in predicting support for the Religious Right.

ACU support during the GOP House takeover of 1994 appears to be similar to that enjoyed by the Christian Coalition, but there are important differences nevertheless. In the 103rd Congress, the southern/nonsouthern distinction was, just as it was with the coalition, the most important variable in terms of predicting support for the American Conservative Union. But support for the ACU grew 8.63 points as a result of the regional variable, which is two full points less than CC growth along the same lines. Just as before, the Jewish block was an important counterweight to the regional distinctions, for it meant a 19-point drop in support, as compared to a 20-point drop for the coalition. The primary difference is that the largest negative influence on the ACU's support came from Catholic Republicans. Unlike the pattern which is present with the CC, the Catholic variable borders on significance in explaining ACU support in the 103rd Congress.

In the 104th Congress, the magnitude of the regional variable was diminished, just as it was in the analysis of the coalition's support. The drop here, however, was smaller: around 41 percent, as compared to a 68 percent drop in support for the coalition. The levels of freshman Republican support for the CC again rose to prominence in the 104th Congress—which is particularly noteworthy given their lack of a strong relationship with ACU issue positions during the 103rd Congress. Catholicism in the latter House was also strongly and negatively related to support for the ACU. When the coefficient was standardized, in fact, it became the second most powerful predictor of ACU support, just .0033 behind the freshman variable.

The validity of hypothesis 3 was confirmed by the analysis of data; safe districts played no role in support for either the coalition or the ACU. Additionally, results of the regression analysis show that freshman status was strongly related to support for the ACU during the 104th Congress, while it was nonexistent in the 103rd Congress. The southern/regional variable in turn shows that southern Republicans are supportive of the Christian Coalition and of a conservative agenda, lending credence to hypotheses 5 and 7, respectively. The null hypothesis for H_8, on the other hand, could not be safely rejected—representatives of districts in which the coalition was active did not significantly display CC support that distinguished them from their colleagues in non-CC districts. Perhaps, as Kingdon (1989) suggests, this is because of the role of member cue-taking from colleagues on the floor; it may also reflect an idea of the Christian Coalition as a *national* agenda-setting power which has not yet translated itself into a particularly credible *local* threat to electorally safe House members. In any case, what is clear from the rejection of hypothesis 8 is that CC influence on GOP House members is a field of study that requires substantial future research.[5]

CONCLUSIONS

Several conclusions flow naturally from the preceding analysis. Constituency effects, when measured by safe districts and the presence of the Christian Coalition within a district, had no discernible influence on legislative support for either the Christian Coalition or the American Conservative Union.[6] This finding slightly contradicts Kingdon (1989), but this could be due to poor measurements of the concepts. Possibly, for example, the data provided by the People for the American Way was inaccurate or not expansive enough. Regardless of the explanation, more empirical work must be done on the Christian Coalition's presence in congressional districts before strong conclusions about the group's impact can be drawn. The analysis in this study, however, supports previous claims that safe districts are not crucial determinants of a legislator's voting behavior (Fiorina 1973; Kingdon 1989). It is possible and even probable, of course, that House leadership exercised a great deal of control during the 104th Congress. This, in addition to the fact that House Republicans of the 1980s and early 1990s were very disciplined as the loyal opposition, may explain the reduced effect of constituency during these congresses. Constituency concerns appear to have been greatest in the South.

The effects of religious affiliation get a mixed review based upon the results of the analysis in this essay. In every regression equation, at least one religious variable was statistically significant. Historically, Jews and Catholics have been politically liberal, for both were cogs in the New Deal machine. While Republican Catholics and Jews nevertheless tend to be more conservative than their Democratic counterparts, they are still more liberal than other factions within the House Republican caucus. As such, they are harder for the CC to bring within a "payback collective," so to speak, and they are likely to remain a thorn in the Religious Right's side in any future attempts of the CC to exact legislative rewards out of the House Republican caucus. The primary culprit behind religion's poor showing in this study, however, is likely to be the data itself. Broad categories like "Protestant" have little explanatory power, for there are many stripes of Protestantism. More refined information, similar to that of Benson and Williams (1982), is needed before religion and its relationship to legislative voting behavior can be adequately treated. There may be a simmering religious schism brewing within the Republican Congress, but examination of the phenomenon requires proper operationalization of an inherently tricky and subjective variable.

Finally, support for the Religious Right may be unique. Perhaps the faction is such a cornerstone in the Republican Party that it is getting legislative payback. The evidence above certainly leans toward that conclusion. The source of this support, it seems, is due to the "freshman effect" suggested earlier in this essay, particularly in the 104th Congress. These freshmen may have been naturally more conservative than their legislative forebears, or they may have been more closely attached to the new House leadership of their time, but either way they clearly outdistanced the freshmen from the preceding class in their support of the Religious Right and the conservative agenda. This is one instance where seniority—or, more precisely, the lack of it—clearly played a role in legislative behavior. The revolutionary nature of the 1994 election may be making its presence felt in this finding; perhaps the class of 1994 felt that a clear mandate had been expressed by the voters, and that the Contract with America was a national mandate that supplanted the traditional wisdom of constituency service. The learning curve for 1994 GOP freshmen, in other words, was not steep enough to teach them the merits of constituency service before they had committed to the will of the Republican leadership—and its extracongressional allies.

Future research may wish to concentrate on exploring elements of the CC-GOP legislative alliance, particularly insofar as the effects of freshman support and religious affiliation are concerned. This essay concludes far from being able to answer all of the important questions about this alliance, but it has demonstrated that Republican conservativism in the 103rd and 104th Congresses was not a unidimensional political lockstep. Of particular note in the face of the results from the 1998 congressional elections, in which the GOP actually experienced a reverse "midterm slump" which benefitted the president's party, is the possibility that payback is a phenomenon that is of limited use for a limited time in the maelstrom of a revolution.

NOTES

1. Generally considered to be a liberal interest group, founded by television producer Norman Lear among others. Information obtained from this group came from their World Wide Web site at www.pfaw.org.

2. Two such variables, staff and party leadership, are covered by Kingdon (1989) and are not of primary importance when things like party and constituency are used as controls. Besides, there are no staff data concerning congressional support for the Religious Right. Also, since general party support is the concern, looking at party leaders is fraught with problems. The party leaders themselves have support scores for the Religious Right, and, given the lack of interview data, those scores are the only way to know the party's position on the Religious Right's agenda. So, if the leaders' support scores are included in a statistical analysis, votes of leaders would be used to predict the simultaneous votes of others, which results in a causal calamity. As such, party leaders will be left out of this analysis.

3. The ACU is an organization committed to the furtherance of a conservative agenda in government. The group's conservatism is wide-ranging, and the issues they used to compute their support scores reflect both religious and secular items of conservative interest.

4. The ACU scores were based on approximately 24 votes in each year of both terms. The coalition scores were based on 14 votes during each term. Upon review, the

votes did overlap some, but not much. This is probably an accurate reflection of the agendas being put forth by each organization, for the ACU has a much broader conservative agenda when compared to the more narrow, family-driven program avowed by the Christian Coalition. The fact that some overlap exists reflects reality, so the scores were not recomputed to include only mutually exclusive positions. This would have divorced conservatism from support from the Religious Right, and that could have led to very different conclusions for this chapter. Also, the scores were calculated so that absences did not punish the legislator. Therefore, scores are simply a percentage (votes for the agenda divided by total votes cast in relation to the agenda, multiplied by 100).

5. There is some concern, understandably, that the Christian Coalition's ranking of legislators is not as established as other organizations like the ACU. This concern is well-founded in some respects, for if the legislation used to rank the House of Representatives differs dramatically from the 103rd to the 104th Congress, then the case for payback may be weakened. To combat this possibility, issues that were used in both the 103rd and the 104th Congress were analyzed. There were five issues prominently used in each set of rankings. They included the balanced budget amendment, the use of federal money for abortion (both foreign and domestic), family tax relief, federal intervention in abortion protests (which the coalition was against), and the reduction in government spending (which was manifested in an amendment to cut federal spending by certain amounts and in an amendment that would require a 3/5 majority to raise taxes or engage in deficit spending). If support for these core issues increased, the case for payback would be even stronger. These issues were analyzed just as the full agenda was inspected above.

The results were remarkably similar to the analysis of the coalition's entire agenda. The coalition's support still manages to go up a solid 6.7 percent (from 88.523 in the 103rd to 94.530 in the 104th Congress). The variation in the group's support also tightens dramatically (the standard deviation went from 18.946 to 12.326), and each of these differences were significant. The difference in mean support yielded a p-value of .0002, while the difference in the variances posted a value of .0000. As a result, the coalition received more, and more consistent, support for what could be termed its core agenda in the 104th Congress. This should allay fears that an increase in the coalition's support, from the 103rd to the 104th Congress, is merely an artificial product of the group's tinkering with the issues it selected for the rankings.

6. The analysis was performed with only the safe-district variable and again with only the coalition presence variable, and there was no change in the outcome.

Epilogue: The South and Congress in 2000 and Beyond

As the chapters in this volume attest, the twentieth century saw dramatic change in the South and in Congress. In a number of important ways, these changes have been interrelated. For example, the change in the southern party system in the post–World War II period—perhaps a realignment as suggested by the data presented by Gaddie and Hoffman—was triggered in part by actions taken by a reforming and somewhat liberalized Congress (for example, the Civil Rights Act of 1964, the Voting Rights Act of 1965) that contributed to disaffection with the national Democrats and ultimately assisted the Republicans in expanding their tenuous foothold and rising to competitive status. In turn, this transformation of the party system has contributed to changing the partisan balance in Congress, especially in the 1990s. In this process, as Rae and Glaser have argued in their chapters, newly elected southern Republicans and former southern Democrats who switched parties have been particularly important in helping to define the Republican agenda and in helping to establish the Republican congressional image. Similarly, as addressed in the chapters by Hayes and Wink and Sharpe, changes in the shape and composition of congressional districts in the South in response to the 1982 amendments to the Voting Rights Act simultaneously affected southern parties and elections and the makeup of Congress in important ways by increasing both black and Republican representation. Now that the future of majority-minority districting has been called into serious question by the Supreme Court, resulting changes are certain to affect further both regional political practices and congressional composition and operations.

The changes examined in this book are not necessarily unusual—in a very real sense, politics typically involves change of various sorts—so we cannot claim they are special because they are unique. They are, nevertheless, important and interesting because they help alert us to a variety of factors associated with political change and, perhaps even more importantly, because they clarify our understanding of contemporary southern and congressional politics. Peters's excellent historical overview, for example, highlights some of the key reasons for congressional change in the past half century (and that is of interest in and of itself) and illuminates the events, personalities, and processes that have given us the current Congress; he argues, in the process, that the contemporary Congress is affected by the South (particularly southern Republicans), but in ways that differ significantly from that region's effect as recently as the 1960s. His conclusion that southern Republicans are more important in the current directions of Congress as Republicans who are similar to other Republicans in other regions rather than as southerners is broadly congruent with those who have argued that there has been a nationalization of American politics (or, in one version of the thesis, a southernization of American politics).

A key point is that understanding change is important for understanding the product of that change, even if the change is ongoing. The foregoing essays tell a great deal about where Congress stands currently, they offer some useful insights into how the South contributed to making Congress what it is, and they suggest some possibilities about future directions.

For example, as regards the South's future contribution to maintaining the Republicans' current majority, Berard and Rohde make a convincing case that further Republican gains in the region are likely to be scarce. In fact, the possibility is greater that Democrats will make some modest gains in the wake of the Supreme Court's recent rulings on majority-minority redistricting. Similarly, the importance of party switching as a factor in Republican growth is likely to diminish, if for no other reason than the smaller numbers of Democratic officeholders remaining, many of whom were elected in largely Democratic districts. At the same time, with the possible exception of Republican losses resulting from redistricting and/or the occasional locally based or personality-based Democratic defeat of a Republican incumbent (or, ironically, Democrat victories in the open seats resulting from the retirements of those members of the class of 1994 who promised self-imposed term limits), chances are quite good that southern Republicans in Congress will continue to be an important part of the party's national coalition. The elections of 1998, discussed briefly by Berard and Rohde and more extensively by Bullock, generally confirm these points. As Peters argues convincingly, however, this is not evidence of a regional orientation so much as it is evidence of the nationalization of the Republican Party; southern Republicans in Congress are part of the party's ideological mainstream to a degree sufficient to diminish regional impact. While the southerners may well have provided a substantial part of the driving force that produced this ideological center of gravity for the party, as Rae argues, the goal of that effort has clearly been focused on a national coalition developed around ideological and issue concerns rather than on the pursuit of narrower regional gain. Again, Peters's analysis of the Gingrich revolution, its aftermath, and the more recent House leadership changes and Rae's discussion of the orientations and motivations of new Republicans in Congress are instructive in this regard.

A second observation, closely related to the first, is that Congress has become more regionally and ideologically polarized along partisan lines than it was two decades ago. Feigert and Ault point out that over the past twenty-five years both parties have exhibited less intraparty ideological division along regional lines but greater interparty ideological differences; southern Republicans have tended to become more like other Republicans in Congress, and southern Democrats have become more like their nonsouthern congressional colleagues. Glaser's analysis identifies party switchers as one contributing factor in this process of greater ideological differentiation between the congressional parties as former-Democrats-turned-Republican tend to move further to the right once the switch has been made while simulataneously lessening the conservatism of the remaining Democratic aggregate, a process similar to the party sorting that has been reported in studies of party activists at the state and local levels in the South. Along the same lines, the analyses by Hayes and Wink and by Smith demonstrate that majority-minority districting and affinity for the Religious Right, especially among the Republican class of 1994, contributed to this ideological differentiation as well. One consequence of this development is the possible erosion of political moderation in the Congress as the parties divide more widely along ideological lines. A second consequence is that the party leadership in Congress can become more regionalized at the very time that congressional politics is becoming less regionalized; Peters advances this point by noting that the House party leadership has actually become more regionalized (with southerners becoming leaders of the Republican Party in the House and nonsoutherners becoming leaders of the Democratic Party in the House—a result made possible by the reduction of regional interests in both parties in recent years).

As the nation enters a new millennium, then, the sweeping transformations of southern politics and of Congress have come together in ways that have reduced the impact of regionalism on Congress. This is not to say that region is unimportant—it remains a crucial part of the equation in understanding Congress—but it is clearly different than it previously was. Indeed, some have contended that it is not the South that has become captive to the GOP, but rather the Republicans who have become captive to the South. In the June 1998 issue of the conservative publication *The Weekly Standard*, senior writer Christopher Caldwell argued that

> [S]outhern interests diverge from those of the rest of the country, and the southern presence in the Republican Party has passed a "tipping point," at which it began to alienate voters from most other regions. . . . The most profound clash . . . is a cultural one. It arises from the southern tradition of putting values—particularly Christian values—at the center of politics. This is not the same as saying that the Republican Party is "too far right"; Americans consistently tell pollsters that they are conservative on values issues. It is, rather, that the Republicans have narrowly defined "values" as the folkways of one regional subculture, and have urged their imposition on the rest of the country. . . . Southerners now wag the Republican dog.

During the 2000 GOP presidential primaries, the profundity of these comments became all too apparent to George W. Bush and his strategic planners after a visit to Bob Jones University during the important South Carolina primary. Bob Jones University, a strictly evangelical private university in the "bible belt" upstate, was a token for religious Christian conservatives—a constituency that Bush badly needed to counter what was thought to be a potentially devastating "Democrats for John McCain" vote in the state's open primaries. Its policies in the past have painted it as an anti-gay, anti-race mixing, anti-Catholic institution; it even lost its tax-exempt status as an institution of higher education in the now-famous "private discrimination" case of *Bob Jones University v. United States,* 461 U.S. 574 (1983). While Bush's campaign speech there endeared him to South Carolina's rock-solid evangelical conservative vote and ultimately played a part in his solid primary win of the state, the candidate found it hard to recover from the impression that he had been painted into the corner of the southern Religious Right—a point which the McCain campaign used aggressively 48 hours later to score big primary wins in Arizona and Michigan. Moderates in South Carolina, according to numerous stories in the Charleston *Post and Courier* and other leading newspapers across the region, were dismayed by the moralistic tone the Republican campaign took in the Palmetto State, to the detriment of a more issues-oriented effort.

What of the impact of this morals-first conservative approach in Congress? Mark Caleb Smith, in the concluding chapter of this volume, provided at least part of the answer by suggesting that there were important differences—albeit still not explained to the degree we need to understand them—between freshman GOP support for the American Conservative Union and the Christian Coalition; southern members, in particular, appear to know the power of these constituents back in their home districts. With disappointing results of the 1998 congressional elections and the subsequent resignation of Newt Gingrich as Speaker of the House late that year, House Republicans turned to yet another southerner—Robert Livingston of Louisiana, whose rapid rise to power was eclipsed by his even faster fall after revelations of a longtime extramarital affair. Livingston's departure was in large part due to the "morals trap" that the GOP had loosed upon itself; having used it as a winning theme in the vastly successful 1994 elections to become the majority, House Republicans in particular also prosecuted the same line of argumentation in their impeachment of President Bill Clinton four years later. The Republican battle cry during Clinton's impeachment centered around themes like hypocrisy and lying; it was ironically those same themes that were enunciated by *Hustler* magazine publisher Larry Flynt when he took out the one-million-dollar-bounty advertisement for information about members of Congress who had engaged in immoral or illicit activity. When several individuals came forward to name Livingston as an adulterer, the tables had been successfully turned (Cohen 1998). The details of a private life that did not necessarily bother economic conservatives—or to some extent, even secular social ones—became Livingston's Achilles' heel among religiously charged conservative Christians who had finally arrived in the halls of Capitol Hill power. His respect, tenure of service, and leadership abilities were moot at that point; his moral failing became the sum total of his aborted campaign for the Speakership.

Gingrich, too, was felled to some extent by the morals-centered demand of the revolution he helped to create and bring to power. Richard Cohen (1999) points out that Gingrich was finally done in by a slipping away of support from critically important members of the Republican House "inner circle," and that his level of activity and need to dominate the legislative process were factors in this destruction. Nevertheless, a "particularly grave self-inflicted wound was Gingrich's ethics trouble . . . including teaching, book-writing and an active speaking schedule" which netted him considerable outside revenue and often blurred the line between neutral scholarship and partisan pandering. He also dramatically underestimated Clinton's resiliency against a Congress that had been seen increasingly as more a set of vandals than of revolutionaries by the general public, noting privately to one anonymous lawmaker that "everything will be OK because Clinton will collapse" when the Contract with America's favorability ratings began to wane in 1997.

The Republican "revolution" of 1994, to use Gingrich's characterization, has turned out to be less than advertised. Although the majority managed to push through several major planks of the Contract with America, the most highly visible and salient issues to the voting public—including the impeachment battle with Clinton and the December 1995 budget impasse with him that effectively shut down the federal government for four weeks—wound up being losing battles. In November of 1996, Republicans lost an additional nine seats in the House as Gingrich continued arguing the appeal from abstract virtue—telling his colleagues after the election that they had "an absolute moral obligation to make this system work" (Cohen 1999). One year later, however, Gingrich himself was the target of a morals investigation; the House Ethics Committee recommended a reprimand for violating chamber rules in his use of money from GOPAC, his private political action committee. He won reelection as Speaker in January of 1997 with only 216 of 431 votes cast; two weeks later, the House formally reprimanded him as the Ethics Committee had suggested. Far from licking his wounds and retreating into the comfort of noncontroversiality, however, Gingrich began quietly taking revenge against coup-plotters within his own party in July of 1997 that had attempted to replace him as Speaker (Cohen 1999).

It is little wonder, then, that by the fall of 1998, after this maelstrom of controversy, House Republicans lost another five seats in that year's elections, spurring Gingrich's resignation from both the Speakership and the House. It is also of little wonder, after surviving the rambunctious southerner and his tempestuous ways—only to have to survive still more morals charges against Speaker-Elect Livingston that brought down his budding regime—that the majority elected the relatively obscure, quiet, and nonsouthern Dennis Hastert of Illinois as Speaker in 1999. Hastert immediately promised to be a "workhorse" in the Tip O'Neill mold (albeit far from O'Neill's ideological persuasion) and told members that "solutions to problems cannot be found in a pool of bitterness." According to Matt Bai (1999), Republican "ideologues trusted Hastert's strongly conservative voting record; moderates liked his inclusive style." Above all—and as perhaps House members learned during the tempest of rejections of well-known, fiery, and controversial nominees to the Supreme Court that eventually resulted in the appointment of the widely unknown David Souter—Hastert did not begin his job with the kind of ethical baggage that had embarrassed the Republican Party in the last days of Gingrich and Livingston. He represented, to the contrary, perhaps an ideal candidate to succeed to the Speakership after a maelstrom of morals-oriented battling; he had solid party credentials for insiders, and the general public and media knew little to nothing about him.

While Hastert has yet to develop completely his leadership style in the House, it is nevertheless clear that southerners continue to remain both an important part of the Republican coalition and the leadership in Congress. Trent Lott of Mississippi remains majority leader in the Senate. Majority leader Dick Armey and firebrand majority whip Tom DeLay in the House both represent their native Lone Star state in classically conservative style, at the same time representing at least with some vigor the interests of evangelicals across Dixie who have become so important in guaranteeing that GOP slippages in the early 2000s abate or reverse themselves. The Senate, of course, has traditionally been more attuned to compromise and cooperation as the self-perceived body of great statesmen and stateswomen who can put ideological cleavages aside for bipartisan policy progress (notwithstanding the fact that the unanimous consent rules and threat of filibuster make it more of a body of equals). In the House of Representatives, however, increased partisan and ideological divisions—related in numerous ways directly to the changes in southern politics discussed in the preceding chapters of this volume—are likely to continue to characterize the federal legislative process at the beginnings of the twenty-first century. More liberal northeastern Democrats and conservative southern ones seem to have found a temporary truce to their historic ideological division in order to fight to regain their majority status, but it is an uneasy truce at best. With the internal battles of numerous Republican factions consistently trying to determine whether their conservativism should be economically, socially, or even theocratically based to maintain their appeal to voters, it has become increasingly clear that the GOP cannot palliate one faction notably without endangering themselves among the others. Through the fog of this legislative strife, it remains the South—with its notably but well-documented eccentric political and social issues—that raises the most considerable concerns of the dangers inherent in attempting to be a national governing party. It is also the South that appears poised to remain the eye of the congressional storm for the near future.

References

Editor's Note: where text references have no specific author listed in *Congressional Quarterly Weekly Report*, they have been omitted from this list in favor of providing full date citation in-text with the parenthetical note accompanying the reference.

Abramowitz, Alan I. 1980a. "Is the Revolt Fading? A Note on Party Loyalty Among Southern Democratic Congressmen." *Journal of Politics* 42: 568–72.

Abramowitz, Alan I. 1980b. "A Comparison of Voting for U.S. Senator and Representatives in 1978." *American Political Science Review* 74: 633–40.

———. 1983. "Partisan Redistricting and the 1982 Congressional Elections." *Journal of Politics* 45: 767–70.

Abramowitz, Alan I., and Jeffrey Segal. 1993. *Senate Elections.* Ann Arbor: University of Michigan Press.

Abramson, Paul R., John H. Aldrich, and David W. Rohde. 1995. *Change and Continuity in the 1992 Elections.* Rev. ed. Washington, D.C.: CQ Press.

Aistrup, Joseph A. 1990. "Republican Contestation of U.S. State Senate Elections in the South." *Legislative Studies Quarterly* 15: 227–45.

———. 1996. *The Southern Strategy Revisited.* Lexington: University Press of Kentucky.

Aldrich, John H. 1995. *Why Parties?* Chicago: University of Chicago Press.

Altemus, Vaughn. 1977. "Party Leadership Changes in the House of Representatives: 1910–76." *American Political Science Review* 71: 587–88.

Alvarez, Lizette. 1998. "Democratic Caucus in the House Elects Veterans to 2 Top Posts." *New York Times.*

American Political Science Association, Committee on Political Parties. 1950. "Toward a More Responsible Two-Party System." *American Political Science Review* 44:3 (supplement).

Anderson, R. Bruce. 1994. "Electoral Competition and the Structure of Southern State Legislatures: Party Building and Organizational Complexity." Paper presented at the Ninth Citadel Symposium on Southern Politics, Charleston, SC, March 2–3, 1994.

Armey, Richard. 1995. *The Freedom Revolution*. New York: Regnery Press.

Asher, Herert B., and Herbert F. Weisberg. 1978. "Voting Change in Congress: Some Dynamic Perspectives on an Evolutionary Process." *American Journal of Political Science* 22: 391–425.

Bader, John B. 1996. *Taking the Initiative: Leadership Agendas in Congress and the "Contract with America."* Washington, D.C.: Georgetown University Press.

Bai, Matt. 1999. "'Coach! Coach! Coach!': An Unassuming Speaker Struggles to Find His Voice." *Newsweek*, August 9.

Baker, Tod A., Robert P. Steed, and Laurence W. Moreland. 1991. "Preachers and Politics: Jesse Jackson, Pat Robertson, and the 1988 Presidential Nomination Campaign in South Carolina." In *The Bible and the Ballot Box: Religion and Politics in the 1988 Election*. Edited by James L. Guth and John C. Green. Boulder, CO: Westview Press.

———. 1998. "Culture Wars and Religion in the South: The Changing Character of the Party Struggle." In *Political Party Activists in Southern Politics: Mirrors and Makers of Change*. Edited by Charles D. Hadley and Lewis Bowman. Knoxville, TN: University of Tennessee Press.

———, eds. 1983. *Religion and Politics in the South: Mass and Elite Perspectives*. New York: Praeger.

Baltagi, Badi H., and Qi Li. 1990. "A Lagrange Multiplier Test for the Error Components Model with Incomplete Panels." *Econometric Review* 9: 103–7.

Balz, Dan, and Ceci Connolly. 1997. "House Leadership Battle Mirrors Deeper Conflict." *Washington Post*, July 20.

Barnes, Fred. 1997. "Tough Love for Newt." *The Weekly Standard*, May 5.

Barone, Michael, and Grant Ujifusa. 1993. *The Almanac of American Politics, 1992*. Washington, D.C.: National Journal.

———. 1995. *The Almanac of American Politics, 1994*. Washington, D.C.: National Journal.

———. 1997. *The Almanac of American Politics, 1998*. Washington, D.C.: National Journal.

Barry, John M. 1989. *The Ambition and the Power*. New York: Viking Press.

Bartley, Numan V., and Hugh D. Graham. 1975. *Southern Politics and the Second Reconstruction*. Baltimore: Johns Hopkins University Press.

Bass, Jack, and Walter DeVries. 1995. *The Transformation of Southern Politics: Social Change and Political Consequence Since 1945*. Athens: University of Georgia Press.

Bass, Jack, and Thomas E. Terrill, eds. 1986. *The American South Comes of Age*. New York: Alfred A. Knopf.

Beck, Paul Allen. 1977. "Partisan Dealignment in the Postwar South." *American Political Science Review* 71: 477–97.

Benson, Peter L., and Dorothy L. Williams. 1982. *Religion on Capitol Hill: Myths and Realities*. San Francisco: Harper and Row.

Berke, Richard L. 1998. "Without a New Tune to Whistle, G. O. P. Kept Humming 'Scandal.'" *New York Times*, November 5.

Black, Earl. 1976. *Southern Governors and Civil Rights*. Cambridge, MA: Harvard University Press.

Black, Earl, and Merle Black. 1987. *Politics and Society in the South*. Cambridge, MA: Harvard University Press.

Black, Merle, and Earl Black. 1990. "The South in the Senate: Changing Patterns of Representation on Committees." In *The Disappearing South? Studies in Regional Change and Continuity*. Edited by Robert P. Steed, Laurence W. Moreland, and Tod A. Baker. Tuscaloosa: University of Alabama Press.

———. 1992. *The Vital South: How Presidents are Elected.* Cambridge, MA: Harvard University Press.

Bolling, Richard. 1968. *Power in the House: A History of the Leadership of the U.S. House of Representatives.* New York: Dutton Books.

Bond, Jon R., Cary Covington, and Richard Fleisher. 1985. "Explaining Challenger Quality in Congressional Elections." *Journal of Politics* 47: 510–29.

Born, Richard. 1976. "Cue-Taking within State Party Delegations in the U.S. House of Representatives." *Journal of Politics* 38: 71–94.

———. 1985. "Partisan Intentions and Election Day Realities in the Congressional Redistricting Process." *American Political Science Review* 84: 377–93.

Bowman, Lewis, William E. Hulbary, and Anne E. Kelley. 1990. "Party Sorting at the Grass Roots: Stable Partisans and Party-Changers Among Florida's Precinct Officials." In *The Disappearing South?* Edited by Robert P. Steed, Laurence W. Moreland, and Tod A. Baker. Tuscaloosa: University of Alabama Press.

Bradley, Jennifer, and Jim Vande Hei. 1997. "Disaster Bill Disaster Engulfs House GOP." *Roll Call*, June 18.

Brady, David W. 1978. "Critical Elections, Congressional Parties, and Clusters of Policy Changes." *British Journal of Political Science* 8: 79–99.

———. 1988. *Critical Elections and Congressional Policymaking.* Stanford, CA: Stanford University Press.

Brady, David W., and Phillip Althoff. 1974. "Party Voting in the U.S. House of Representatives, 1890–1910: Elements of a Responsible Party System." *Journal of Politics* 36: 753–75.

Brady, David W., Joseph Cooper, and Patricia A. Hurley. 1979. "The Decline of Party in the U.S. House of Representatives, 1887–1968." *Legislative Studies Quarterly* 4: 381–407.

Brady, David W., and Charles S. Bullock, III. 1980. "Is There a Conservative Coalition in the House?" *Journal of Politics* 42: 549–52.

———. 1981. "Coalition Politics in the House of Representatives." In *Congress Reconsidered*, 2d ed. Edited by Lawrence C. Dodd and Bruce I. Oppenheimer. Washington, DC: Congressional Quarterly Press.

Broder, David S. 1972. *The Party's Over: The Failure of Politics in America.* New York: Harper.

Brown, Lynne P., and Robert L. Peabody. 1990. "Patterns of Succession in House Democratic Leadership: Foley, Gephardt, and Gray, 1989." Paper presented at the 1990 meeting of the American Political Science Association, Washington, D.C.

Bullock, Charles S., III. 1975. "Redistricting and Congressional Stability." *Journal of Politics* 37: 569–75.

———. 1981. "Congressional Voting and the Mobilization of a Black Electorate in the South." *The Journal of Politics* 43: 662–82.

———. 1983. "The Effects of Redistricting on Black Representation in Southern State Legislatures." Paper presented at the 1983 meeting of the American Political Science Association, Chicago, IL.

———. 1985. "Congressional Roll Call Voting in a Two-Party South." *Social Science Quarterly* 66: 789–804.

———. 1987. "Redistricting and Changes in the Partisan and Racial Composition of Southern Legislatures." *State and Local Government Review* 19: 62–67.

———. 1988a. "Regional Realignment from an Officeholding Perspective." *Journal of Politics* 50: 553–74.

———. 1988b. "Creeping Realignment in the South." In *The South's New Politics: Realignment and Dealignment.* Edited by Robert H. Swansbrough and David M. Brodsky. Columbia: University of South Carolina Press.

———. 1995a. "Winners and Losers in the Latest Round of Redistricting." *Emory Law Review* 44: 943–77.

———. 1995b."The Impact of Changing the Racial Composition of Congressional Districts on Legislators' Roll Call Behavior." *American Politics Quarterly* 23: 141–58.

———. 1995c. "Affirmative Action Districts: In Whose Faces Will They Blow Up?" *Campaigns and Elections*, April 22–23.

Bullock, Charles S., III, and Charles Lamb. 1985. *Implementation of Civil Rights Policy.* New York: HarperCollins.

Bullock, Charles S., III, and Mark J. Rozell, eds. 1998. *The New Politics of the Old South: An Introduction to Southern Politics.* Lanham, MD: Rowman and Littlefield.

Bullock, Charles S., III, and David J. Shafer. 1997. "Party Targeting and Electoral Success." *Legislative Studies Quarterly* 22: 573–84.

Burnham, Walter Dean. 1970. *Critical Elections and the Mainspring of American Politics.* New York: Norton.

Campbell, Angus, Philip E. Converse, Warren E. Miller, and Donald E. Stokes. 1960. *The American Voter.* Chicago: University of Chicago Press.

Campbell, Bruce A. 1977. "Patterns of Change in the Partisan Loyalties of Native Southerners." *Journal of Politics* 39: 730–61.

Campbell, James E. 1982. "Cosponsoring Legislation in the U.S. Congress." *Legislative Studies Quarterly* 7: 415–22.

———. 1986a. "Presidential Coattails and Midterm Losses in State Legislative Elections." *American Political Science Review* 80: 45–64.

———. 1986b. "On the Structure and Sequence of Issue Evolution." *American Political Science Review* 80: 901–20.

———. 1989. *Issue Evolution.* Princeton, NJ: Princeton University Press.

———. 1997. *The Presidential Pulse of Congressional Elections.* Lexington: University Press of Kentucky.

Canon, David T., Matthew M. Schousen, and Patrick J. Sellers. 1996. "The Supply Side of Congressional Redistricting: Race and Strategic Politicians 1972–1992." *Journal of Politics* 58: 846–62.

Carmines, Edward G., and Harold W. Stanley. 1990. "Ideological Realignment in the Contemporary South." In *The Disappearing South?* Edited by Robert P. Steed, Laurence W. Moreland, and Tod A. Baker. Tuscaloosa: University of Alabama Press.

Carmines, Edward G., and James A. Stimson. 1980. "The Two Faces of Issue Voting." *American Political Science Review* 74: 78–91.

———. 1989. *Issue Evolution: Race and the Transformation of American Politics.* Princeton, NJ: Princeton University Press.

Carr, Rebecca. 1997. "Subcommittee Lays out Details of Gingrich Ethics Violations." *Congressional Quarterly Weekly Report*, January 4.

Ceaser, James, and Andrew W. Busch. 1997. *Losing to Win: The 1996 Elections and American Politics*. Lanham, MD: Rowman and Littlefield.

Champagne, Anthony. 1984. *Congressman Sam Rayburn*. New Brunswick, NJ: Rutgers University Press.

Chappell, David L. 1994. *Inside Agitators: White Southerners in the Civil Rights Movement*. Baltimore, MD: Johns Hopkins University Press.

Chen, Edwin. 1998. "GOP Sees Chance to Alter 'Mean White-Guy' Image." *New York Times*, November 11.

Chubb, John. 1988. "Institution, the Economy, and the Dynamics of State Elections." *American Political Science Review* 82: 133–54.

Clausen, Aage. 1973. *How Congressmen Decide: A Policy Focus*. New York: St. Martin's.

Clubb, Jerome M., William H. Flanigan, and Nancy H. Zingale. 1990. *Partisan Realignment: Voters, Parties, and Government in American History*. Boulder, CO: Westview.

Clubb, Jerome M., and Santa A. Traugott. 1977. "Partisan Cleavage in the House of Representatives, 1861–1974." *Journal of Interdisciplinary History* 7: 375–401.

Cohen, Adam. 1998. "The Speaker Who Never Was." *Time*, December 28.

Cohen, Richard E. 1999. "The Rise and Fall of Newt." *National Journal*, March 6.

Cohodas, Nadine. 1984."Prayer Issue Engulfs Congress as Senate Embarks on Debate." *Congressional Quarterly Weekly Report*, March 10.

Coleman, John J. 1996. *Party Decline in America: Policy, Politics, and the Fiscal State*. Princeton, NJ: Princeton University Press.

Collie, Melissa P. 1985. "Voting Behavior." In *Handbook of Legislative Research*. Edited by Gerhard Loewenberg, Samuel C. Patterson, and Malcolm E. Jewell. Cambridge, MA: Harvard University Press.

———. 1988. "The Rise of Coalition Politics: Voting in the U.S. House, 1933–1980." *Legislative Studies Quarterly* 13: 321–42.

———. 1989. "Electoral Patterns and Voting Alignments in the U.S. House, 1886–1986." *Legislative Studies Quarterly* 14:107–27.

Conway, M. Margaret. 1991. *Political Participation in the United States*. Washington, D.C.: Congressional Quarterly Press.

Cook, Charles E. 1997. "Political Surveyor." *Roll Call*, June 19.

Cooper, Joseph, and David Brady. 1981. "Institutional Context and Leadership Style: The House from Cannon to Rayburn." *American Political Science Review* 75: 411–25.

Cosman, Bernard. 1966. *Five States for Goldwater: Continuity and Change in Southern Presidential Voting Patterns*. Tuscaloosa: University of Alabama Press.

Cox, Gary W., and Matthew D. McCubbins. 1993. *Legislative Leviathan: Party Government in the House*. Berkeley: University of California Press.

Davidson, Roger H., and Walter J. Oleszek. 1977. *Congress against Itself*. Bloomington: Indiana University Press.

Dionne, E.J. 1997. "The Plot against Gingrich." *The Washington Post*, July 20.

Doherty, Carroll L., and Jeffrey L. Katz. 1998. "Firebrand GOP Class of '94 Warms to Life on the Inside." *Congressional Quarterly Weekly Report*, January 24.

Downs, Anthony. 1957. *An Economic Theory of Democracy*. New York: Harper and Row.

Drew, Elizabeth. 1997. *Whatever It Takes: The Real Struggle for Political Power in America*. New York: Viking Press.

Duncan, Philip D. 1993. *Politics in America: The 103rd Congress.* Washington, D.C.: Congressional Quarterly Press.

Duncan, Philip D., and Christine C. Lawrence. 1995. *Politics in America: The 104th Congress.* Washington, D.C.: Congressional Quarterly Press.

———. 1996. *Politics in America, 1996.* Washington, D.C.: Congressional Quarterly Press.

———. 1997. *Politics in America, 1998: The 105th Congress.* Washington, D.C.: Congressional Quarterly Press.

Edwards, George C., III. 1989. *At the Margins: Presidential Leadership of Congress.* New Haven, CT: Yale University Press.

Eilperin, Juliet, and Jim Vande Hei. 1997a. "Speaker May Return to a Smaller Leadership." *Roll Call,* June 17.

———. 1997b. "Some Wounds Never Heal: Today's GOP Leadership Struggle Has Roots in 'Guerilla' Warriors of the 1980s." *Roll Call,* October 2.

———. 1997c. "'Contract' High to Coup Low: How It Fell Apart." *Roll Call,* October 6.

———. 1997d. "House GOP Leadership's Fractured Present: Gingrich-Armey Alliance against DeLay-Paxon." *Roll Call,* October 9.

Elving, Ronald D., and Andrew Taylor. 1997. "A Balanced-Budget Won, A Defining Issue Lost." *Congressional Quarterly Weekly Report,* August 2.

Epstein, Leon. 1986. *Political Parties in the American Mold.* Madison: University of Wisconsin Press.

Erikson, Robert, and Kent Tedin. 1981. "The 1928–1936 Partisan Realignment: The Case for the Conversion Hypothesis." *American Political Science Review* 75: 951–62.

———. 1986. "Voter Conversion and the New Deal Realignment." *Western Political Quarterly* 39: 729–32.

Erikson, Robert S., Gerald C. Wright, and John P. McIver. 1993. *Statehouse Democracy: Public Opinion and Policy in the American States.* New York: Cambridge University Press.

Espo, David. 1995. "Wavering Democrat Giving Back Party Money," *Associated Press Wire Service,* July 25.

Fairclоth, Adam. 1995. *Race and Democracy: The Civil Rights Struggle in Louisiana, 1915–1972.* Athens: University of Georgia Press.

Farley, Christopher John. 1994. "Prodding Voters to the Right." *Time,* November 21.

Fenno, Richard. 1978. *Home Style.* Boston: Little, Brown and Company.

Ferejohn, John. 1977. "On the Decline of Competition in Congressional Elections." *American Political Science Review* 71: 166–76.

Fineman, Howard. 1994. "Revenge of the Right." *Newsweek,* November 21.

Fiorina, Morris P. 1973. "Electoral Margins, Constituency Influence, and Policy Moderation: A Critical Assessment." *American Politics Quarterly* 1: 479–98.

———. 1974. *Representatives, Roll Calls, and Constituencies.* Lexington, MA: Lexington Books.

———. 1977. "The Case of the Vanishing Marginals: The Bureaucracy Did It." *American Political Science Review* 71: 177–81.

———. 1996. *Divided Government.* Needham Heights, MA: Allyn and Bacon.

Fleisher, Richard. 1993."Explaining the Change in Roll-Call Voting Behavior of Southern Democrats." *Journal of Politics* 55: 327–41.

Gimpel, James. 1996. *Legislating the Revolution: The Contract with America in Its First Hundred Days.* Boston, MA: Allyn and Bacon.

Gingrich, Newt. 1995. *To Renew America.* New York: HarperCollins.

Glaser, James M. 1994. "Back to the Black Belt: Racial Environment and White Racial Attitudes in the South." *Journal of Politics* 56: 21–41.

———. 1996. *Race, Campaign Politics, and the Realignment in the South*. New Haven, CT: Yale University Press.

Graham Jr., Cole Blease, and Kenny J. Whitby. 1989. "Party-Based Voting in a Southern State Legislature." *American Politics Quarterly* 17: 181–93.

Green, John C., and James L. Guth. 1990. "The Transformation of Southern Political Elites: Regionalism among Party and PAC Contributors." In *The Disappearing South?* Edited by Robert P. Steed, Laurence W. Moreland, and Tod A. Baker. Tuscaloosa: University of Alabama Press.

Green, John C., James L. Guth, Lyman A. Kellstedt, and Corwin E. Smidt. 1995. "Evangelical Realignment: The Political Power of the Christian Right." *The Christian Century*, July 5.

Greenblatt, Alan. 1998. "Re-Energized New Deal Coalition boosts Democrats for 2000." *Congressional Quarterly Weekly Report*, November 7.

Gruenwald, Julianna. 1995. "Deal's Switch to GOP Exposes Erosion in Once Solid South." *Congressional Quarterly Weekly Report*, April 15.

Gruenwald, Julianna, and Robert Marshall Wells. 1996. "At Odds with Some Workers, AFL-CIO Takes Aim at GOP." *Congressional Quarterly Weekly Report*, April 13.

Gugliotta, Guy. 1998. "Democrats Hope to Translate Latino Distrust of GOP into Votes." *Washington Post*, January 5.

Guth, James L., and John C. Green. 1991. *The Bible and the Ballot Box*. Boulder, CO: Westview Press.

Hadley, Charles D., and Lewis Bowman, eds. 1995. *Southern State Party Organizations and Activists*. Westport, CT: Praeger.

———, eds. 1998. *Party Activists in Southern Politics: Mirrors and Makers of Change*. Knoxville: University of Tennessee Press.

Hardeman, D.B., and Donald C. Bacon. 1987. *Rayburn: A Biography*. Austin: Texas Monthly Press.

Heard, Alexander. 1952. *A Two-Party South?* Chapel Hill: University of North Carolina Press.

Hedlund, Ronald D., and H. Paul Friesma. 1972. "Representatives' Perceptions of Constituency Opinions." *Journal of Politics* 34: 730–52.

Herrnson, Paul S. 1998. *Congressional Elections: Campaigning at Home and in Washington*. Washington, D.C.: Congressional Quarterly Press.

Hibbing, John R. 1982. "Voluntary Retirement from the U.S. House: Who Quits?" *American Journal of Political Science* 26: 467–84.

———. 1991. *Congressional Careers: Contours of Life in the U.S. House of Representatives*. Chapel Hill: University of North Carolina Press.

Hill, Kevin A. 1995. "Does the Creation of Majority Black Districts Aid Republicans? An Analysis of the 1992 Congressional Elections in Eight Southern States." *Journal of Politics* 57: 384–401.

Hill, Kevin A., and Nicol C. Rae. Forthcoming. "What Happened to the Democrats in the South? U.S. House Elections, 1992–1996." *Party Politics*.

Hill, Samuel S., Jr., ed. 1972. *Religion and the Solid South*. Nashville, TN: Abington Press.

Hinckley, Barbara. 1971. *The Seniority System in Congress*. Bloomington: University of Indiana Press.

Hoadley, John F. 1980. "The Emergence of Political Parties in Congress, 1789–1803." *American Political Science Review* 74: 757–79.

Hood, M.V., III, Quentin Kidd, and Irwin L. Morriss. 1996. "Of Byrd[s] and Bumpers: A Pooled Cross-Sectional Study of the Roll-Call Voting Behavior of Democratic Senators from the South, 1955–1996." Paper presented at the 1996 meeting of the Southern Political Science Association, Atlanta, GA.

Hoppe, Layne. 1997. "Increasing Liberalism among Southern Members of Congress, 1970–1990, with an Analysis of the 1994 Congressional Elections." In *Southern Parties and Elections.* Edited by Robert P. Steed, Laurence W. Moreland, and Tod A. Baker. Tuscaloosa: University of Alabama Press.

Hunter, James Davidson. 1991. *Culture Wars: The Struggle to Define America.* New York: Basic Books.

Hurley, Patricia A., and Rick K. Wilson. 1989. "Partisan Voting Patterns in the U.S. Senate, 1877-1986." *Legislative Studies Quarterly* 14: 225–50.

Jacobsin, Louis. 1998. "The Rise and Fall of a Think Tank." *National Journal*, August 22.

Jacobson, Gary C. 1981. "Congressional Elections: The Case of the Vanishing Challengers." In *Congressional Elections.* Edited by Louis Sandy Maisel and Joseph Cooper. Beverly Hills, CA: Sage Publications.

———. 1990. *The Electoral Origins of Divided Government.* Boulder, CO: Westview Press.

———. 1997. "Reversal of Fortune: The Transformation of U.S. House Elections in the 1990s." Paper presented at the Conference on the Congressional Elections in the Post–World War II Era, The Hoover Institutions, Stanford, CA.

Jacobson, Gary C., and Samuel Kernell. 1983. *Strategy and Choice in Congressional Elections.* New Haven, CT: Yale University Press.

Katz, Jeffrey L. 1998a. "Supporters of Campaign Finance Overhaul Grow Wary as House GOP Leaders Signal a Summer of Protracted Debate." *Congressional Quarterly Weekly Report*, May 23.

———. 1998b "Politically Charged Vote Sets Tone for Impeachment Inquiry." *Congressional Quarterly Weekly Report*, October 10.

———. 1998c. "Shakeup in the House." *Congressional Quarterly Weekly Report*, November 7.

Katz, Jeffrey L., and Carroll J. Doherty. 1998. "New GOP Leaders' Watchword is Realism, Not Revolution." *Congressional Quarterly Weekly Report*, November 21.

Kazee, Thomas. 1994. *Who Runs for Congress?: Ambition, Context, and Candidate Emergence.* Washington, D.C.: Congressional Quarterly Press.

Kessel, John H. 1964. "The Washington Congressional Delegation." *Midwest Journal of Political Science* 8: 1–21.

Key, V.O., Jr. 1949. *Southern Politics in State and Nation.* New York: Knopf Books.

———. 1955. "A Theory of Critical Elections." *Journal of Politics* 17: 3–18.

———. 1959. "Secular Realignment and the Party System." *Journal of Politics* 21: 198–210.

———. 1966. *The Responsible Electorate.* Cambridge, MA: Harvard University Press.

Kingdon, John W. 1977. "Models of Legislative Voting." *Journal of Politics* 39: 563–95.

———. 1989. *Congressmen's Voting Decisions.* Ann Arbor: University of Michigan Press.

Koszcuk, Jackie. 1997a. "Gingrich's Friends Turn to Foes as Frustration Builds." *Congressional Quarterly Weekly Report*, March 22.

———. 1997b. "Gingrich under Fire as Discord Simmers from Rank to Top." *Congressional Quarterly Weekly Report*, June 21.

———. 1997c. "Coup Attempt Throws GOP off Legislative Track." *Congressional Quarterly Weekly Report*, July 19.

———. 1997d. "Party Stalwarts Will Determine Gingrich's Long-Term Survival." *Congressional Quarterly Weekly Report*, July 26.

———. 1998. "Gingrich, Leading Attack on Clinton, Takes off Gloves, Goes out on Limb." *Congressional Quarterly Weekly Report*, May 2.

Koszcuk, Jackie, and Rebecca Carr. 1997. "Committee Votes for Reprimand, $300 000 Fine for Gingrich." *Congressional Quarterly Weekly Report*, January 18.

Krasno, Jonathan S., and Donald Philip Green. 1988. "Preempting Quality Challengers in House Elections." *Journal of Politics* 50: 920–36.

Krehbiel, Keith. 1991. *Information and Legislative Organization*. Ann Arbor: University of Michigan Press.

———. 1995. "Cosponsors and Wafflers from A to Z." *American Journal of Political Science* 39: 906–23.

Kristol, William. 1998a. "The Democrats' Fate." *The Weekly Standard*, October 19.

———. 1998b. "Cheer Up!" *The Weekly Standard*, October 26.

Kuzenski, John C. 1997a. "South Carolina: The Heart of GOP Realignment in the South." In *The New Politics of the Old South*. Edited by Charles S. Bullock, III and Mark J. Rozell. Lanham, MD: Rowman and Littlefield.

———. 1997b. "The Four—Yes, Four—Types of Primary Systems. *PS: Political Science and Politics* 30: 207–8.

———. 1998. "Evangelicals among the Elephants: Threat and Schism Assessments of the Religious Right within Southern State Republican Executive Committees." Paper presented at the 1998 meeting of the Southern Political Science Association, Atlanta, GA.

Ladd, Everett C. 1990. "Like Waiting for Godot: The Uselessness of Realignment for Understanding Change in Contemporary American Politics." *Polity* 22: 511–25.

Lamis, Alexander P. 1984. *The Two-Party South*. New York: Oxford University Press.

———, ed. 1999. *Southern Politics in the 1990s*. Baton Rouge: Louisiana State University Press.

Lawson, Steven F. 1976. *Black Ballots: Voting Rights in the South, 1944–1969*. New York: Columbia University Press.

Layman, Geoffrey C. 1999. "'Culture Wars' in the American Party System." *American Politics Quarterly* 27: 89–101.

Leege, David C., and Lyman A. Kellstedt, eds. 1993. *Rediscovering the Religious Factor in American Politics*. Armonk, NY: M.E. Sharpe.

Leogrande, William M., and Alana S. Jeydel. 1997. "Using Presidential Election Returns to Measure Constituency Ideology: A Research Note." *American Politics Quarterly* 25: 3–18.

Lewis-Beck, Michael S., and John R. Alford. 1980. "Can Government Regulate Safely? The Coal Mine Example." *American Political Science Review* 74: 745–56.

Lipset, Seymour Martin, and Stein Rokkan. 1967. *Party Systems and Voter Alignments*. New York: Free Press.

Loewenberg, Gerhard, Samuel C. Patterson, and Malcolm E. Jewell, eds. 1985. *Handbook of Legislative Research*. Cambridge, MA: Harvard University Press.

Lublin, David Ian. 1994. "Quality, Not Quantity: Strategic Politicians in U.S. Senate Elections 1952–1990." *Journal of Politics* 56: 228–41.

———. 1997. *Gerrymander for Justice? Racial Redistricting and Black and Latino Representation*. Princeton, NJ: Princeton University Press.

Maney, Patrick J. 1998. "Hale Boggs: The Southerner as National Democrat." In *Masters of the House*. Edited by Roger H. Davidson, Susan Webb Hammond, and Raymond W. Smock. Boulder, CO: Westview Press.

Manley, John F. 1973. "The Conservative Coalition." *American Behavioral Scientist* 17: 223–48.

———. 1977. "The Conservative Coalition in Congress." *In Congress Reconsidered*. Edited by Lawrence C. Dodd and Bruce I. Oppenheimer. New York: Praeger.

Mann, Thomas E., and Raymond E. Wolfinger. 1980. "Candidates and Parties in Congressional Elections." *American Political Science Review* 74: 617–32.

Mayhew, David. 1974a. *Congress: The Electoral Connection*. New Haven, CT: Yale University Press.

———. 1974b. "The Case of the Vanishing Marginals." *Polity* 6: 295–317.

McAllister, Bill. 1998. "Wisconsin Backers of Gingrich Termed Hill's Biggest Patrons." *Washington Post*, September 10.

McSeveney, Samuel T. 1991. "No More Waiting for Godot." In *The End of Realignment?* Edited by Byron E. Shafer. Madison: University of Wisconsin Press.

Meyerson, Harold. 1992. "The Election: Impending Realignment?" *Dissent* 39: 421–24.

Miller, Warren E. 1991. "Party Identification, Realignment, and Party Voting: Back to the Basics." *American Political Science Review* 85: 557–68.

Miller, Warren E., and the National Election Studies. 1991. *American National Election Studies Cumulative Data File* [Computer File], 6th release. Ann Arbor: University of Michigan Center for Political Studies.

Miller, Warren E., and Donald E. Stokes. 1963. "Constituency Influence in Congress." *American Political Science Review* 57: 45–56.

Moen, Matthew C. 1989. *The Christian Right and Congress*. Tuscaloosa: University of Alabama Press.

Moreland, Laurence W., and Robert P. Steed, eds. 1998. *The 1996 Presidential Election in the South: Southern Party Systems in the 1990s*. Westport, CT: Praeger.

Murphy, Reg, and Hal Gulliver. 1971. *The Southern Strategy*. New York: Charles Scribners' Sons.

Nadeau, Richard, and Harold W. Stanley. 1993. "Class Polarization in Partisanship among Native Southern Whites." *American Journal of Political Science* 37: 900–919.

Nardulli, Peter F. 1995. "The Concept of Critical Realignment, Electoral Behavior, and Political Change." *American Political Science Review* 89: 10–23.

Nesbit, Dorothy Davidson. 1988. "Changing Partisanship among Southern Party Activists." *Journal of Politics* 50: 322–34.

New Orleans *Times-Picayune*. 1995. "Defeated Democrat Joins GOP." New Orleans *Times-Picayune*, December 1.

Nie, Norman H., Sidney Verba, and John R. Petrocik. 1976. *The Changing American Voter*. Cambridge, MA: Harvard University Press.

Nixon, C.H. 1946. "The Politics of the Hills." *Journal of Politics* 8: 123–33.

Norpoth, Helmut. 1987. "Under Way and Here to Stay: Party Realignment in the 1980s?" *Public Opinion Quarterly* 51: 376–91.

Norpoth, Helmut, and Jerrold G. Rusk. 1982. "Partisan Dealignment in the American Electorate: Itemizing the Deductions since 1964." *American Political Science Review* 17: 522–37.

Oppenheimer, Bruce I., James A. Stimson, and Richard W. Waterman. 1986. "Interpreting U.S. Congressional Elections: The Exposure Thesis." *Legislative Studies Quarterly* 11: 227–48.

Ornstein, Norman J., Thomas E. Mann, and Michael J. Malbin. 1998. *Vital Statistics on Congress, 1997–98*. Washington, D.C.: Congressional Quarterly Press.

Ota, Alan K. 1998. "Congress Clears Huge Transportation Bill, Restoring Cut-off Funding to States." *Congressional Quarterly Weekly Report*, May 23.

Parker, Glenn R., ed. 1985. *Studies of Congress*. Washington, D.C.: Congressional Quarterly Press.

Patterson, Samuel C., and Gregory A. Caldeira. 1988. "Party Voting in the United States Congress." *British Journal of Political Science* 17: 111–31.

Peabody, Robert L. 1976. *Leadership in Congress*. Boston: Little, Brown and Company.

Peters, Ronald M., Jr. 1997. *The American Speakership: The Office in Historical Perspective,* 2d ed. Baltimore, MD: Johns Hopkins University Press.

———. 1999. "Institutional Context and Leadership Style: The Case of Newt Gingrich." In *New Majority or Old Minority: The Impact of the Republicans on Congress*. Edited by Nicol C. Rae and Colton C. Campbell. Lanham, MD: Rowman and Littlefield.

Petrocik, John R. 1981. *Party Coalitions: Realignments and the Decline of the New Deal Party System*. Chicago: University of Chicago Press.

———. 1987. "Realignment: New Party Coalitions and the Nationalization of the South." *Journal of Politics* 49: 347–75.

Pew Research Center. 1996. *The Diminishing Divide: American Churches, American Politics*. Washington, D.C.: Pew Research Center Publications.

Polsby, Nelson W. 1968. "The Institutionalization of the House of Representatives." *American Political Science Review* 62: 144–68.

Polsby, Nelson W., Miriam Gallagher, and Barry Spencer Rundquist. 1969. "The Growth of the Seniority System in the U.S. House of Representatives." *American Political Science Review* 63: 787–807.

Poole, Keith T., and Steven Daniels. 1985. "Ideology, Party, and Voting in the U.S. Congress, 1959-1980." *American Political Science Review* 79: 373–99.

Poole, Keith T., and Howard Rosenthal. 1984. "The Polarization of American Politics." *Journal of Politics* 46: 1061–79.

Pope, Charles. 1998. "McCain-Feingold Bill on Campaign Financing Proves Dead on Revival." *Congressional Quarterly Weekly Report*, September 12.

Prysby, Charles. 1992. "Realignment among Southern Party Activists." Paper presented at the annual meeting of the American Political Science Association, Chicago, Illinois.

Rae, Nicol C. 1996a. Interview with Congressman David Funderburk, March 28.

———. 1996b. Interview with Congressman Mark Foley, April 30.

———. 1996c. Interview with Congressman J.C. Watts, May 2.

———. 1996d. Interview with Congressman Tom Davis, May 14.

———. 1996e. Interview with Congressman Joe Scarborough, May 28.

———. 1996f. Interview with Congressman Mark Sanford, June 12.

———. 1996g. Interview with Congressman Bob Barr, June 18.

———. 1996h. Interview with Congressman Lindsay Graham, July 18.

———. 1996i. Interview with Congressman Zach Wamp, July 17.

———. 1996j. Interview with Congressman Van Hilleary, July 18.

———. 1996k. Interview with Congressman Ed Whitfield, July 31.

———. 1998. *Conservative Reformers: The Republican Freshmen and the Lessons of the 104th Congress*. Armonk, NY: M.E. Sharpe.

Rees, Matthew. 1997a. "Chaos on Capitol Hill." *The Weekly Standard*, July 28.

———. 1997b. "Rebel for a Day." *The Weekly Standard*, August 4.

Rieselbach, Leroy N. 1986. *Congressional Reform*. Washington, D.C.: Congressional Quarterly Press.

Ripley, Randall B. 1988. *Congress: Process and Policy*. New York: W.W. Norton.

Roberts, Steven V. 1994. "Squaring Off Over Values." *U.S. News and World Report*, November 21.

Rodgers, Harrell R., Jr., and Charles S. Bullock, III. 1976. *Coercion to Compliance*. New York: Lexington Books.

Rohde, David W. 1991a. "The Electoral Roots of the Resurgence of Partisanship among Southern Democrats in the House of Representatives." Paper presented at the annual meeting of the American Political Science Association, Washington, D.C.

———. 1991b. *Parties and Leaders in the Post-Reform Congress*. Chicago: University of Chicago Press.

———. 1992. "Electoral Forces, Political Agendas, and Partisanship in Congress." In *The Post-Reform Congress*. Edited by Roger Davidson. New York: St. Martin's.

———. 1996. "The Inevitability and Solidity of the 'Republican Solid South.'" *American Review of Politics* 17: 23–46.

Rosin, Hannah. 1996. "Whiplash." *The New Republic*, February 19.

———. 1997. "The Men Who Would Be Newt." *The New Republic*, April 28.

Rovere, Richard H. 1965. *The Goldwater Caper*. New York: Harcourt, Brace and World.

Rozell, Mark J., and Clyde Wilcox. 1995. *God at the Grass Roots: The Christian Right in the 1994 Elections*. Lanham, MD: Rowman and Littlefield.

———, eds. 1997. *God at the Grassroots, 1996: The Christian Right in the 1996 Elections*. Lanham, MD: Rowman and Littlefield.

———. 1996. "Second Coming: The Strategies of the New Christian Right." *Political Science Quarterly* 111: 271–94.

Salant, Jonathan D. 1995a. "House Votes to Toughen Gift Restrictions." *Congressional Quarterly Weekly Report*, November 18.

———. 1995b. "Bill Would Open Windows on Lobbying Efforts." *Congressional Quarterly Weekly Report*, December 2.

Scammon, Richard, and Alice V. McGillivray. 1996. *America Votes*. Washington, D.C.: Congressional Quarterly Press.

Schamel, Charles E., et al. 1989. *Guide to the Records of the United States House of Representatives at the National Archives: 1789–1989 Bicentennial Edition*. Washington, D.C.: United States House of Representatives.

Scher, Richard K. 1997. *Politics in the New South: Republicanism, Race and Leadership in the Twentieth Century*. Armonk, NY: M.E. Sharpe.

Scher, Richard K., Jon L. Mills, and John J. Hotaling. 1997. "Voting Rights in the South After *Shaw* and *Miller*: The End of Racial Fairness?" In *Southern Parties and Elections: Studies in Regional Political Change*. Edited by Robert P. Steed, Laurence W. Moreland, and Tod A. Baker. Tuscaloosa: University of Alabama Press.

Schlesinger, Joseph. 1966. *Ambition and Politics: Political Careers in the United States*. Chicago: Rand McNally.

Schneider, Jerrold E. 1979. *Ideological Coalitions in Congress*. Westport, CT: Greenwood Press.

Schneider, Paige. 1997. "Factionalism in the Southern Republican Party: The Impact of the Christian Right." Paper presented at the annual meeting of the Southern Political Science Association, Atlanta, GA.

Seagull, Louis M. 1975. *Southern Republicanism*. New York: Wiley.

Shaffer, Steven D., and David Breaux. 1992. "Generational Differences among Southern Grassroots Party Workers." Paper presented at the annual meeting of the American Political Science Association, Chicago, IL.

Shaffer, William R. 1980. *Party and Ideology in the United States Congress*. Lanham, MD: University Press of America.

Shannon, W. Wayne. 1972. "Revolt in Washington: The South in Congress." In *The Changing Politics of the South*. Edited by William C. Havard. Baton Rouge: Louisiana State University Press.

Sharp, J. Michael. 1997. *Directory of Congressional Voting Scores and Interest Group Ratings*. Washington, D.C.: Congressional Quarterly Press.

Sharpe, Christine LeVeaux, and James C. Garand. 1995. "Race, Roll Calls, and Redistricting: The Impact of Majority-Minority Districts on Congressional Roll-Call Voting." Paper presented at the 1995 meeting of the Midwest Political Science Association, Chicago, IL.

Sheffner, Benjamin. 1995. "Parker Quits Coalition, Inching toward GOP." *Roll Call*, July 20.

Sheppard, Burton D. 1985. *Rethinking Congressional Reform: The Reform Roots of the Special Interest Congress*. Cambridge, MA: Schenkman Press.

Sinclair, Barbara Deckard. 1977. "Party Realignment and the Transformation of the Political Agenda: The House of Representatives, 1925–1938." *American Political Science Review* 71: 940–53.

———. 1978. "From Party Voting to Regional Fragmentation: The House of Representatives, 1933–1956." *American Politics Quarterly* 6: 125–46.

———. 1983. *Majority Party Leadership in the U.S. House*. Baltimore, MD: Johns Hopkins University Press.

———. 1985. "Agenda, Policy, and Alignment Change: From Coolidge to Reagan." In *Congress Reconsidered*. Edited by Lawrence Dodd and Bruce Oppenheimer. Washington, D.C.: Congressional Quarterly Press.

———. 1992. "The Emergence of Strong Leadership in the 1980s House of Representatives." *Journal of Politics* 54: 657–83.

———. 1997. *Unorthodox Lawmaking: New Legislative Processes in the U.S. Congress*. Washington, D.C.: Congressional Quarterly Press.

Sinclair, Barbara Deckard, and John Stanley. 1974. "Party Decomposition and Region: The House of Representatives, 1945–1970." *Western Political Quarterly* 27: 249–64.

Smith, Stephen S. 1981. "The Consistency and Ideological Structure of U.S. Senate Voting Alignments, 1957–1976." *American Journal of Political Science* 25: 780–95.

Smith, Steven S., and Christopher J. Deering. 1984. *Committees in Congress*. Washington, D.C.: Congressional Quarterly Press.

Smith, Steven S., and Bruce A. Ray. 1983. "The Impact of Congressional Reform: House Democratic Committee Assignments." *Congress and the Presidency* 10: 219–40.

Snowiss, Leo M. 1966. "Congressional Recruitment and Representation." *American Political Science Review* 60: 627–39.

Sprague, John. 1981. "One-Party Dominance in Legislatures." *Legislative Studies Quarterly* 6: 259–85.

Squire, Peverill. 1989a. "Competition and Uncontested Seats in U.S. House Elections." *Legislative Studies Quarterly* 14: 281–95.

———. 1989b. "Challengers in U.S. Senate Elections." *Legislative Studies Quarterly* 14: 531–45.

Stacks, John. 1994. "Stampede." *Time*, November 21.

Stanley, Harold W. 1987. *Voter Mobilization and the Politics of Race*. New York: Praeger.

———. 1988. "Southern Partisan Change: Dealignment, Realignment, or Both?" *Journal of Politics* 50: 64–88.

———. 1992. "Southern Republicans in Congress: Have They Fallen and They Can't Get Up?" *Social Science Quarterly* 73: 136–40.

———. 1994. "The South and the 1992 Presidential Election." In *The 1992 Presidential Election in the South: Current Patterns of Southern Party and Electoral Developments*. Edited by Robert P. Steed, Laurence W. Moreland, and Tod A. Baker. Westport, CT: Praeger.

———. 1998. "The South and the 1996 Presidential Election: Republican Gains among Democratic Wins." In *The 1996 Presidential Election in the South: Southern Party Systems in the 1990s*. Edited by Laurence W. Moreland and Robert P. Steed. Westport, CT: Praeger.

Starobin, Paul. 1995. "True Believer." *National Journal*, January 7.

Stedman, Murray S., and Herbert Sonthoff. 1951. "Party Responsibility: A Critical Inquiry." *Western Political Quarterly* 4: 454–68.

Steed, Robert P. 1990. "Party Reform, the Nationalization of American Politics, and Party Change in the South." In *Political Parties in the Southern States: Party Activists in Partisan Coalitions*. Edited by Tod A. Baker, Charles D. Hadley, Robert P. Steed, and Laurence W. Moreland. New York: Praeger.

———. 1997. "Introduction: Changing Electoral and Party Politics in the South." In *Southern Parties and Elections: Studies in Regional Political Change*. Robert P. Steed, Laurence W. Moreland, and Tod A. Baker. Tuscaloosa: University of Alabama Press.

Steed, Robert P., John A. Clark, Lewis Bowman, and Charles D. Hadley, eds. 1998. *Party Organization and Activism in the American South*. Tuscaloosa: University of Alabama Press.

Steed, Robert P., Laurence W. Moreland, and Tod A. Baker, eds. 1997. *Southern Parties and Elections Studies in Regional Political Change*. Tuscaloosa: University of Alabama Press.

Stern, Mark. 1987. "The Democratic Presidency and Voting Rights in the Second Reconstruction." In *Blacks in Southern Politics*. Edited by Laurence W. Moreland, Robert P. Steed, and Tod A. Baker. New York: Praeger.

Stimson, James A. 1985. "Regression in Time and Space: A Statistical Essay." *American Journal of Political Science* 29: 914–47.

Stokes, Melvyn, and Rick Halpern, eds. 1994. *Race and Class in the American South since 1890*. Oxford, UK: Berg Publishers.

Strong, Donald S. 1956. *The 1952 Presidential Election in the South*. Tuscaloosa: University of Alabama Bureau of Public Administration.

———. 1960. *Urban Republicanism in the South*. Tuscaloosa: University of Alabama Bureau of Public Administration.

Sundquist, James L. 1973. *Dynamics of the Party System: Alignment and Realignment of Political Parties in the United States*. Washington, D.C.: The Brookings Institution.

———. 1981. *The Decline and Resurgence of Congress.* Washington, D.C.: Brookings Institution.

Swansbrough, Robert H., and David M. Brodsky, eds. 1988. *The South's New Politics: Realignment and Dealignment.* Columbia: University of South Carolina Press.

Tate, Katherine. 1993. *From Protest to Politics: The New Black Voters in American Elections.* Cambridge, MA: Harvard University Press.

Taylor, Andrew. 1997. "Clinton Signs 'Clean' Disaster Aid after Flailing GOP Yields to Veto." *Congressional Quarterly Weekly Report*, June 14.

———. 1998. "Congress Wraps up and Heads Home on a Trail of Broken Budget Caps." *Congressional Quarterly Weekly Report*, October 24.

Theilemann, Gregory S. 1992. "The Rise and Stall of Southern Republicans in Congress." *Social Science Quarterly* 72: 123–35.

Truman, David B. 1951. *The Governmental Process.* New York: Knopf.

Turner, Julius. 1950. "Responsible Parties: A Dissent from the Floor." *American Political Science Review* 45: 143–52.

———. 1951. *Party and Constituency: Pressures on Congress.* Baltimore, MD: Johns Hopkins Press.

U.S. Census. 1984. *Congressional Districts* [series]. Washington, D.C.: United States Government Printing Office.

Van Doren, Peter M. 1990. "Can We Learn the Causes of Congressional Decisions from Roll-Call Data?" *Legislative Studies Quarterly* 15: 311–40.

Vande Hei, Jim. 1998. "DeLay Secretly Aided Gingrich Foe in California." *Roll Call*, January 19.

Vega, Arturo, and Ronald M. Peters, Jr. 1996. "Principal-Agent Theories of Party Leadership under Preference Homogeneity: The Case of Simpson-Mazzoli." *Congress and the Presidency* 23: 15–32.

Vobejda, Barbara. 1998. "In Turn Back, Blacks Moving to the South." *Washington Post*, January 29.

Voss, D. Stephen. 1996. "Beyond Racial Threat: Failure of an Old Hypothesis in the New South." *Journal of Politics* 58: 1156–70.

Wahlke, John C., Heinz Eulau, William Buchanan, and Leroy C. Ferguson. 1962. *The Legislative System: Explorations in Legislative Behavior.* New York: John Wiley and Sons.

Wattenburg, Martin P. 1987. "The Hollow Realignment: Partisan Change in a Candidate-Centered Era." *Public Opinion Quarterly* 51: 58–74.

Watters, Pat, and Reese Cleghorn. 1967. *Climbing Jacob's Ladder: The Arrival of Negroes in Southern Politics.* New York: Harcourt, Brace and World.

Welch, Susan, and John G. Peters, eds. 1977. *Legislative Reform and Public Policy.* New York: Praeger.

Williams, Juan. 1987. *Eyes on the Prize: America's Civil Rights Years, 1954–1965.* New York: Penguin.

Wolfinger, Ray, and Michael G. Hagen. 1985. "Republican Prospects: Southern Comfort." *Public Opinion* 8: 8–13.

Woodward, C. Vann. 1960. *The Burden of Southern History.* New York: Vintage Books.

———. 1966. *The Strange Career of Jim Crow.* New York: Oxford University Press.

Wright, Frederick D. 1987. "The History of Black Political Participation to 1965." In *Blacks in Southern Politics.* Edited by Laurence W. Moreland, Robert P. Steed, and Tod A. Baker. New York: Praeger.

Wright, Gerald. 1977. "Contextual Models of Electoral Behavior: The Southern Wallace Vote." *American Political Science Review* 71: 497–508.

Yang, John E. 1997. "House GOP Leadership Comes Apart at the Seams." *Washington Post*, July 19.

Index

About the Editors and Contributors

EDITORS

JOHN C. KUZENSKI is Associate Professor of Political Science at The Citadel and co-director of The Citadel Symposium on Southern Politics.

LAURENCE W. MORELAND is Professor of Political Science at The Citadel and co-director of The Citadel Symposium on Southern Politics.

ROBERT P. STEED is Professor of Political Science at The Citadel and co-director of The Citadel Symposium on Southern Politics.

CONTRIBUTORS

MICHAEL AULT is Assistant Professor of Political Science at California State University at Bakersfield.

STANLEY P. BERARD is Assistant Professor of Political Science at Lock Haven University of Pennsylvania.

CHARLES S. BULLOCK III is Richard B. Russell Professor of Political Science at the University of Georgia.

FRANK B. FEIGERT is Regents Professor of Political Science at the University of North Texas.

RONALD KEITH GADDIE is Associate Professor of Political Science at the University of Oklahoma.

James M. Glaser is Associate Professor of Political Science at Tufts University.

Allison L. Hayes is Assistant Professor of Political Science at Western Carolina University.

Donna R. Hoffman is a doctoral student in political science at the University of Oklahoma.

Ronald M. Peters, Jr., is Professor of Political Science and Director of the Carl Albert Center for Legislative Studies at the University of Oklahoma.

Nicol C. Rae is Professor of Political Science at Florida International University.

David W. Rohde is University Distinguished Professor of Political Science at Michigan State University.

Christine LeVeaux-Sharpe is Assistant Professor of Political Science at the University of Houston.

Mark Caleb Smith is a doctoral student in political science at the University of Georgia.

Kenneth A. Wink is Assistant Professor of Political Science/Public Administration at the University of Texas at Tyler.

www.ingramcontent.com/pod-product-compliance
Ingram Content Group UK Ltd.
Pitfield, Milton Keynes, MK11 3LW, UK
UKHW041638031026
15587UKWH00001B/364

9 780275 971144